SAT®
Critical Reading Workbook
Third Edition

RELATED TITLES FOR COLLEGE-BOUND STUDENTS

SAT Comprehensive Program
SAT Premier Program
SAT Strategies for Super Busy Students
SAT 2400
SAT Critical Reading Workbook
SAT Writing Workbook
SAT Vocabulary Prep Level 1
SAT Vocabulary Flashcards Prep Level 2
SAT in a Box

SAT Subject Test: Biology E/M
SAT Subject Test: Chemistry
SAT Subject Test: Literature
SAT Subject Test: Mathematics Level 1
SAT Subject Test: Mathematics Level 2
SAT Subject Test: Physics
SAT Subject Test: Spanish
SAT Subject Test: U.S. History
SAT Subject Test: World History

The Ring of McAllister: An SAT Score-Raising Mystery
Frankenstein: A Kaplan SAT Score-Raising Classic
The Tales of Edgar Allan Poe: A Kaplan SAT Score-Raising Classic
Dr. Jekyll and Mr. Hyde: A Kaplan SAT Score-Raising Classic
The War of the Worlds: A Kaplan SAT Score-Raising Classic
Wuthering Heights: A Kaplan SAT Score-Raising Classic
Domina El SAT: Preparate para Tomar el Examen para Ingresar a la Universidad

AP Biology
AP Calculus AB/BC
AP Chemistry
AP English Language & Composition
AP English Literature & Composition
AP Environmental Science
AP European History
AP Human Geography
AP Macroeconomics/Microeconomics
AP Physics B & C
AP Psychology
AP Statistics
AP U.S. Government & Politics
AP U.S. History
AP U.S. History in a Box
AP World History

SAT®

Critical Reading Workbook

Third Edition

The Staff of Kaplan Test Prep and Admissions

PUBLISHING

New York

Published by Kaplan Publishing, a division of Kaplan, Inc.
1 Liberty Plaza, 24th Floor
New York, NY 10006

Printed in the United States of America

July 2008
10 9 8 7 6 5 4 3 2 1

ISBN-13: 978-1-4195-5212-0

Kaplan Publishing books are available at special quantity discounts to use for sales promotions, employee premiums, or educational purposes. Please email our Special Sales Department to order or for more information at kaplanpublishing@kaplan.com, or write to Kaplan Publishing, 1 Liberty Plaza, 24th Floor, New York, NY 10006.

Table of Contents

Section Three: Reading Comprehension

Short Reading Comprehension Practice Sets

Long Reading Comprehension Practice Sets

Section Four: Practice Tests and Explanations

Section Five: SAT Vocabulary

Note for International Students

AVAILABLE ONLINE

FOR ANY TEST CHANGES OR LATE-BREAKING DEVELOPMENTS

kaptest.com/publishing

The material in this book is up-to-date at the time of publication. However, the College Board may have instituted changes in the test after this book was published. Be sure to carefully read the materials you receive when you register for the test. If there are any important late-breaking developments—or any changes or corrections to the Kaplan test preparation materials in this book—we will post that information online at kaptest.com/publishing.

FEEDBACK AND COMMENTS

kaplansurveys.com/books

We'd love to hear your comments and suggestions about this book. We invite you to fill out our online survey form at **kaplansurveys.com/books.** Your feedback is extremely helpful as we continue to develop high-quality resources to meet your needs.

How to Use This Book

Welcome to the SAT's Critical Reading section. To get a higher score, you'll need to practice, practice, and practice. That's what this book will help you do. It gives you hundreds of sample Critical Reading questions to work on.

Practice Sets

Most of this workbook is divided into practice sets corresponding to the three Critical Reading question types. Circle your answers directly in the book.

Explanations

Explanations are included for every question in this workbook. Use these to figure out why you got questions wrong and how to avoid making the same mistakes in the future. You'll also want to use these explanations for questions you got right—especially if you weren't sure and guessed—to reinforce the best approach.

Kaplan's Word and Root List

At the end of the book, you'll find a listing of 500 frequently seen SAT words, along with a word root list. It is important that you learn as many vocabulary words as possible before test day. A strong vocabulary is particularly useful on Sentence Completions, but it is also important for the Reading Comprehension questions. Some questions ask about the use of a specific word, and while you can often use the context around the word to help you understand it, you will be better prepared if you are familiar with that word before test day.

Sample Tests

Finally, there are two sample Critical Reading tests at the end of the book. Try to take these under timed, testlike conditions.

OTHER KAPLAN PROGRAMS

Since 1938, more than 3 million students have come to Kaplan to advance their studies, prepare for entry to American universities, and further their careers. In addition to the above programs, Kaplan offers courses to prepare for the ACT, GMAT®, GRE®, MCAT®, DAT®, USMLE®, NCLEX®, and other standardized exams at locations throughout the United States.

Applying to Kaplan English Programs

To get more information, or to apply for admission to any of Kaplan's programs for international students and professionals, contact us at:

Kaplan English Programs

700 South Flower, Suite 2900
Los Angeles, CA 90017, USA
Phone (if calling from within the United States): 800-818-9128
Phone (if calling from outside the United States): 213-452-5800
Fax: 213-892-1364
Website: www.kaplanenglish.com
Email: world@kaplan.com

*Kaplan is authorized under federal law to enroll nonimmigrant alien students. Kaplan is accredited by ACCET (Accrediting Council for Continuing Education and Training).

FREE Services for International Students

Kaplan now offers international students many services online—*free of charge*!
Students may assess their TOEFL skills and gain valuable feedback on their English
language proficiency in just a few hours with Kaplan's TOEFL Skills Assessment.
Log onto www.kaplanenglish.com today.

SAT Critical Reading Essentials

Chapter One: **Strategy Overview**

There are three sections on the SAT: Critical Reading, Writing, and Math.

Each section is scored on a 200–800 point scale. The three scores are then added together to get your cumulative score. A perfect score is 2400.

FORMAT AND TIME

The three SAT topic areas are divided into eight sections. (Actually, there will be nine sections on the test, but one of them is an experimental section that won't count. You won't know which section that is, however, so you'll have to work through all sections alike.) Here's how they break down:

The Math Section

There are two kinds of questions on the Math section: **Regular Math** questions, which are straightforward multiple-choice questions, and **Grid-Ins**, which require you to write your response in a little grid. Both types of question test the same math concepts—they're just in different formats.

The Critical Reading Section

The Critical Reading section contains three types of questions: **Sentence Completions** test your ability to see how the parts of a sentence relate to each other. They are basic fill-in-the-blank questions—with either one blank or two blanks. **Short Reading Comprehension** questions test your ability to understand a very brief passage, and **Long Reading Comprehension** questions test your know-how with a longer text. For the reading comprehension questions, you are asked about such things as the main idea, contextual references, and vocabulary.

The Writing Section

The Writing section is broken into two parts: a **written essay** and multiple-choice questions in **Usage**, **Sentence Correction**, and **Paragraph Correction**. Both sections are meant to test your grasp of grammar, usage, and vocabulary.

The essay assignment will come first. You'll have 25 minutes to write the essay, and if you finish early, you'll be allowed to move on directly to the multiple-choice questions. (But once the 25 minutes are up for the essay, you won't be allowed to go back to it.)

GENERAL SAT STRATEGIES

Now that you know some basics about how the test is set up, you can approach the multiple-choice questions with a plan. Having a plan is the key to success on the SAT. Here's the Kaplan plan of attack. The focus here is for the Critical Reading questions, but these strategies apply to the other sections as well.

1. Think about the question first.
2. Pace yourself.
3. Know when a question is supposed to be easy or hard.
4. Move around within a section.
5. Be a good guesser.
6. Be a good gridder.
7. Two-minute warning: locate quick points.
8. Fear not. Quell your stress.

1. Think about the Question First

The people who write the SAT put distractors among the answer choices. Distractors are answer choices that look right, but aren't. If you jump into the answer choices without thinking about what you're looking for, you're more likely to fall for a trap. So always think about the question for a couple of seconds before you look at the answers.

2. Pace Yourself

The SAT gives you a lot of questions to answer in a short period of time. To get through a whole section, you can't spend too much time on any one question. Keep moving through the test at a good speed. If you run into a hard question, circle it in your test booklet, skip it, and come back to it later if you have time.

3. Know When a Question Is Supposed to Be Easy or Hard

Some sections have their multiple-choice questions arranged in order of difficulty. In other words, the questions get harder as you move through the problem set. Here's a breakdown:

		Arranged Easiest to Hardest?
Math	Regular Math	Yes
	Grid-Ins	Yes
Critical Reading	Sentence Completion	Yes
	Short Reading Comprehension	No
	Long Reading Comprehension	No
Writing	Usage	No
	Sentence Correction	No
	Paragraph Correction	No

As you can see, all question sets in Math are arranged in order of difficulty, as are sentence completions in Critical Reading. As you work through a set that is organized this way, *be aware of where you are in a set*. When working on the easy problems, you can generally trust your first impulse—the obvious answer is likely to be right. As you get to the end of the set, you need to be more suspicious of "obvious" answers, because the answer should not come easily. If it does, look at the problem again because the obvious answer is likely to be wrong. It may be one of those distractors—a wrong answer choice meant to trick you.

Hard SAT questions are usually tough for two reasons:

1. Their answers are not immediately obvious
2. The questions do not ask for information in a straightforward way

Here's an easy question.

> Known for their devotion, dogs were often used as symbols of _____ in Medieval and Renaissance painting.
>
> (A) breakfast
> (B) tidal waves
> (C) fidelity
> (D) campfires
> (E) toothpaste

The correct answer, *fidelity* (C), probably lunged right out at you. This question would be at the beginning of a problem set. Easy questions are purposely designed to be easy, and their answer choices are purposely obvious.

Here is virtually the same question, made hard.

> Known for their _____, dogs were often used as symbols of _____ in Medieval and Renaissance painting.
>
> (A) dispassion . . . bawdiness
> (B) fidelity . . . aloofness
> (C) monogamy . . . parsimony
> (D) parity . . . diplomacy
> (E) loyalty . . . faithfulness

This question would be at the end of a problem set. This time the answer is harder to find. For one thing, the answer choices are far more difficult. In addition, the sentence contains two blanks.

The correct answer is (E). Did you fall for (B) because the first word is *fidelity*? (B) is a good example of a distractor.

4. Move Around Within a Section

On a test at school, you probably spend more time on the hard questions than you do on the easy ones, since hard questions are usually worth more points. *Do not do this on the SAT.*

Easy problems are worth as many points as tough problems, so do the easy problems first. Don't rush through the easy problems just to get to the hard ones. When you run into questions that look tough, circle them in your test booklet and skip them for the time being. (Make sure you skip them on your answer grid too.)

Then, if you have time, go back to them AFTER you have answered the easier ones. Sometimes, after you have answered some easier questions, troublesome questions can get easier, too.

5. Be a Good Guesser

The SAT says there is a penalty for guessing on the SAT. This is not true. There is only a "wrong answer penalty"—if you guess WRONG, you get penalized. Here's how the wrong answer penalty works:

If you get an answer wrong on a multiple-choice question, which have five answer choices, you lose a fraction of a point. These fractions of points are meant to offset the points you might get "accidentally" by guessing the correct answer.

If you get an answer wrong on a Grid-in Math question, for which you write in your own answers, you lose NOTHING.

If you can eliminate one or more wrong answer choices, you turn the odds in your favor, and you will actually come out ahead by guessing. Take a look at this question:

> After spending countless hours helping the needy children in their community, the basketball players were as recognized for their acts of _____ as they were for their slam dunks.
>
> (A) breakfast
> (B) tidal waves
> (C) charity
> (D) campfires
> (E) toothpaste

Chances are, you recognized that choice (A), *breakfast*, was wrong. You then looked at the next answer choice, and then the next one, and so on, eliminating wrong answers to find the correct answer. This process is usually the best way to work through multiple-choice SAT questions. If you don't know the right answer but can eliminate one or more wrong answers, *you should guess.*

6. Be a Good Gridder

Don't make mistakes filling out your answer grid. When time is short, it's easy to get confused skipping around a section and going back and forth between your test book and your grid. If you misgrid a *single* question, you can misgrid several others before realizing your error—if you realize it at all. You can lose a *ton* of points this way.

To avoid mistakes on the answer grid:

- Always circle the answers you choose. Circling your answers in the test booklet makes it easier to cross-check with your grid later.
- Grid five or more answers at once. Don't transfer your answers to the grid after every question. Transfer your answers after every five questions, or, in the Critical Reading section, at the end of each reading passage. That way, you won't keep breaking your concentration to mark the grid. You'll save time and improve accuracy.

Important Exception

When time is running out at the end of a section, start gridding one by one so you don't get caught at the end with ungridded answers.

- Circle the questions you skip. Put a big circle in your test booklet around the number of any questions you skip, so they'll be easy to locate when you return to them. Also, if you realize later that you accidentally skipped a box on the grid, you can more easily check your grid against your booklet to see where you went wrong.
- Write in your booklet. Take notes, circle hard questions, underline things, etcetera. Proctors collect booklets at the end of each testing session, but the booklets are not examined or reused.

7. Two-Minute Warning: Locate Quick Points

When you start to run out of time, locate and answer any of the quick points that remain. For example, some Critical Reading questions will ask you to identify the meaning of a particular word in the passage. These can be done at the last minute, even if you haven't read the passage.

8. Fear Not. Quell Your Stress

- Keep moving forward instead of getting bogged down in a difficult question or passage. You don't have to get everything right to achieve a fine score. So, don't linger out of desperation on a question that is going nowhere even after you've spent considerable time on it. The best test takers skip difficult material temporarily in search of the easier stuff. They mark the ones that require extra time and thought. This strategy buys time and builds confidence so you can handle the tough stuff later.

- Don't be thrown if other test takers seem to be working more busily and furiously than you are. Continue to spend your time patiently but doggedly thinking through your answers; it's going to lead to higher-quality test taking and better results. Don't mistake the other people's sheer activity as signs of progress and higher scores.

- *Keep breathing!* Weak test takers tend to share one major trait: They forget to breathe properly as the test proceeds. They start holding their breath without realizing it, or they breathe erratically or arrhythmically. Improper breathing hurts confidence and accuracy. Just as important, it interferes with clear thinking.

- Some quick isometrics during the test—especially if concentration is wandering or energy is waning—can help. Try this: Put your palms together and press intensely for a few seconds. Concentrate on the tension you feel through your palms, wrists, forearms, and up into your biceps and shoulders. Then, quickly release the pressure. Feel the difference as you let go. Focus on the warm relaxation that floods through the muscles. Now you're ready to return to the task.

Chapter Two: **Introduction to Critical Reading**

The questions on the Critical Reading section test your knowledge of genre, cause and effect, comparative arguments, and your ability to assess relationships among parts of a text. In total, you will spend 70 minutes on Critical Reading questions, presented in three sections.

There are three kinds of questions on this section:

Sentence Completion questions test your ability to see how the parts of a sentence relate. About half have one word missing from a sentence; the rest have two words missing. Both types test vocabulary and reasoning skills.

Sentence Completions will be arranged in order of difficulty. The first few questions in a set are meant to be fairly easy. The middle few questions will be a little harder, and the last few are the most difficult. Keep this in mind as you work.

To solve a Sentence Completion, use the following method:

1. **Read the sentence for clue words.** Words such as *but*, *although*, *however*, and *on the other hand* tell you that there is a contrast within the sentence.

2. **Anticipate the answer.** Before you look at the answer choices, fill in the missing pieces yourself. Predict what goes in the blank. It doesn't have to be precise; you just need a rough idea.

3. **Compare your prediction with each answer choice, and pick the best match.** Scan every answer choice before deciding upon an answer. Don't pick an answer choice just because it sounds hard. Sometimes, hard vocab words are included just to trick you.

4. **Read the sentence with your answer choice in the blank(s).** Only one choice should make sense in the sentence.

Short Reading Comprehension questions are based on passages of around 100 words. For each short passage, there are two questions or so.

Long Reading Comprehension questions are based on longer passages of 450–800 words. Around 6–12 questions follow each passage. These require the same set of skills as the Short Reading Comp questions.

Reading Comprehension questions are *not* arranged by order of difficulty. If you find yourself spending too much time on a Reading Comp question, you should skip it and come back to it later.

To solve a Reading Comprehension question—Short or Long—use the following method:

1. **Read the text.** Skim, but skim carefully. Don't pay attention to the details. Just try to get the overall idea of the passage.

2. **Read the question stem.** Read the question carefully so that you understand what is being asked. The meaning of an entire question can change with just one word.

3. **Locate the material you need.** If you are given a line reference, read the material surrounding that text. It will clarify exactly what the question is asking.

4. **Come up with an idea of the right answer.** Don't spend time making up a precise answer. You need only a general sense of what you're after, so that you can recognize the correct answer quickly when you read the choices.

5. **Scan the answer choices.** Scan the choices, looking for the one that fits your idea of the right answer. If you don't find an ideal answer, quickly eliminate wrong choices. Rule out choices that are too extreme or go against common sense. And get rid of answers that sound reasonable but don't make sense in the context of the passage.

6. **Select your answer.** You've eliminated the obvious wrong answer choices. One of the remaining choices should fit your ideal. If you're left with more than one contender, consider the main idea of the text and make an educated guess.

| SECTION TWO: |

Sentence Completions

Chapter Three: **Introduction to SAT Sentence Completions**

Sentence Completions test your ability to read carefully and think logically. They also test your knowledge of college-level vocabulary.

The Structure

A Sentence Completion is simply a fill-in-the-blank question. You might think this section would be a breeze. Well, some of these questions are, but many others are tough. Either the sentence or the choices will contain words that are completely unfamiliar to you.

The Format

Though the real SAT directions and sample question will look slightly different, they'll mean the same thing as what follows. Learn now what you'll need to do when you open your booklet to Sentence Completions. Don't waste time reading the directions on Test Day.

Select the lettered word or set of words that best completes the sentence.

> **Example:**
>
> Today's small, portable computers contrast markedly with the earliest electronic computers, which were - - - - - .
>
> (A) effective
> (B) invented
> (C) useful
> (D) destructive
> (E) enormous

In the example, the new computers, which are small and portable, are contrasted with old computers. You can infer that the old computers must be the opposite of "small and portable", so (E) *enormous* is right.

Sentence Completions are arranged in order of difficulty. The hardest questions are at the end of each set, so pace yourself accordingly. Work quickly on these questions, and save the bulk of your time for Reading Comprehension questions.

If a question stumps you, mark it in your test booklet, skip it on your answer sheet, and come back to it later if you have time. But first finish all the other questions in Sentence Completions, Analogies, and Critical Reading.

HINT: Don't get hung up on any one question. Your goal is to get as many questions right as possible.

Like everything else on the SAT, Sentence Completions come in a standard format. Once you get used to solving them, they can be quite easy. So if you're having trouble, practice.

Dealing with Hard Words

You'll find hard words in the sentences and the answer choices. That's why it's important to study our Word and Root Lists. But what if you still don't know some words? Don't give up. Try these suggestions for working around unknown words:

- Look in the sentence itself for clues to a word's meaning.
- Think about where you might have heard the word before.
- Try to spot familiar roots or prefixes that can help you understand the word's meaning.
- If all else fails, eliminate answers you think are wrong, and guess.

Dealing with Hard Sentences

It's important to read the sentences and answer choices carefully, especially near the end of the set. Follow the twists and turns of the sentence, and be sure you understand what it says. Then you won't get caught by tricky answers that the test makers like to include.

- Don't pick an answer just because it sounds hard. Be sure the answer you choose makes sense.
- Don't choose an answer choice that is the opposite of the correct answer. Read the sentence carefully.

Dealing with Two-Blank Sentences

Two-blank sentences can be easier than one-blankers. In two-blankers you can:

- Scan the sentence and start with the easier blank.
- Eliminate all answer choices that won't work for that blank.
- Try only the remaining choices in the second blank.

HINT: In two-blankers, don't pick a choice that fits one blank but not the other.

Practice Set One

1. Joseph's employees were ---- by the ---- manner in which he dealt with them.

    (A) repulsed . . . placid
    (B) irritated . . . curt
    (C) incensed . . . droll
    (D) perturbed . . . amiable
    (E) weakened . . . sullen

2. It is sometimes customary to view rain as ---- sign; many believe that if it rains on the day of your wedding, you will enjoy financial prosperity.

    (A) an inopportune
    (B) a meager
    (C) an auspicious
    (D) an untimely
    (E) a modest

3. Once a ---- population center, the city gradually lost residents to the factory towns of the North.

    (A) bustling
    (B) manufactured
    (C) rural
    (D) seedy
    (E) deserted

4. The scene was even ---- than Rebecca had ----; dead trees and patchy brown grass seemed to stretch on forever under a leaden sky.

    (A) uglier . . . feigned
    (B) drearier . . . envisioned
    (C) lazier . . . divulged
    (D) scantier . . . desired
    (E) keener . . . perceived

5. Proponents of a bill requiring each home to keep a firearm and ammunition sought to placate their opponents by including ---- for those who did not ---- gun possession.

    (A) a penalty . . . frown upon
    (B) an exemption . . . support
    (C) a theory . . . relish
    (D) an addendum . . . continue
    (E) a waiver . . . abolish

6. Otis ---- agreed to ---- his partner's decision, misguided though he thought it was.

    (A) gracefully . . . rail at
    (B) maliciously . . . compromise on
    (C) wistfully . . . bargain with
    (D) grudgingly . . . abide by
    (E) cynically . . . reign over

KAPLAN

7. The name of the housing development is a ----;
   although it is called "Forest Hills," it is located in a
   ---- valley.

   (A) dilution . . . river
   (B) fallacy . . . neglected
   (C) misnomer . . . treeless
   (D) retelling . . . contented
   (E) fault . . . barren

8. Far from being ----, today's television advertising,
   with its constant barrage of last-minute sales and
   new-and-improved products, practically ---- the
   viewer.

   (A) subtle . . . assaults
   (B) engaging . . . titillates
   (C) utilitarian . . . assists
   (D) obtuse . . . ridicules
   (E) informative . . . ignores

9. Unfortunately, the treasurer's plan to get the company out of debt ---- gaining access to certain
   funds that may never become available.

   (A) speaks to
   (B) treats with
   (C) delves into
   (D) metes out
   (E) hinges on

10. A true ascetic, Jorge ---- luxuries and other world-
    ly pleasures in an effort to ---- his spiritual side.

    (A) spurns . . . fortify
    (B) embraces . . . emulate
    (C) relishes . . . assist
    (D) condones . . . reclaim
    (E) lambastes . . . interpret

ANSWERS AND EXPLANATIONS

1.   B

Getting to the Answer: The two words here must reinforce each other. Either the employees were *pleased* by the *nice* manner in which Joseph dealt with them, or they were *displeased* by the *not nice* manner in which he dealt with them.

(A) is out, as *placid* and *repulsed* are unrelated. *Placid* means "calm," and *repulsed* means "repelled." With (C) and (D), the words are almost opposites. (B) is a good match. *Curt* means "rudely brief in speech," so it makes sense that employees would be *irritated* by their employer's curt manner.

2.   C

Getting to the Answer: "Financial prosperity" is a strong clue. Since it's a good thing, *rain* must be a sign of good fortune.

Scanning the answer choices, the closest match is (C), *auspicious*. It means "foretelling good fortune."

3.   A

Getting to the Answer: Clue words here are *once* and *lost residents*.

Since it *lost residents*, the city once must have been a large *population center*. That sense is conveyed by (A) *bustling*. Bustling means "crowded and busy." It certainly is not conveyed by deserted, seedy, manufactured, or rural.

4.   B

Getting to the Answer: The semicolon offers a clue. The words that go in the blanks must fit the gloomy description after the semicolon. Your phrase might be: The scene was even *worse* than Rebecca had *imagined*.

In the first blank, *lazier*, *keener*, and *scantier* aren't close to *worse*, and they don't fit, so you're left with (A) and (B). Since either *uglier* or *drearier* would fit the first blank, you have to decide between (A) and (B) based on their second words. *Feigned*, which means "pretended," doesn't make sense, but *envisioned* works fine.

5.   B

Getting to the Answer: This one's tough if you don't know the vocabulary. The *proponents* were trying to get the bill passed by the legislature. They wanted firearm possession to be mandatory. A *proponent* is a supporter, and to *placate* is to soothe or appease. Presumably, their opponents didn't favor keeping guns, so the second blank should be filled by something that means *supported*. The first blank might be filled by something like *a loophole*, a way for people who don't want to obey the law to avoid its requirements.

(A) is out because *penalty* doesn't fit the first blank, and *frown upon* is the opposite of what we want for the second blank. In (C), it doesn't make sense for a theory to be included in a bill. Moreover, *relish*, which means "to enjoy greatly," is totally at odds with our description for the second blank. An *addendum* is usually "attached to" something, rather than "included" in it. With (D), *continue* makes no sense in the second blank. In (E), a *waiver* precisely matches our word *loophole* for the first blank, but it doesn't make sense to talk about exempting those who do not *abolish* gun possession. (B) fits. An *exemption* is a waiver or an exception from a requirement.

6.   D

Getting to the Answer: Your clue here is *misguided*. Since Otis thought his partner's decision was misguided, he obviously "reluctantly" *agreed to* "go along with it."

(D) fits both descriptions. *Otis* grudgingly *agreed to abide by* his partner's decision. The other choices don't make sense. In (E), *cynically* might fit, but *reign* over is wrong.

7.   C

Getting to the Answer: The sentence suggests that the housing development's name is misleading. It may have been called *Forest Hills,* but it was actually constructed *in a—valley*, not in the *Hills*. So you need a word such as *mistake*, or even *fraud*, for the first blank. And for the second blank, you're looking for something that contrasts with *Forest*.

Start with the first blank. (B) and (C) are the only two possible choices. A *fallacy* means a "logical error," and a *misnomer* means a "wrong name." Now check the second blanks. *Neglected* doesn't fit, but *treeless* does. (C) is correct.

8. A

Getting to the Answer: The clue here is *far from being*. It tells you that you're dealing with two contrasting sentence parts. *Far from* being—, today's television—the viewer. We're also told that today's television advertising consists of a constant *barrage* of information. The implication is that today's television advertising "attacks" the viewer. So look for a second word that's similar to *attacks*, and a first word that contrasts with it.

The only second word that means "attacks" is *assaults*, in (A). The advertising practically assaults the viewer in a heavy-handed way. *Subtle*, or indirect, is a good opposite, so this fits. In (B), *engaging* and *titillates* are not opposites; engaging commercials might very well titillate (excite) the viewer. (C) *utilitarian*, or functional, makes no sense. *Obtuse* in (D) means "dull" or "stupid," and has little to do with ridicules. In (E), *informative* might be right, but the *barrage* of television advertising certainly doesn't ignore the viewer.

9. E

Getting to the Answer: Your clue is *unfortunately*. The treasurer's plan unfortunately may not work because it—*gaining access to* certain funds that may not become available. To fill the blank, look for a phrase such as *relies on* or is *based on*.

The closest choice is (E). *Hinges on* means "depends on." The other four phrases don't make sense. *Delves into* means "digs deeply," and *metes out* means "gives out small rations."

10. A

Getting to the Answer: Since *Jorge* is a *true ascetic,* the word in the first blank must support that description. An *ascetic* is one who practices self-denial. You could say: A true ascetic *gives up* luxuries. To make sense, the second blank has to reinforce that. He gives up luxuries in order to *strengthen* his spiritual side.

Checking the first blank, (A) works best. *Spurn* means "reject." Now for the second blank. A true ascetic spurns luxuries in an effort to fortify his spiritual side. That makes sense. The other choices contain some difficult words. If you don't know them all, eliminate choices when one word doesn't make sense. You probably knew that *embraces* and *relishes* mean almost the opposite of "gives up," so you could eliminate (B) and (C). You also know that *interpret* has nothing to do with "strengthen," so you could eliminate (E). Then you could guess between (A) and (D).

Practice Set Two

Directions: Select the lettered word or set of words that best completes the sentence.

1. Barbara Walters distinguished herself as a journalist by asking famous people the kinds of ---- questions that other reporters shied away from.

   (A) discreet
   (B) intriguing
   (C) pointed
   (D) gentle
   (E) indirect

2. Ozone in the upper layers of Earth's atmosphere is beneficial, ---- animal and plant life from dangerous ultraviolet radiation.

   (A) reflecting
   (B) withdrawing
   (C) displacing
   (D) thwarting
   (E) protecting

3. All of today's navel oranges are ---- of a single mutant tree that began producing seedless fruit nearly 200 years ago.

   (A) progenitors
   (B) hybrids
   (C) descendants
   (D) conglomerations
   (E) spores

4. So ---- was the saleswoman's pitch about the value of the used car that Hallie nearly missed the ---- in its logic.

   (A) convincing . . . fallacy
   (B) inept . . . liability
   (C) relieving . . . reason
   (D) tired . . . persuasiveness
   (E) sarcastic . . . rejoinder

5. Certain members of the pack viciously ---- others, ---- the hierarchical structure of the group.

   (A) venerate . . . destroying
   (B) bully . . . reinforcing
   (C) coax . . . subsidizing
   (D) terrorize . . . memorizing
   (E) pass . . . reacting

6. After inventing a sign language for the deaf in the mid-1700s, Giacobbo Rodriguez Pereira ---- his business activities in order to ---- all his energies to humanitarian work.

   (A) shouldered . . . donate
   (B) elicited . . . transmit
   (C) abandoned . . . devote
   (D) ceased . . . attach
   (E) ceded . . . sell

7. Investigators are trying to determine whether the recent rash of fires is the work of ---- or simply a ---- of unfortunate accidents.

   (A) a pyromaniac . . . source
   (B) an accomplice . . . consequence
   (C) a criminal . . . premonition
   (D) an arsonist . . . series
   (E) an assortment . . . string

8. Despite his physical disability, the soccer player was ---- in helping his country's team capture the World Cup.

   (A) ungainly
   (B) accessible
   (C) rampant
   (D) instrumental
   (E) unvarying

9. Doing much more than was expected of her, Henrietta ---- the responsibilities of a department supervisor's position for eight months before she finally received the title.

   (A) undertook
   (B) procured
   (C) entreated
   (D) bestowed
   (E) precipitated

10. The poet received room, board, and ---- from the university in return for leading two seminars.

   (A) an impetus
   (B) an amulet
   (C) a writ
   (D) a niche
   (E) a stipend

ANSWERS AND EXPLANATIONS

1. C

Getting to the Answer: Barbara Walters earned a reputation for herself as a journalist by doing what other reporters shied away from or "avoided." The clue lies in the kinds of questions she asked—the kind others shied away from.

You can predict that Ms. Walters asked personal, probing questions about controversial subjects. The only answer that describes such questions is (C). A journalist wouldn't shy away from *gentle* or *indirect* questions, so (D) and (E) are out. As for (B), all reporters try to make their questions *intriguing*. *Discreet*, in (A), means "modestly quiet" or " circumspect."

2. E

Getting to the Answer: In the upper layers of the earth's atmosphere, ozone is said to be beneficial or "helpful," so it must do something good for animal and plant life.

(E) fits the bill. The ozone *protects* animal and plant life. *Thwart*, in (D), means to "hinder" or "obstruct."

3. C

Getting to the Answer: You have to predict a relationship between all of today's navel oranges and a single mutant tree that produced seedless fruit a long time ago.

Today's navel oranges are (C) *descendants* or *offspring* of that first tree. *Mutant* may confuse you into selecting (B), but the sentence does not suggest that today's navel oranges are offspring of two different species. (A) *Progenitors* or ancestors, describe a mutant tree, but not today's navel oranges. Likewise, (D), *conglomerations* or a mixture of various things, doesn't describe navel oranges.

4. A

Getting to the Answer: The saleswoman's pitch is her sales talk. We need a word such as *persuasive* for the first blank and something like *flaw* for the second.

(A) is the only choice that matches either prediction. A *fallacy* in (A) is an error in logic. *Inept* in (B) means "incompetent."

5. B

Getting to the Answer: If you didn't know some of the tough words here, you could eliminate wrong choices and guess. The only two choices whose first words can reasonably be modified by *viciously* are (B) and (D). Checking the second blank, (B) makes sense and (D) doesn't. The aggressive behavior of these pack animals was reinforcing the *structure of the group* rather than memorizing it. So you could arrive at (B) by process of elimination.

Had you known the vocabulary words, you could have reached the same conclusion more quickly and with more certainty. The first part of the sentence indicates that some *members of the pack* get away with *viciously* attacking *others*. The second part implies that these attacks have something to do with the group's *hierarchical structure*. (B) best fits the meaning of the sentence, since the aggressive members of the pack control the weaker members.

6. C

Getting to the Answer: Try examining the main clause alone: *Pereira —— his business activities in order to —— all his energies to humanitarian work*. In other words, he wanted to spend less time on *business activities* and more on *humanitarian work*. In the second blank, (A) and (C) are the only choices that fit. You can't transmit, attach, or sell your energies to a project. To *shoulder* is to take on a responsibility. So (A) and (C) are the only possibilities.

For the second blank, since he wanted to spend less time on business activities, he probably abandoned them, so (C) is correct. He abandoned *his business activities in order to* devote *all his energies to humanitarian work*.

7. D

Getting to the Answer: In this context, a *rash* is not a skin irritation but a large number of instances within a short period of time. Here we're talking about a recent series of fires. For the first blank, we'll need a person or thing that might have caused the fires.

The best options for the first blank are (A), *pyromaniac*, or (D), *arsonist*. Though a *criminal*, (C), might have started the fires, a criminal does not have as specific a connection with fires. And (B), *accomplice*, would by definition have helped set the fires, rather than set them himself.

Now look at the words that (A) and (D) offer for the second blank. *The recent rash of fires* could not have been *a source of unfortunate accidents* unless it caused accidents, which we are not told. But series *of accidents* fits well with the idea of a *rash of fires.*

8. D

Getting to the Answer: *Despite* is the clue word.

In spite of his disability, the soccer player was important to his team. The only choice that comes close to that prediction is (D). *Instrumental* means "contributing to promote, helpful."

9. A

Getting to the Answer: A long time elapsed between the time when Henrietta—the responsibilities of a department supervisor's position and the time when she finally received the title.

You might predict *assumed* or *shouldered*. The closest choice is (A). *Undertook* means "took upon oneself." As for (B), Henrietta eventually procured the title, but first she undertook the responsibilities. *Procured* means "obtained or achieved by some effort."

10. E

Getting to the Answer: What might the university have given *the poet* as compensation *for leading two seminars*?

We know that *the poet received room* and *board,* or living quarters and meals. The other obvious form of compensation would be money. (E) is the only choice that has anything to do with monetary compensation. A *stipend* is a wage or other form of compensation to offset expenses. An *impetus* is a stimulus or driving force.

Practice Set Three

1. The first primitive fish had lungs; in most of their descendants, these ---- have ----- into swim bladders.

    (A) animals . . . merged
    (B) organs . . . evolved
    (C) ancients . . . combined
    (D) organisms . . . stretched
    (E) functions . . . barged

2. Martha's wardrobe looked as though it had been ---- from a rag bin; her expensive boots were her sole ---- fashion.

    (A) swiped . . . agreement with
    (B) compartmentalized . . . return to
    (C) beguiled . . . contribution to
    (D) salvaged . . . concession to
    (E) bought . . . interruption from

3. John Price was ---- from the slave-hunters who had abducted him by the citizens of Oberlin and the neighboring towns; 37 of these citizens were then ---- under the Fugitive Slave Act.

    (A) kidnapped . . . legislated
    (B) recovered . . . deemed
    (C) rescued . . . indicted
    (D) serenaded . . . jailed
    (E) pressured . . . penalized

4. The 150-year-old church had been ---- for demolition until architects and neighborhood residents ---- to have it declared an historic landmark.

    (A) scheduled . . . declined
    (B) excommunicated . . . prayed
    (C) slated . . . rallied
    (D) exchanged . . . paid
    (E) repaired . . . sought

5. In 1883, ---- eruption of Mount Krakatoa killed many thousands of people and ---- havoc on the coasts of Java and Sumatra.

    (A) a fateful . . . diminished
    (B) an inoffensive . . . spawned
    (C) an immoral . . . reigned
    (D) a blistering . . . authorized
    (E) a disastrous . . . wreaked

6. The contractor first quoted an outrageous figure to repair the roof but appeared willing to ---- when Ben ---- at the price.

    (A) negotiate . . . balked
    (B) bargain . . . floundered
    (C) participate . . . recoiled
    (D) reconsider . . . waived
    (E) intensify . . . fainted

7. Because the ancient Egyptians ---- the hour as one-twelfth of the time from dawn to dusk, its length varied during the ---- of the year.

    (A) measured . . . remainder
    (B) revered . . . occurrence
    (C) imagined . . . dates
    (D) defined . . . course
    (E) idealized . . . seasons

8. The candidate answered tough questions with ---- candor, winning over many viewers who had previously supported her rival.

    (A) presumptuous
    (B) impatient
    (C) unintentional
    (D) dogmatic
    (E) disarming

9. Henry Louis Gates Jr. believes that Frederick Douglass ---- patterned his 1845 autobiography after the ---- of former slave Olaudah Equiano, whose life story was published in 1789.

    (A) patronizingly . . . reminder
    (B) consciously . . . narrative
    (C) anxiously . . . capture
    (D) expectantly . . . epitaph
    (E) belatedly . . . antiquity

10. It was difficult to imagine George, ---- man, as a psychiatrist; listening while others talked was not his style.

    (A) a voluble
    (B) an insensitive
    (C) a pessimistic
    (D) a truculent
    (E) a depressed

ANSWERS AND EXPLANATIONS

1. B

Getting to the Answer: You don't need a science background to complete this sentence. You just need to understand the logic of the sentence.

For the first blank, the phrase *these*—must refer to lungs. Apparently the lungs have developed into *swim bladders* in most of today's fish. So you might predict a word like *structures* for the first blank, and *developed* for the second blank. (B) is the best choice: The organs *have* evolved *into swim bladders*.

2. D

Getting to the Answer: The first blank needs something like *taken*.

(B) and (C) make no sense: You might *beguile*, or try to win over, someone in order to take something from him, but *beguiled* doesn't mean "taken." The remaining three choices have first words that mean "taken," but only one of them matches up with *a bin* that contains worthless rags and clothes. (A) and (E) won't work, because no one would have *swiped* or *bought* anything from a rag bin. But *salvaged* makes perfect sense. It also makes sense to say that "*her expensive boots were her sole concession*" to *fashion*. A *concession* is an "acknowledgment, admission," so the only acknowledgment to fashion in Martha's wardrobe were her *expensive boots*.

3. C

Getting to the Answer: Since the citizens must have "taken" *John Price* away from *the slave-hunters*, (A), (B), and (C) might fit the first blank.

(D) and (E) are out, because *serenaded* and *pressured* have no meaning in this context. Now check the second blanks of (A), (B), and (C). You have to decide between three tough second words. In (A), one can *legislate* behavior, but not people. (B) *deemed* doesn't work either, since the word has to be followed by an adjective or noun. One is deemed "something." But they could have been *indicted* for helping a runaway slave, so (C) is correct.

4. C

Getting to the Answer: Your clue is the conjunction *until,* which divides this sentence into two time periods. In the first period, the *church* was scheduled *for demolition;* in the second, people banded together to *have it declared an historic landmark.* You can rule out (B) immediately. People can be *excommunicated*; an old *church* cannot. (D) and (E) are also wrong, since the church couldn't have been *exchanged* or *repaired* for demolition.

On the other hand, *scheduled* and *slated* match our prediction, so (A) and (C) both fit the first blank. But in (A), *declined* doesn't fit the second blank. If people had declined or refused to have it declared an historic landmark, the church would presumably still have been demolished. Instead, they must have *rallied* on its behalf.

5. E

Getting to the Answer: An eruption that kills *many thousands of people* must be *bad* or *severe*. That's what you need in the first blank.

(E) *disastrous* is the obvious choice for the first blank, though *fateful* and *blistering* are possible. (B) is clearly wrong, and it doesn't make sense to describe a natural disaster as *immoral*, so (C) is out as well. For the second blank, check out (A), (D), and (E). It makes no sense to say the eruption *diminished* or *authorized* havoc. Clearly, (E) *wreaked* is our answer. It means "inflicted."

6. A

Getting to the Answer: The clue word *but* suggests that the contractor was willing to lower his price because of Ben's response, so the first word should mean something like *lower his price* or *bargain*.

(A), (B), and (D) would all work in the first blank, but now try the second blanks. These words are challenging. (B) doesn't work well. Why would Ben have floundered (or struggled to move) *at the price*? In (D), *waived* means "voluntarily gave up a claim or right"; that makes no sense because it should be *the contractor* who waived *the price*, not Ben. But *balked* in (A) makes sense. It means "stopped short, failed to." The *outrageous figure* stopped Ben cold, and he refused to complete the transaction unless *the contractor* was *willing to* negotiate.

7.   D

Getting to the Answer: This one's hard to predict, but we need a word that describes an hour.

Looking at the first words, *measured* and *defined* seem more likely than *revered*, *imagined*, or *idealized*. *Revered* means "honored, held in high esteem." So focus on the second words in (A) and (D). The only one that makes sense is *course*. If you plug (D) into the blanks, the logic of the sentence becomes clear. A summer's day is longer than a winter's day; therefore, *one-twelfth of the time from dawn to dusk* is not constant through the year. So the *length* of an ancient Egyptian hour *varied during the course of the year because* it was defined in terms of the total length of a day.

8.   E

Getting to the Answer: Though it would be helpful to know the meaning of *candor* here, it isn't necessary. (It means "frankness, honesty, openness.") The fact that *the candidate's candor* earned her many new supporters suggests that it was a good trait, so the word in the blank should be positive.

Presumptuous, impatient, and *dogmatic* are all negative. *Presumptuous* means "overstepping the bounds of one's position," and *dogmatic* means "dictatorial, insisting on one's own beliefs." *Unintentional* isn't inherently negative, but it certainly isn't positive. The only positive word here is (E) *disarming*, which means "easing or neutralizing criticism or hostility." *The candidate's candor* disarmed or won over voters *who had previously supported her rival.*

9.   B

Getting to the Answer: If *Frederick Douglass . . . patterned his . . . autobiography after* something, he must have modeled it on another literary work.

The type of work should go in the second blank. Only (B) and (D) work with the second words. It would be hard to model an entire autobiography on a simple epitaph (a brief saying about a dead person), so you can pick (B) as the answer on the basis of the second blank alone. But in any two-blank sentence, make sure that both words fit. *Consciously* fits fine in the first blank, so (B) is indeed correct.

10.   A

Getting to the Answer: Ignore the phrase *as a psychiatrist.* The main hint lies in the contrast between the distinct parts of the sentence: *George was—*; and *listening while others talked was not his style.*

In the sentence, it is difficult to imagine George in a certain way; that is, *not* the way he actually is. Look for a word that means *noisy* or *talkative*. The only choice that has anything to do with talking or not talking is (A). *Voluble* means "talkative." *Truculent*, (D), means "disposed to fight, fierce."

Practice Set Four

Directions: Select the lettered word or set of words that best completes the sentence.

1. Happy ---- have replaced the ---- outcomes of some stories in the updated English translations of Hans Christian Andersen's fairy tales.

   (A) plots . . . silly
   (B) endings . . . gloomy
   (C) characters . . . mythical
   (D) results . . . lanky
   (E) moods . . . historic

2. A report that the corporation was precariously close to the ---- of bankruptcy caused panic among its creditors and stockholders.

   (A) cessation
   (B) deficit
   (C) brink
   (D) absorption
   (E) absence

3. Gary was ---- about the ---- of his family heirlooms and personal mementos in the fire.

   (A) depressed . . . meaning
   (B) noncommittal . . . eradication
   (C) incensed . . . recovery
   (D) mournful . . . insurance
   (E) distraught . . . destruction

4. Julio's good mood was ----; within minutes, his normally ---- partners were grinning and choking back laughter.

   (A) promiscuous . . . glum
   (B) genial . . . famished
   (C) ghastly . . . intolerable
   (D) pretentious . . . forlorn
   (E) infectious . . . stolid

5. Many novels by the Brontë sisters and other nineteenth-century female authors were initially published under masculine ---- in the belief that works by ---- authors would meet more favorable reception.

   (A) monikers . . . patriarchal
   (B) aliases . . . established
   (C) rubrics . . . famous
   (D) pseudonyms . . . male
   (E) criteria . . . talented

6. Moira forced herself to eat every morsel on her plate; although she found the food practically ----, she wanted to avoid offending her kind hosts.

   (A) egregious
   (B) nourishing
   (C) inedible
   (D) overheated
   (E) sodden

7. Architect Tadao Ando's penchant for placing ----
concerns above technical practicalities sometimes
---- unsettling, even precarious, structures.

    (A) artistic . . . results in

    (B) monetary . . . clashes with

    (C) mundane . . . replaces

    (D) lofty . . . cuts down

    (E) social . . . supports

8. With his army already ---- in the snow, Napoleon's
retreat from the outskirts of Moscow turned into a
rout after Russian troops began to ---- his soldiers.

    (A) vacillating . . ravage

    (B) jangling . . harass

    (C) plummeting . . insinuate

    (D) foundering . . assault

    (E) tottering . . upbraid

9. Traditionally, any citizen is entitled to be tried by a
jury of her peers; however, the law does not ----
how or to what extent the jurors must ---- the
defendant.

    (A) monitor . . . assess

    (B) specify . . . resemble

    (C) indicate . . . charge

    (D) necessitate . . . enable

    (E) predict . . . mirror

10. The features of Noh, the oldest form of Japanese
drama, are highly ----; verse sections must be
sung, and the vocal style in the prose passages
has to be based on the chanting of specific
Buddhist prayers.

    (A) prescribed

    (B) undertaken

    (C) ineffectual

    (D) frugal

    (E) absolute

ANSWERS AND EXPLANATIONS

1. B

Getting to the Answer: The first blank must have something to do with *outcomes,* because you can't replace *outcomes* with a word that serves an entirely different function.

The second blank seems to refer to mood: If happy outcomes replaced the original outcomes, the original outcomes were probably sad. (B) or (D) might work in the first blank, but only *gloomy* in (B) fits the second blank. *Lanky,* in (D), means "tall and thin, ungraceful."

2. C

Getting to the Answer: You don't need to know what *precariously* means here to find the answer, though it means "marked by unstability and uncertainty." Something caused panic among the creditors.

The word that fills the blank must be something like *point* or *edge.* A *brink,* (C), is an "edge of a steep place or concept," such as a cliff or a disaster, so it's correct. A *cessation* means "a stopping," and a *deficit* means "a shortage or shortfall."

3. E

Getting to the Answer: Gary must have been upset because *his family heirlooms and personal mementos* had been lost in the fire. So the first word must mean *upset,* and second word, *loss.*

(A), (D), and (E) work well for the first blank. *Mournful* in (D) means "sorrowful." *Distraught* in (E), means "extremely upset or agitated." And since *destruction* fits the second blank best, (E) is correct. In (B), *eradication* is related to destruction but isn't usually applied to concrete objects. Besides, Gary certainly wasn't *noncommittal* about the loss, so the first blank for (B) doesn't fit.

4. E

Getting to the Answer: It sounds as though Julio's colleagues don't usually go around grinning and laughing, so the second blank probably means "stern" or "glum."

To explain why Julio's partners suddenly found themselves in such a good mood, we can predict that Julio's good mood was *contagious. Infectious* is a good fit, and *stolid* means "unemotional," so (E) is correct. *Genial* in (B) means "kindly," and *forlorn* in (D) means "alone, isolated, miserable."

5. D

Getting to the Answer: The major contrast in this sentence is one of gender: *female authors* versus *masculine* pen names.

The second blank seems to require something along the lines of *masculine.* That means only (A) and (D) are possible. *Monikers* in (A) are *nicknames,* but *patriarchal* (ruled by men) seems a bit overspecialized in this context. Just to be sure, check the first word in (D) to make sure it's the better choice. *Pseudonyms* are used by people who don't want their work published under their real names. Overall, (D) makes the internal logic tighter: The *novels* written by *female authors were initially published under masculine* pseudonyms because *works by* male *authors* generally received more favorable reviews.

6. C

Getting to the Answer: Moira didn't want to eat the food, but she also didn't want to offend her hosts. The word *practically* suggests she must have disliked the food very much, so the answer will be a very negative word like *revolting.*

(B) is positive, and (D) doesn't seem negative enough. (A), *egregious,* or *conspicuously bad,* doesn't quite fit. You can say "egregious errors" but not "egregious food." *Sodden* means "soaked," but that isn't necessarily bad, so (E) is wrong. The best answer is (C), *inedible,* which means "uneatable."

7. A

Getting to the Answer: If Ando places (A) *artistic,* or (B) *monetary,* or any other interests *above technical practicalities,* the building he designs could be *precarious.*

Most choices would fit in the first blank, but only (A) provides a suitable answer for the second blank: If Ando places artistic interests above *technical practicalities,* it results in *precarious structures. Precarious* means "uncertain, unstable." A *penchant* means "a tendency."

8. D

Getting to the Answer: We can predict that *Napoleon's army* was stuck *in the snow* and "doing badly" as they tried to *retreat* from Moscow. As a result, the retreat became a *rout*, a humiliating retreat.

(D) *foundering* and (E) *tottering* are the best options. (A) *vacillating* means the army was "wavering," which doesn't fit. For the second blank, it makes sense to say the *Russian troops began to* assault the *soldiers,* so (D) is the logical choice. To *upbraid* is to "criticize verbally."

9. B

Getting to the Answer: The *citizen* who is *tried*, or brought to court on criminal charges, is the *defendant*. A jury of your *peers* is a jury of your equals. So it sounds as though *the law does not* dictate the exact way in which *the jurors* should be the equals of *the defendant*.

In (A), *monitor* is not quite what we had predicted, but it might still fit. But *assess* doesn't match the predicted meaning at all. If we plug it into the second blank, the two halves of the sentence no longer connect to each other. An SAT Sentence Completion generally has tight internal logic, but choice (A) doesn't. Choice (C) has the same problem. (D) just doesn't make sense when you plug it into the blanks. That leaves (B) and (E). (B) works better; the function of *the law* is to *specify*, not *predict*. (B) explains that though tradition dictates that a *defendant* be judged by *a jury of her peers,* the law doesn't specify in what way *the jurors* should resemble, or be *peers* of, *the defendant.*

10. A

Getting to the Answer: At first glance, you might think that the blank should be filled by a word like *musical* or *vocal*. But no such word appears in the answer choices. The only choice that tightens up the internal logic of the sentence when you plug it in is *prescribed*. The words *must be* and *has to be* indicate that aspects of *Noh* are strictly dictated or prescribed.

Practice Set Five

Directions: Select the lettered word or set of words that best completes the sentence.

1. Because of the ---- and prolonged nature of the ----, water must be carefully conserved and rationed.

   (A) arid . . . reservoir
   (B) dire . . . forecast
   (C) severe . . . drought
   (D) negligible . . . emergency
   (E) miserly . . . supply

2. The spectacular ---- of the Grand Canyon cannot be fully captured by a two-dimensional ---- such as a photograph.

   (A) periphery . . . benchmark
   (B) vista . . . opportunity
   (C) foliage . . screening
   (D) topography . . representation
   (E) graphics . . likeness

3. Until his defeat by the newcomer, the veteran boxer won most of his bouts by knockouts and had achieved an ---- series of wins.

   (A) inconsequential
   (B) exaggerated
   (C) able-bodied
   (D) unbroken
   (E) observable

4. Although the whale shark is found in equatorial waters around the world, it is ---- encountered by divers because of its low numbers and ---- nature.

   (A) persistently . . . reluctant
   (B) successfully . . . aggressive
   (C) anxiously . . . unfortunate
   (D) constantly . . . indifferent
   (E) rarely . . . solitary

5. Some of the paintings formerly ---- the Italian Renaissance artist are now thought to have been created by one of his students.

   (A) exhibited with
   (B) submitted to
   (C) adapted from
   (D) attributed to
   (E) denied by

6. Although both plants control soil erosion, kudzu disrupts the local ecology by displacing native fauna, while vetiver has no ---- effects.

   (A) foreseeable
   (B) adverse
   (C) domestic
   (D) permanent
   (E) advantageous

KAPLAN

7. Because its bookkeepers altered some figures and completely fabricated others, the company's financial records were entirely ----.

   (A) spurious
   (B) disseminated
   (C) singular
   (D) concealed
   (E) cursory

8. The journalist's ---- to accurately describe events in the region was not attributable to a lack of effort, but to a dearth of ---- and unbiased information.

   (A) willingness . . . prevalent
   (B) failure . . . reliable
   (C) training . . . universal
   (C) hesitation . . . dominant
   (E) incentive . . . clear

9. As ---- as she is original, choreographer Twyla Tharp has created dances for mainstream ballet, Hollywood films, and commercial theater, as well as more offbeat venues.

   (A) charming
   (B) redundant
   (C) versatile
   (D) polished
   (E) rarefied

10. Peach pits, which contain small amounts of the poisonous compound cyanide, are not usually harmful, but, if consumed in sufficient quantities, can be ----.

   (A) acerbic
   (B) superfluous
   (C) virulent
   (D) unpalatable
   (E) multifarious

ANSWERS AND EXPLANATIONS

1. C

Getting to the Answer: You're told that *water must be carefully conserved and rationed because of the prolonged nature of the —*, so the word in the second blank will be something like *water shortage*.

Drought in (C) seems like a perfect match. *Emergency* might also work, so check out the first blanks for (C) and (D). The word in the first blank is connected by *and* to the phrase *prolonged nature*. So the word should be consistent with *prolonged*. You need a word like *serious*. The first word in (C), *severe*, means the same thing as *serious*. Our other contender, (D), has *negligible* in the first blank. *Negligible* means "not serious," so (C) is correct. If you checked out the first blanks in the other choices, you might have been tempted by (A) and (B), *arid* and *dire*. But these two choices don't make sense when you plug the second blank into the sentence. (A) isn't logical because if a reservoir were arid, or completely dry, there would be no water to ration. (B) doesn't explain why water must be rationed. A dire forecast isn't necessarily a forecast of drought;—a forecast of a violent thunderstorm would also be dire.

2. D

Getting to the Answer: What could be *spectacular* about the Grand Canyon? You know it can't be the *foliage* or the *graphics*. After all, there are no trees or graphics in the Grand Canyon. So (C) and (E) are out.

The only choice that makes sense is (D). A *representation* is a "presentation or depiction." One could say that a two-dimensional representation can't capture the spectacular topography of the Grand Canyon.

3. D

Getting to the Answer: Since *the veteran boxer* had *won most of his bouts by knockouts,* you can assume that he was pretty successful.

(D) is the only choice that describes his *series of wins* in a way that suggests success; an unbroken series of victories would be a winning streak with no losses. (A) and (B) are contradicted by information in the sentence itself. (C) may seem to fit in a sentence about a boxer, but what's an *able-bodied series of wins*? (E) makes some sense, since

you could watch someone win lots of fights, but we have to reject it because the sentence is about a boxer who, after winning many fights, finally loses to a newcomer.

4. E

Getting to the Answer: The clue word *although* sets up a contrast between the whale shark's appearance all over the world and the way it's *encountered by divers.* A word like *seldom* would set up the needed contrast. (E) *rarely* is the best fit.

For the second blank, the word should explain why the shark's *nature* makes it hard for humans to spot. *Shy* or *tending to avoid people* would work. (E) *solitary* fits the bill. *Reluctant*, in (A), could be a longshot to fill the second blank, but we don't need to spend time thinking about the other choices, since only (E) fits the first blank.

5. D

Getting to the Answer: This sentence tests your understanding of the word *attributed*, a word often followed by *to*. A painting that's attributed to a Renaissance painter is one "credited to" him, or generally thought to have been painted by him.

The sentence contains a virtual definition of *attributed* in the phrase *thought to have been created by*. The clue words *formerly* and *now* in the sentence signal a contrast between the past and present: The paintings were *formerly* attributed to the artist, but *now* they're thought to have been painted by one of his students.

6. B

Getting to the Answer: *Although* sets up a contrast between *kudzu*, which *disrupts the local ecology*, and *vetiver*, which *has no —effects*. The sentence is comparing the consequences of the two plants.

The missing word refers to kudzu's disruptive ecological effects. Look for a word like *bad* or *negative*. (B) most closely matches. (E) is the opposite of what's needed, and (A) and (D) make no sense. (C) is completely out of context.

7.   A

Getting to the Answer: A good vocabulary will help you figure out this one. The bookkeepers *altered some financial records and completely fabricated others,* so you need a word like *altered* or *falsified*. (A) *spurious* is the only choice that matches. It means false, lacking authenticity. It makes no sense to say the financial records were entirely disseminated or entirely singular, so rule out (B) and (C).

8.   B

Getting to the Answer: The second blank may be easier to fill here, so start with that. The clue word *and* tells you that the missing word in the phrase—*and unbiased information* will be consistent with *unbiased*. So you can predict that the missing word will have a meaning similar to *unbiased,* such as the word *impartial*. (B) reliable and (E) clear are both pretty close to *unbiased,* so let's try them in the first blank.

For the first blank, *the journalist's—to accurately describe events* results from a *dearth* or "lack" of good information. A lack of good information might prevent someone from describing a situation accurately. We can predict a word like *inability* for this blank. The first word in (E), *incentive,* means "motivation," which doesn't match. The first word in (B), *failure,* matches perfectly. *Unbiased* means "impartial, unprejudiced."

9.   C

Getting to the Answer: Since *Twyla Tharp has created* a wide range of *dances* ranging from movies and *mainstream ballet* to *more offbeat* forms, she's a (C) versatile *choreographer*.

Though her work may also be polished, the sentence concerns the range of her activities, not their quality, so (D) is wrong. Someone who works in several *mainstream* areas wouldn't be termed *rarefied,* so (E) is out. Even though several kinds of dance production are mentioned, nothing suggests that they are redundant, so (B) is wrong, too; moreover, *redundant* is a negative term, but the sentence is positive—it praises Tharp's work. Choice (A)'s *charming* sounds okay with the word *original,* but the sentence talks about Tharp's accomplishments as a choreographer, not about her personality.

10.   C

Getting to the Answer: The sentence hinges on knowing what (C) *virulent* means. You're told that certain *poisonous compounds* in *peach pits* are *usually not harmful. But,* the sentence continues, if you eat enough of them, they are—. So you need a word that means "poisonous" or "harmful."

(C) *virulent* fits that definition. If you couldn't figure that out, you could have tried eliminating answer choices. (A) *acerbic* means "sour, harsh," and (D) *unpalatable* means "distasteful," so neither one means *poisonous.* Neither (B) nor (E) makes sense in the blank. If you didn't know *virulent,* you might have known the related word *virus,* a disease-causing agent. So *virulent* might have something to do with disease and harm.

Practice Set Six

Directions: Select the lettered word or set of words that best completes the sentence.

1. Once ----, wolves have been hunted almost to extinction.

   (A) nonexistent
   (B) numerous
   (C) garrulous
   (D) captive
   (E) natural

2. The benefits of the exchange program are ----, with both countries acquiring new technical insights and manufacturing techniques.

   (A) promised
   (B) inclusive
   (C) blatant
   (D) mutual
   (E) applicable

3. The author monotonously catalogues the ---- points of fashion history, while omitting the details that might ---- the reader's interest.

   (A) vital . . . acquire
   (B) trivial . . . enhance
   (C) salient . . . offend
   (D) undisputed . . . limit
   (E) essential . . . rescind

4. The Morgan Library in New York provides a ---- environment in which scholars work amidst tapestries, paintings, stained-glass windows, and hand-crafted furniture.

   (A) realistic
   (B) frugal
   (C) sumptuous
   (D) friendly
   (E) practical

5. The eruption ---- tons of mineral-rich volcanic ash, restoring to the soil nutrients long since ---- by decades of farming.

   (A) deposited . . . depleted
   (B) clumped . . . harvested
   (C) removed . . . secreted
   (D) displaced . . . entrenched
   (E) regained . . . fertilized

6. The fullest edition of the letters of H. P. Lovecraft consists of five volumes; however, only a small fraction of Lovecraft's ---- correspondence has ever been published.

   (A) laconic
   (B) unknown
   (C) voluminous
   (D) verbal
   (E) popular

7. The candidate denounced as ---- his rival's solution to the problem of unemployment, but offered no ---- alternative.

    (A) arbitrary . . . altruistic

    (B) elitist . . . virulent

    (C) salutary . . . absolute

    (D) convoluted . . . provincial

    (E) unworkable . . . viable

8. The government decided against ---- assemblies and strikes organized by the opposition, fearing that such a measure might ---- armed conflict.

    (A) continuing . . . multiply

    (B) intimidating . . . interrupt

    (C) banning . . . precipitate

    (D) granting . . . reapportion

    (E) welcoming . . . voice

9. Prime Minister Neville Chamberlain of Great Britain adopted a ---- approach to Hitler, even accepting Germany's annexation of Austria.

    (A) hasty

    (B) precarious

    (C) haughty

    (D) conciliatory

    (E) dependent

10. Medieval kings customarily gave away valuables and property, expecting that their ---- would ensure the ---- of their vassals.

    (A) imprudence . . . probity

    (B) largess . . . fidelity

    (C) adaptation . . . integrity

    (D) formality . . . sophistry

    (E) haste . . . mirth

ANSWERS AND EXPLANATIONS

1. B

Getting to the Answer: *Once,* the first word in the sentence, is an important structural clue. It signals that there's a contrast between the status of wolves at an earlier time (before excessive hunting) and the status of wolves now (almost extinct).

To set up the contrast, the word in the blank has to mean something like *abundant*. Choice (B) *numerous* is the most logical option.

2. D

Getting to the Answer: Since both countries are acquiring new technical insights and manufacturing techniques in their exchange program, they are benefiting from each other. We can predict that the blank word should mean something like *shared* or *reciprocal*, since the benefits go both ways.

Choice (D) *mutual* matches this prediction perfectly. Don't be fooled by (E) *applicable*. The technical insights and techniques may well be applicable somewhere, but we're being asked to describe the success of the exchange program, not the status of the manufacturing techniques.

3. B

Getting to the Answer: The clue word here is *monotonously*. It means "without variety or variation." If the author is *monotonously cataloguing the—points of fashion history,* we can safely predict that those points are going to be *boring* or another such negative word.

(B) *trivial* best fits the description. In the second part of the sentence, *while* is another clue. It signals a contrast between the boring *cataloguing* and the omitted details that *might* have—*the reader's interest.* Look for a second-blank word that means something like *increased.* (B) again makes the most sense: *The author monotonously catalogues the* trivial *points while omitting the details that might* enhance *the reader's interest. Salient* (C) means "striking, prominent," and *rescind* (E) means "to take back."

4. C

Getting to the Answer: What word would you use to describe an environment that's full of tapestries, paintings, stained-glass windows, and hand-crafted furniture? Probably something like *fancy* or *elegant.*

The closest choice to this prediction is (C) *sumptuous.* It doesn't make sense to describe such an environment as (A) *realistic* or (B) *frugal.* And, while the library's atmosphere may well be (D) *friendly* or (E) *practical,* those choices don't make sense in the context. *Sumptuous* in (C) means "luxurious."

5. A

Getting to the Answer: When a volcano erupts, it ejects lava, ash, and other material. So it's unlikely that the volcano (B) *clumped* or (C) *removed* tons of volcanic ash.

Choice (E) *regained* means the volcano was sucking ash into itself instead of spewing it out—an unlikely situation. This leaves (A) and (D). Choice (A) sounds good: The eruption *deposited* mineral-rich ash, restoring to the soil nutrients long since *depleted* by decades of farming. In (D), the eruption could conceivably *displace* ("push out or move") ash, but the second-blank word doesn't make sense. If nutrients were long since *entrenched* ("established, settled") in the ground, there would be no need to restore them to the soil. (A) is the best answer.

6. C

Getting to the Answer: The clue word *however* sets up a contrast between *the fullest edition* and the *small fraction of correspondence* that's *been published.* This tells us that a great deal of *Lovecraft's—correspondence* remains unpublished, so fill the blank with a word like *abundant.*

(C) *voluminous* best completes the sentence's meaning. (E) *popular* is a weak second best. (A) *laconic* means "uncommunicative, using few words."

7. E

Getting to the Answer: If the candidate denounced his rival's solution as—, the first blank will be negative. Since four of the five answer choices have negative first words, it will be hard to eliminate possibilities. In a two-blank sentence, you can choose which blank to do first, so start with the blank that's easier to fill. Here, that's the second blank.

If the candidate offered no—alternative, we can infer that the candidate offered no good or workable alternative. (E) *viable* ("workable, achievable") best matches this prediction. Plugging the first word of (E) into the sentence, we see that it makes sense too: The candidate denounced as *unworkable* his rival's solution, but offered no *viable* alternative himself. No other choice makes as much sense.

8. C

Getting to the Answer: The second half of the sentence follows directly from the first: The government decided against doing something because it feared armed conflict.

(C) best completes the logic of the sentence: The government decided against *banning* assemblies and strikes because they feared such a move would *precipitate* armed conflict. *Precipitate* means "instigate, bring about."

9. D

Getting to the Answer: Since *Chamberlain even accepted Germany's annexation of* Austria, he probably adopted a nonaggressive, accepting approach to Hitler. His approach to German aggression would not have been tough or militant.

The choice that comes closest to this prediction is (D) *conciliatory*. It means "tending to pacify or accommodate." Choice (B) *precarious*, means "uncertain," so that word wouldn't work.

10. B

Getting to the Answer: The *kings gave away valuables and property, expecting* something back from their subjects. The first blank relates to the action of giving away all these nice things, so we can predict a word like *generosity*. As for what they expected in return, we might predict something like *respect*, *happiness*, or *loyalty*. So the two words need to be positive.

Choice (B) has two distinctly positive words: *largess* and *fidelity*. *Largess* means "generosity," and *fidelity* means "faithfulness, loyalty." Plugging them in, they work perfectly: *The kings gave away property, expecting that their* largess *would ensure the* fidelity *of their subjects.* You may have been tempted by (D) *formality*, since the kings' generosity could be seen as a formal exercise. But that's a stretch. Besides, if you check out the second blank, *sophistry* ("misleading argumentative style") doesn't make sense.

Practice Set Seven

Directions: Select the lettered word or set of words that best completes the sentence.

1. Unlike her first novel, which received kudos for its ----, her second effort was widely criticized as uninventive and predictable.

   (A) monotony
   (B) originality
   (C) conventionality
   (D) prudence
   (E) literacy

2. Medieval alchemists tried to attain wealth by ---- lead and other base metals into gold.

   (A) transforming
   (B) encouraging
   (C) replicating
   (D) displacing
   (E) copying

3. The dance critic was ---- in her praise of the company, describing the choreography in glowing terms and ---- the poise and elegance of every dancer.

   (A) agreeable . . . insulting
   (B) vague . . . demonstrating
   (C) conciliatory . . . relating
   (D) timorous . . . describing
   (E) effusive . . . extolling

4. The British social philosopher Thomas Malthus predicted that population growth would eventually ---- world food production, resulting in massive famine and political unrest.

   (A) pressure
   (B) forbid
   (C) resist
   (D) surpass
   (E) confront

5. Bird species ---- to this island were exterminated by feral cats, ---- of pets abandoned here decades ago by sailors.

   (A) provincial . . . competitors
   (B) harmless . . . liberators
   (C) indigenous . . . descendants
   (D) unusual . . . signals
   (E) benign . . . ancestors

6. Soon after adopting a syllabic system of writing, the Greeks made the final step to a phonetic alphabet, dividing the consonants from the vowels and writing each ----.

   (A) formally
   (B) abstractly
   (C) separately
   (D) mysteriously
   (E) accurately

7. In the early nineteenth century, some British agricultural workers felt that newly invented farm machinery threatened their jobs, and they ---- their fear of ---- by smashing machines.

    (A) lessened . . . injustice

    (B) aggravated . . . landlords

    (C) displayed . . . technology

    (D) accommodated . . . equipment

    (E) magnified . . . exploitation

8. The restaurant manager, who had ---- provided crayons and paper tablecloths for the amusement of small children, found that adult patrons were equally ---- the opportunity to express themselves.

    (A) aggressively . . . delighted by

    (B) impulsively . . . anxious about

    (C) warily . . . shrewd about

    (D) initially . . . enthralled with

    (E) imaginatively . . . alarmed by

9. Before it became involved in the Second World War, the United States held to a policy of neutrality, setting up legislation explicitly ---- the sale of weapons to ---- nations.

    (A) repealing . . . expatriate

    (B) forbidding . . . belligerent

    (C) enacting . . . dependent

    (D) prompting . . . arbitrary

    (E) defending . . . isolated

10. By 1918, the painter André Derain had ---- both Cubism and the new abstract art in favor of a more ---- approach based on the example of the old masters.

    (A) compiled . . . reticent

    (B) vexed . . . indulgent

    (C) thwarted . . . expressive

    (D) discarded . . . tentative

    (E) repudiated . . . traditional

ANSWERS AND EXPLANATIONS

1. B

Getting to the Answer: This sentence contains the word *kudos,* which might have thrown you. It means "praise, honor." But, as in most Sentence Completions, you can get the answer if you focus on the logic of the sentence.

Notice the clue word *unlike.* It signals a contrast. If her first novel is *unlike* her *uninventive and predictable* second novel, her first novel must be the opposite. It must have had (B) *originality*.

2. A

Getting to the Answer: You've got a tough vocabulary word in the sentence: *alchemists*. (In the Middle Ages, alchemists combined chemistry and philosophy to turn base metals into gold. "You can work around it, though, if you don't know what it means. The *alchemists tried to attain wealth by — lead into gold*.

Choices (C) and (E) won't work because you don't replicate or copy *lead into gold,* you transform it. The only logical answer is (A) *transforming*.

3. E

Getting to the Answer: The clue here is the word *glowing*. Since *the critic described the choreography in glowing terms,* she was —— *in her praise.* Look for a positive word in the first blank that means *enthusiastic.*

You can quickly eliminate (B) *vague*, (C) *conciliatory*, and (D) *timorous*. *Conciliatory* means appeasing, and *timorous* means meek. That leaves (A) *agreeable* and (E) *effusive*, so let's try (A) and (E) in the second blank. In the second part of the sentence, the connecting word *and* indicates consistency, so the second blank must also be positive. Look for an answer choice that means she praised the poise and elegance of the dancers. (A) *insulting* is obviously wrong, but *extolling* is a positive word, so (E) is correct.

4. D

Getting to the Answer: Don't be intimidated by the serious subject matter. Just take the sentence apart and look for clues.

The biggest clue is the word *famine*. When the relationship between *population growth* and *world food production* changes in some way, the result is *famine*. You know that *famine* happens when there's not enough food for a large number of people to live on. Or, as the sentence puts it, *population growth would eventually* exceed *food production, resulting in massive famine.* The answer choice that best matches this prediction is (D) *surpass*. It means "to exceed."

5. C

Getting to the Answer: Don't give up if you don't know the word *feral*. Instead, read this two-blank sentence looking for one blank that leaps out as predictable. Start working with that one, and use it to rule out choices for the second blank.

Start with the second blank. You're told that *bird species were exterminated by cats.* These cats had something to do with *pets abandoned here decades ago by sailors.* That probably means the cats were (C) *descendants* of pets. But check out the other choices. Since the pets were abandoned on the island decades ago, the cats couldn't logically be (B) *liberators*, (D) *signals*, or (E) *ancestors* of pets. And it's unlikely they'd be (A) *competitors*, either. (C) makes the most sense in the second blank. Now try the first blank. "Bird species indigenous to the island were exterminated by the descendants of abandoned pets"—that seems to make sense. A quick glance at the other choices confirms that (C) is right.

6. C

Getting to the Answer: This fairly easy sentence contains the clue word *and*. Since the phrase *dividing the consonants from the vowels* is joined to *writing each* with the word *and,* the two phrases must agree with each other. So whatever goes in the blank must go along with the idea of dividing consonants and vowels.

The choice that makes sense is (C) *separately*: *The Greeks divided consonants from vowels and wrote each separately.* The rest of the choices don't fit the context. For instance, (E) *accurately* might have seemed sensible, but the whole point is that the Greeks divided up their letters, not that they wrote precisely.

7. C

Getting to the Answer: Again the clue word *and* indicates consistency throughout the sentence: The workers felt threatened, *and* their fear led them to smash machines. Their fear of what? Probably a fear of (C) *technology*. (C)'s first blank works well, too: The farm *workers* displayed *their fear of* technology *by smashing machines.*

Check the other answers just to make sure they don't work. (A) *injustice* and (E) *exploitation* might seem to go along with the subject. But there's nothing in the sentence to indicate the workers *fear* those things. Besides, in both cases the first blanks don't fit. (C) works best.

8. D

Getting to the Answer: In the first half, you read that *the crayons and paper tablecloths* had been *provided for the amusement of small children.* In the last half, you read that adults were *equally —— about the opportunity to express themselves.* The clue word *equally* tells you the adults felt the same way as the kids. So the adults must have been equally (A) *delighted* by the opportunity, or (D) *enthralled* ("enchanted, captivated") with the opportunity.

Now try the first words in (A) and (D). In (A), *aggressively* doesn't fit. Why would a restaurant aggressively provide crayons and paper to kids? But (D) *initially* works fine. The restaurant, which had initially *provided crayons and paper* just for kids, *found that adults were equally* enthralled with *the opportunity to express themselves.*

9. B

Getting to the Answer: If the United States is practicing *neutrality*, you can predict it would forbid *the sale of weapons* to *nations* taking part in the war.

The answer choice that matches that prediction is (B): *Holding to its policy of neutrality,* the United States *set up legislation* forbidding *the sale of weapons to* belligerent *nations.* (C) *enacting*, (D) *prompting*, and (E) *defending* suggest that the United States was encouraging the sale of weapons. (A) *repealing* implies that legislation already existed and was being overturned.

10. E

Getting to the Answer: Two important phrases clue you in to the sentence's meaning: *in favor of* and *based on the example of the old masters.* The second blank looks easier, so let's deal with it first.

If Derain's new approach is *based on the example of the old masters,* you can predict it must be old-fashioned. That looks like (E) *traditional*. (C) *expressive* might seem to work, but you're not told that the old masters were expressive—you just know they were old. Let's try (C) and (E) in the first blank to make sure. (C) *thwarted* ("obstructed") won't work. It's not clear how Derain was hindering or obstructing Cubism and abstract art, and it's not correct English to say he hindered one style of art *in favor of* another. Looking at (E) *repudiated* ("rejected"), this makes sense. Derain rejected abstract art *in favor of* a more traditional approach.

Practice Set Eight

> **Directions: Select the lettered word or set of words that best completes the sentence.**

1. Rosa embarked on a ---- of strenuous exercise to build up the ---- to complete a marathon.

   (A) program . . . lethargy
   (B) regimen . . . endurance
   (C) pursuit . . . stamina
   (D) commitment . . . strength
   (E) complex . . . rhythm

2. An editorial praised the generosity of an anonymous ----, who had donated over a million dollars and several priceless paintings to the college.

   (A) mercenary
   (B) agnostic
   (C) curmudgeon
   (D) benefactor
   (E) harbinger

3. Some historians claim that the concept of courtly love is a ---- that dates from the age of chivalry, while others believe it has more ---- origins.

   (A) relic . . . simultaneous
   (B) notion . . . ancient
   (C) memento . . . discovered
   (D) period . . . documented
   (E) suitor . . . amorous

4. The general was ---- of low morale among his troops, but still refused to ---- his command.

   (A) informed . . . bequeath
   (B) appreciative . . . subvert
   (C) fearful . . . proscribe
   (D) wary . . . deprecate
   (E) cognizant . . . relinquish

5. In the wake of several tragic accidents caused by wind shear, major airports installed new radar systems ---- enough to ---- this complex atmospheric phenomenon.

   (A) generalized . . . track
   (B) lamentable . . . honor
   (C) flimsy . . . withstand
   (D) sophisticated . . . detect
   (E) sturdy . . . demolish

6. Although marine engineers claimed that its hull was ----, the Titanic sank after hitting an iceberg.

   (A) amorphous
   (B) equivocal
   (C) preeminent
   (D) impenetrable
   (E) viscous

7. Based on factual ---- rather than conjecture, Dr. Singh's report will ---- previously held views about the nesting habits of the rare species.

(A) conjecture . . . ignore

(B) evidence . . . refute

(C) theory . . . negate

(D) projections . . . corroborate

(E) documentation . . . inspire

8. As they helped the community recover from the storm's devastation, the apparently ---- relief workers worked around the clock with an energy that never seemed to wane.

(A) dexterous

(B) indefatigable

(C) obsequious

(D) syncopated

(E) transcendent

9. Although others found them impressive, Lewis found Senator Gantry's speeches ---- and believed that they ---- the real issues with elaborate but meaningless rhetoric.

(A) bombastic . . . obscured

(B) verbose . . . clarified

(C) captivating . . . defined

(D) exuberant . . . misconstrued

(E) persuasive . . . illuminated

10. The characters in Jane Austen's novels never argue; rather, they employ more subtle verbal weapons: irony and ----.

(A) candor

(B) humility

(C) innuendo

(D) farce

(E) pantomime

ANSWERS AND EXPLANATIONS

1.   B

Getting to the Answer: Let's concentrate on the second blank first. What do you need *to complete a marathon,* a very long race? You need endurance, stamina, or strength, so (B), (C), and (D) are all possibilities.

(A) is out because *lethargy* (sleepiness) would slow you down in a race. Choice (E) *rhythm* might be of some value in a race, but it's not essential. As for the first blank, you embark on a regimen of exercise, but you don't embark on a (C) *pursuit* or a (D) *commitment* of exercise.

2.   D

Getting to the Answer: You're looking for a very positive word, since this anonymous person is being praised for his or her generous donations.

The most positive answer choice is (D) *benefactor*. No other answer choice makes sense. Hint: *Benefactor* contains the roots BENE, "good," and FAC, "make or do." A benefactor is someone who does good things for someone else's sake.

3.   B

Getting to the Answer: The words *while others believe* signal contrast. If *some historians claim that the concept of courtly love dates from* a specific period—*the age of chivalry*—the others must say it has earlier or more recent origins.

Only *ancient* in choice (B) relates to time and provides the necessary contrast. As for the first blank, *the concept of courtly love* can't be a (A) *relic,* (C) *memento,* (D) *period,* or (E) *suitor;* it can only be a notion.

4.   E

Getting to the Answer: *But* is a signal of contrast. If *morale was low among his troops,* what should the general have done about *his command?*

The general might have *relinquished* ("given up") his command, choice (E). No alternative makes sense. Checking out the first blank, if *the general was* cognizant ("aware") *of low morale among his troops,* that would have been reason to do something about it. (E) is the answer.

5.   D

Getting to the Answer: Since *wind shear* is a *complex atmospheric phenomenon,* which caused *several tragic accidents,* the radar systems installed by the airports need to be technologically advanced. They're certainly not (B) *lamentable,* (C) *flimsy,* or (A) *generalized.* They're probably (D) *sophisticated.* But they could also be (E) *sturdy.*

So check out the second word for these two choices. (E)'s second word doesn't work; a radar system can't demolish *wind shear.* You'd expect it to detect *wind* shear, so the answer is (D).

6.   D

Getting to the Answer: *Although* signals a contrast; we want a word that suggests why marine engineers would not have expected the Titanic to sink.

The best answer is (D) *impenetrable.* It means "incapable of being penetrated."

Amorphous in (A) means shapeless, and *equivocal* in (B) means ambiguous, doubtful.

7.   B

Getting to the Answer: In the first blank, something factual is contrasted with conjecture; (B) *evidence* and (E) *documentation* are both possible answers.

In the second blank, (E) doesn't make sense; you can't *inspire* previously held views. But something could certainly *refute* ("to prove false") previously held views, so choice (B) is correct.

8.   B

Getting to the Answer: The definition of the missing word is implicit in the sentence; we're looking for a word that means able to *work around the clock with an energy that never seems to wane.*

That's the meaning of (B) *indefatigable.* More simply put, it means "tireless." (E) *transcendent,* whcih means "supreme," is too vague here. So (B) is the answer.

9.   A

Getting to the Answer: *Although* indicates a contrast with *impressive*. We want negative words for both blanks.

For the first blank, (A) *bombastic* and (B) *verbose* are negative. *Bombastic* means "inflated, pretentious," and *verbose* means "overly wordy." For the second blank, (A) *obscured* and (D) *misconstrued* are negative. Only choice (A) provides suitable negative answers for both blanks, so it's correct.

10. C

Getting to the Answer: The key word is *subtle*.

(D) *farce* is not subtle, it's a form of obvious humor. (A) *candor*, or complete honesty, isn't subtle either. (B) *humility* isn't a verbal weapon, and it's not a subtle alternative to arguing. And (E) *pantomime* isn't verbal at all, it's an art form consisting of silent gestures and movements. The answer is choice (C) *innuendo*. It means "hinting, indirectly stating something."

Practice Set Nine

1. The famous movie star regarded her mountain cabin as ----; she felt safe there from the annoying ---- of reporters and photographers.

    (A) a retreat . . . writings
    (B) a liability . . . prying
    (C) an excuse . . . adulation
    (D) a haven . . . intrusions
    (E) an occupation . . . attentions

2. The congressman promised that he would consider all viewpoints and that he was willing, not only to discuss his proposal, but to ---- it.

    (A) amend
    (B) state
    (C) silence
    (D) accept
    (E) approve

3. The ombudsman was critical of the city's law enforcement agencies for the ---- of their efforts to stem the increase in criminal activity.

    (A) renewal
    (B) inadequacy
    (C) rejection
    (D) ratification
    (E) model

4. The review board ruled that the intern's behavior had been ----; he had violated the high standards required of members of the profession.

    (A) usual
    (B) exemplary
    (C) laudatory
    (D) unethical
    (E) ineffective

5. Critics ---- the play and described the playwright as prolific, brilliant, and ----.

    (A) acclaimed . . . incisive
    (B) berated . . . entertaining
    (C) praised . . . prosaic
    (D) welcomed . . . derivative
    (E) censured . . . imaginative

6. Because of her ---- views, the professor frequently found herself defending traditional values and the status quo in arguments with her more radical students.

    (A) liberal
    (B) extreme
    (C) conservative
    (D) unorthodox
    (E) economic

7. The dramatist lived ---- life and his fame was
   achieved ----; few people had ever heard of him,
   or his works, until several years after his death.

   (A) a hapless . . . effortlessly

   (B) an obscure . . . posthumously

   (C) an infamous . . . gradually

   (D) a monastic . . . publicly

   (E) an eventful . . . prematurely

8. Despite his usual sensitivity to criticism, the commissioner did not ---- his position on the issue,
   even after he was ---- in the press.

   (A) develop . . . approached

   (B) abandon . . . ridiculed

   (C) alter . . . acclaimed

   (D) explain . . . covered

   (E) relinquish . . . substituted

9. In his later work, the artist finally attained a maturity of style utterly ---- his early, amateurish
   pieces.

   (A) descriptive of

   (B) superseded by

   (C) absent from

   (D) celebrated in

   (E) featured in

10. The ambitions of tyrants are not ----, but excited,
    by partial concessions; that is why we must be ----
    in opposing their demands.

    (A) realized . . . clement

    (B) stimulated . . . adamant

    (C) satisfied . . . yielding

    (D) appeased . . . resolute

    (E) inhibited . . . generous

ANSWERS AND EXPLANATIONS

1. D

Getting to the Answer: The semicolon is important here. The clause that follows the semicolon will elaborate on, and possibly help define, what has gone before. The real clue to filling both blanks lies in the phrase *she felt safe there*. It is clear that the first blank means a "safe place," while the second means something negative that the movie star wishes to avoid.

(D) should have jumped out as the answer. The cabin is a haven from the intrusions of reporters and photographers. In (A), *retreat* is good, but then *writings* doesn't work. (B) is wrong because *liability* ("a disadvantage or handicap") doesn't fit the meaning of the sentence. Both words in (C) are way off. (E)'s second word, *attentions*, is fine, but an *occupation* is wrong.

2. A

Getting to the Answer: The structural clue in this sentence is the expression *not only . . . but*. The congressman was willing not only to discuss his proposal, but also to do something else consistent with his promise to consider all viewpoints.

Choice (B) is incorrect. *State* is too close in meaning to *discuss*. (A) *amend* is the answer. It means "to correct or change."

3. B

Getting to the Answer: You don't need to know what an *ombudsman* is to answer this one. (If you're curious, though, it means someone who settles people's complaints against a public agency.) What would *law enforcement* officials be criticized for? Probably their failure to do enough to fight crime.

(C), (D), and (E) do not make sense right off the bat. A *ratification* (D) is a "formal approval." As for (A) *renewal*, it contradicts the meaning of the sentence. (B) is correct: The inadequacy *of their efforts to stem the increase in criminal activity*.

4. D

Getting to the Answer: The semicolon is the clue here. What follows it will elaborate on what came before it.

Clearly, the intern's behavior was very bad; the word *violated* tells you that. You can eliminate (A) because usual behavior is not in violation of standards. Eliminate (B) and (C) also. Being ineffective is bad, but it's not necessarily violating any standards, so (E) is wrong.

5. A

Getting to the Answer: If you noticed the clue word *and*, you might have found it easier to work with the second blank first. *And* tells you that the word in the second blank has to be positive, to go along with *prolific* and *brilliant*.

Once you've established that, you can eliminate (C) *prosaic* and (D) *derivative*. They mean "dull and unimaginative," and "ordinary, derivative: taken from some original source," respectively. The second words in (A), (B), and (E) will work, so let's try their first-blank words. Clearly, the critics liked the play, so we need a positive word here. *Acclaimed*, in (A), is the only positive first-blank choice, and the only one that works when plugged in, so it's correct.

6. C

Getting to the Answer: *Radical* in the political sense means "desiring radical reforms." If the *professor* defended tradition in arguments with *radical students*, her views must be the opposite of radical. They must be conservative. So (C) is correct.

(A) *liberal* is not sufficiently different from *radical* to be the answer. (B) and (D) don't make sense either; a person with *extreme* or *unorthodox* ("unconventional") views may or may not defend tradition. Finally, saying that the professor's views were *economic* (E) doesn't explain why she would defend *the status quo*.

7. B

Getting to the Answer: In sentences whose clauses are separated by a semicolon, read the part that doesn't contain the blanks carefully. Often the clue to filling the blanks lies there. Since *few had heard* of the dramatist, you can predict that he lived a quiet or secluded life. The word in the second blank describes how his fame was achieved, so it will mean something like "after his death."

(A) makes no sense. You wouldn't say that the dramatist lived a *hapless* ("unlucky") life and that his fame was achieved *effortlessly*. When you plug the other choices in, you'll find them equally unworkable.

8. B

Getting to the Answer: The word *despite* tells you what direction the sentence will take. You can predict that, this time, the commissioner wasn't so sensitive to criticism. He did not change his position on the issue just because of the censure it brought him.

For the first blank, we need a word like *change*. (B), (C), and (E) all might work. Of these three choices, let's try to fill the second blank. We're looking here for something like *criticized*. (C) *acclaimed* means "praised," so eliminate it. (E) *substituted* doesn't mean "criticized." By process of elimination, (B) is right. It makes sense to say, *he did not abandon his position, even after he was* ridiculed *in the press.*

9. C

Getting to the Answer: The opening phrase of the sentence, *in his later work*, and the concluding words, *his early, amateurish pieces*, tell us that a comparison is being drawn between the two stages of the artist's career. We are told that he attained a *maturity of style*—something that we might expect to come with age and therefore not to have been present in his early work. (C), *absent from*, is consistent with this idea.

(A) is wrong because it contradicts the sense of the sentence: A mature style wouldn't be *descriptive of* early, amateurish works. In (B), *superseded by* ("replaced by") is clearly wrong. You'd expect more mature art to supersede amateur art, not the other way around.

10. D

Getting to the Answer: The word *not* is an important clue in filling the first blank. It suggests that the missing word will be the opposite of *excited*. So you can predict a word such as *calmed*.

That eliminates (B) at once. (A) and (E) can also be ruled out since their first words aren't anywhere near *calmed*. That leaves (C) *satisfied* and (D) *appeased*. So let's try their second-blank choices. *Yielding* (C) is wrong. The idea is that since *partial concessions* encourage tyrants to push for more, we must be strong *in opposing their demands*. (D)'s *resolute* is the only answer that makes sense. It means "bold, determined."

Practice Set Ten

Directions: Select the lettered word or set of words that best completes the sentence.

1. Generally, fund-raising parties are quite labor-intensive and not very cost-effective; in other words, putting in a great deal of ---- doesn't mean you'll ---- a great deal of income.

   (A) restraint . . . obtain
   (B) effort . . . generate
   (C) management . . . spend
   (D) reception . . . limit
   (E) materials . . . lose

2. The leader of the task force on food quality deplored the fact that her efforts at investigation were ----, largely because of a lack of ---- between task force members and the health departments under investigation.

   (A) final . . . disagreement
   (B) persistent . . . energy
   (C) successful . . . resistance
   (D) challenged . . . discussion
   (E) futile . . . cooperation

3. Scientists had incorrectly assumed that parasites were primitive and ---- life forms; further research has revealed that parasites are actually quite ----.

   (A) uncomplicated . . . complex
   (B) viable . . . unproven
   (C) mobile . . . remote
   (D) vigorous . . . unscientific
   (E) humorous . . . inaccurate

4. Though people often think of them as ---- carnivores, many species of piranha are vegetarian.

   (A) nomadic
   (B) lugubrious
   (C) voracious
   (D) covetous
   (E) exotic

5. On the Serengeti Plain, gazelles ---- from place to place in search of food until forced to run from hungry ---- like lions.

   (A) migrate . . . reprobates
   (B) saunter . . . predators
   (C) ramble . . . insurgents
   (D) falter . . . carnivores
   (E) meander . . . tyrants

6. Inflation has made the cost of consumer goods so ---- that most people can barely afford to buy basic food items.

   (A) insignificant
   (B) dubious
   (C) coercive
   (D) exorbitant
   (E) repugnant

7. In the 19th century, a number of ---- farming communities were founded in the United States by groups of people who sought to create ideal societies.

   (A) utopian
   (B) mawkish
   (C) decorous
   (D) venerable
   (E) surreptitious

8. Although the applicant was well qualified, she wasn't even considered for the job because the ---- way in which she boasted of her past accomplishments seemed ---- to the interviewer.

   (A) awkward . . . haughty
   (B) candid . . . optimistic
   (C) exemplary . . . antagonistic
   (D) pompous . . . excessive
   (E) effusive . . . frugal

9. Yeats's poetry became steadily more elaborate and more ---- during the 1890s; his audience found his poems increasingly difficult to interpret.

   (A) laconic
   (B) inscrutable
   (C) effusive
   (D) lyrical
   (E) euphonious

10. Even if ---- life exists elsewhere in the universe, we humans may never know it, since it may be impossible for us to ---- with these alien beings.

    (A) avaricious . . . confer
    (B) prodigal . . . reside
    (C) sentient . . . communicate
    (D) lachrymose . . . traipse
    (E) extraneous . . . exit

ANSWERS AND EXPLANATIONS

1. B

Getting to the Answer: The suggestion made in this sentence is straightforward: The energy spent on fund-raising parties does not always match the income that results from them. If you have trouble, plug in the answer choices one at a time and listen to the logic of the sentence.

(A) doesn't work: Putting in *restraint* doesn't mean you'll *obtain* income. Move on to (B): *Putting in* effort *doesn't mean you'll* generate *income*. That sounds sensible, and it follows through on the idea expressed in the first part of the sentence. (B) is the answer. But continue to check the others just to make sure. In (C), *putting in* management *and* spend*ing income* sounds funny. In (D), *reception* has nothing to do with limiting income.

2. E

Getting to the Answer: In the first part of the sentence, the verb *deplored* lets us know that the first blank will be a negative word. So, we can predict that the task force leader must have regretted that her efforts were "disregarded" or "useless."

We can immediately rule out (A), (B), and (C), because they're not really negative. That leaves (D) and (E). As for their second words. (D) is too vague: Why would the leader's efforts be challenged because of a lack of *discussion*? (E) makes more sense. *Efforts at investigation were* futile *because of a lack of* cooperation *between task force members and* those *under investigation.*

3. A

Getting to the Answer: You know that the parasites were assumed to be *primitive and —— life forms*. So whatever goes in the first blank must go along with the word *primitive*.

The first word will be something like *simple*. In the second blank, the parasites are *actually quite ——*. So we are looking for a word like *complex*. That means (A) is right. *Life forms* first thought to be *primitive* and uncomplicated have been *revealed* to be quite complex.

4. C

Getting to the Answer: The clue is the word *although*. We need a word that is consistent with the *piranha's* image as a *carnivore,* yet contrasts with the reality that many piranhas eat only plants.

(C) *voracious* works best. It means "greedy, having a huge appetite." No other choice makes sense. If you knew that piranhas were tropical fish, you might have fallen for (E), but piranhas' *exotic* nature has nothing to do with their diet.

5. B

Getting to the Answer: A number of the first-blank words look possible here, so it's easiest to start on the second blank.

Of the second words, only two are real possibilities. The *lions* are either (B) *predators* or (D) *carnivores*. Checking (B) and (D)'s first words, we see that only (B) works, since gazelles wouldn't *falter* from place to place.

6. D

Getting to the Answer: Since *most people can barely afford to buy basic food items,* we can predict that inflation has made the cost of consumer goods extremely expensive.

The best choice is (D) *exorbitant*. It means "excessive or costly." (B) *dubious* means "doubtful."

7. A

Getting to the Answer: A virtual definition of the word in the blank is found in the sentence: "ideal societies."

The only choice that makes sense is (A) *utopian* farming communities. It means "idealistic or visionary." (B) *mawkish* means "sickeningly sentimental."

8. D

Getting to the Answer: *Although* implies contrast. Even though *the applicant was well qualified,* there was something wrong with the way she *boasted* about her *accomplishments*. So the first blank must be filled by a negative word.

Looking at the first words, we can use only (A) *awkward* or (D) *pompous* ("arrogant"). But of these two in the second blank, only (D) makes sense. If she had boasted *awkwardly*, that probably wouldn't have seemed *haughty* to the interviewer. But if she had boasted *pompously*, that could indeed seem *excessive*.

9. B

Getting to the Answer: There are two significant clues here. The first is the word *and,* which tells us that the word in the blank will continue the idea expressed by the adjective *elaborate,* that *Yeats's poetry* became more complex. Secondly, the semicolon suggests that an explanation of the missing word will follow in the second part of the sentence, which goes on to tell us that people had difficulty interpreting his poems. We should look, therefore, for a word that means "difficult to understand."

(B) *inscrutable* is the answer. It means "difficult or impossible to understand or interpret." No other choice makes sense. (A), (C), and (E) would make Yeats's poetry difficult to understand. *Laconic* means "using few words," and *effusive* means "expressing emotions in an unrestrained way."

10. C

Getting to the Answer: Assuming some alien intelligence exists, why might humans never know it? Logically, it must be because we can't (C) *communicate* with the alien life forms.

(C) works: If *sentient* ("conscious") life exists, humans might never know it because we would be unable to communicate with that life. In (A), *confer* might be possible, but *avaricious* ("greedy") wouldn't fit.

Reading Comprehension

Chapter Four: **Introduction to SAT Reading Comprehension**

The Reading Comprehension section of the SAT tests your ability to read passages quickly and perceptively. It also tests your understanding of how words are used in context. You'll be asked questions about the overall point of the passage, the author's point of view, the details, and what's implied. In addition, you'll need to compare and contrast related passages.

THE STRUCTURE

There are two types of reading comprehensive passage on the SAT—short and long—and they appear in all the Critical Reading sections. After each passage, you will be asked a series of questions. For the short passages, it will be 2 or 3 questions. For the long passages, it will be around 6–12 questions. The kinds of questions that appear for both will be the same; it is only the passage length that will differ.

The reading comprehension passages come in four subjects: Humanities, Social Science, Science, and Narrative. As you might expect, Humanities and Social Science passages tend to be easier than Science and Narrative. But don't worry: All the information you'll need to answer the questions will be located in the text.

THE FORMAT

Get familiar with the directions now, so you won't waste precious time on Test Day:

> **Each passage below is followed by questions based on its content. Answer the questions on the basis of what is <u>stated</u> or <u>implied</u> in each passage and in any introductory material that may be provided.**

After the directions, you'll see several reading passages. Some will be very short, while others will be fairly long. You will also see "paired passages," that is, pairs of related passages (short and long), that oppose, support, or otherwise complement each other's point of view. For these, you will be expected to draw comparisons.

The questions that follow these passages will ask about the main idea, an inference you can make based on the text, or a special vocabulary word. For instance:

> **Example**
>
> In line 5, the word *suppress* most nearly means
>
> (A) oppose
>
> (B) vanquish
>
> (C) prohibit
>
> (D) stifle
>
> (E) disguise

Most of the passages will contain a few tough vocabulary words. Don't panic. Most unfamiliar words will be defined. You don't need any outside knowledge to answer the Critical Reading questions.

> **HINT:** A brief introduction precedes the long passages. (The short passages don't include these introductions.) This introduction contains valuable information about the author and the passage. Never skip it, as it will help you earn points.

Reading the Passages

You can tackle the reading passages in any order you wish. Many test takers find it best to complete all the short passages before tackling the longs ones. Before you answer any questions, though, quickly scan all the passages, and start with the passages you find easier.

- Don't read the passage thoroughly—that's a waste of time.
- Do skim the passage to get the drift. If you miss the details, don't worry. The questions will direct you back to important points in the passage.

> **HINT:** The less time you spend reading the passages, the more time you'll have to answer questions, and that's where you score points.

Answering the Questions

All the questions are worth the same number of points, so don't get hung up on any one problem.

Step 1: Read just enough of the passage to figure out the main idea, and to get a sense of how the text is developed.

Step 2: Read the question; if it seems hard, circle it, skip it, and go back to it after. You want to answer the other questions in the set first and then come back to the hard questions.

Step 3: As necessary, go back into the passage to locate the answer to a specific question.

Step 4: Put the answer in your own words.

Step 5: Attack the answer choices, and choose the one that comes closest to the answer you found.

Big Picture questions ask about the overall focus of the passage and the main point. To answer these correctly, you'll need to read actively, asking yourself, "Why did the author write this? What's the point?"

Little Picture questions are usually keyed: They give you a line reference, or refer you to a particular paragraph—a strong clue to where in the passage you'll find your answer. If you're given a line reference, don't read only that line. Read a few lines before and after to get an idea of the context in which that line appears.

Vocabulary-in-Context questions don't test your ability to define hard words. Instead, they ask how a word is used in the passage. The most common meaning of the word is probably *not* the correct answer. Always look back to the passage to see how the word is used in context.

With *paired passages*, the first few questions relate to the first passage, the next few to the second passage, and the final questions ask about the passages as a pair. The best way to do paired passages is:

- Skim the first passage, and do the questions about it.
- Skim the second passage, thinking about how it relates to the first.
- Do the questions about the second passage.
- Do the questions about the relationship between the two passages.

Short Reading Comprehension:
Practice Set One

Questions 1–2 refer to the following passage.

An outstanding feature of Homer's *Iliad* and *Odyssey* is the poet's use of epic similes. In contrast to a simple comparison, an epic simile extends through a number of lines, often present-
(5) ing a dynamic series of images. In the *Iliad,* epic similes often juxtapose the violence of warfare with peacetime scenes or the natural world. The *Odyssey* contains far fewer such comparisons, but the similes in the *Odyssey* are no less important
(10) for the epic's major themes. One telling illustration occurs when the hero strings his bow for the climactic battle: here, he is compared to an epic bard stringing his harp.

1. According to the passage, how does an epic simile differ from a simple comparison?

    (A) Epic similes occur only in the Homeric poems, the *Iliad* and the *Odyssey.*

    (B) Epic similes always occur at the climax of the narrative.

    (C) Epic similes are more important than are simple comparisons for a poem's major themes.

    (D) Epic similes usually deal with the natural world.

    (E) Epic similes are longer than simple comparisons, and they present a number of images.

2. Based on the last sentence of the passage, it is most likely that a major theme in the *Odyssey* is

    (A) the triumph of the hero Odysseus over natural forces

    (B) the suggestion that the hero possesses characteristics in common with the epic bard

    (C) the success of Odysseus in restoring peace to his native land

    (D) the suggestion that Odysseus is godlike

    (E) the praise of Odysseus as resourceful in both peace and war

Questions 3–4 refer to the following passage.

A major story in recent years has been the triumph of electronic mail. Since the early 1990s, e-mail users have multiplied exponentially. Some major corporations have now chosen e-mail as
(5) their primary channel for all communications, internal and external. Yet, however effective and inexpensive e-mail may be, it is not without flaws. The medium is impersonal, lacking the intimacy of a letter or the immediacy of a phone call. As an
(10) interactive medium, e-mail is less than ideal, since messages allow correspondents politely to ignore points they do not wish to address, or indeed not to respond at all.

3. The attitude of the author of the passage could best be described as

   (A) uniformly favorable

   (B) intensely subjective

   (C) harshly critical

   (D) objective and mixed

   (E) casual and indifferent

4. The word *immediacy* in line 9 most nearly means

   (A) quickness

   (B) precision

   (C) closeness

   (D) tragedy

   (E) speed

Questions 5–6 refer to the following passage.

Ecology—the study of the relationships among organisms, and between organisms and their environment—is a relatively new branch of science. The name itself was coined by a German biologist,
(5) Ernst Haeckel, in 1866. Haeckel postulated the living world as a community, where each species has a distinctive role to play. One of the major focuses of ecological study today is fieldwork analyzing relationships within an ecosystem, or a collection
(10) of communities such as a tropical rainforest or a coral reef. The results of such studies have provided conservationists and wildlife managers with important new insights, though many questions remain unanswered.

5. Based on the passage, why might many of the basic questions posed by ecology still remain unanswered today?

   (A) Ecology has received little support from funding agencies and from the general public.

   (B) The areas studied by ecologists are remote and inhospitable.

   (C) Ecologists have found it difficult to enlist the cooperation of other scientists.

   (D) Ecology is a relatively young, developing branch of science.

   (E) Ecologists have been overly concerned with wildlife management.

6. Based on the passage, all of the following might be considered an ecosystem *except*

   (A) a temperate forest

   (B) a coral reef

   (C) an ice crystal

   (D) a tropical rainforest

   (E) a grassy plane

Questions 7–10 refer to the following passages.

Passage 1

As one of the most ethnically diverse countries in the world, the United States should take more vigorous steps to design and support bilingual education programs in our nation's schools. Some
(5) critics object to such programs on the grounds that they are expensive and that they disadvantage students economically by delaying their assimilation into the linguistic mainstream. But maintaining cultural diversity is a value that America,
(10) largely a nation of immigrants, should cherish. Other countries with substantial minority populations, such as Belgium, Canada, and India, have devised bilingual education programs with considerable success. Our school systems would do
(15) well to study examples such as these to see if suitable models can be appropriated for American needs.

Passage 2

One of the most controversial areas in American education today involves bilingual pro-
(20) grams. On the whole, such programs have shown mixed results. If we consider the historical record, generations of immigrants to American shores have prospered economically and socially by assimilating themselves as rapidly as possible into
(25) American life. The fact that children's facility for learning a second language declines as they grow older should argue for the use of English in most courses in primary and secondary schools. Families will always be free to use another lan-
(30) guage at home, but the language of instruction in American schools should be English if the best interests of all students are to be served.

7. The author of Passage 1 believes that bilingual education programs

   (A) delay students' assimilation into the mainstream
   (B) are too expensive to warrant the public's support
   (C) help to maintain cultural diversity
   (D) will encourage people to immigrate to America
   (E) have been unsuccessful in Belgium, Canada, and India

8. The word *grounds* in line 5 of Passage 1 most nearly means

   (A) surface
   (B) soil
   (C) lowest part
   (D) basis
   (E) particles

9. The writer of Passage 2 cites children's ability to learn a second language in order to argue

   (A) in favor of bilingual education programs
   (B) that English as a second language should be taught at home but not in school
   (C) that English is an especially difficult language for children to learn
   (D) that there may soon be a shortage of foreign language teachers
   (E) that children should learn English when they are most able to do so

10. The author of Passage 1 would most likely respond with which of the following statements to the assertion that "On the whole, such programs have shown mixed results," in Passage 2.

    (A) Other programs in several countries have shown quite positive results.

    (B) The programs likely compromised the students' ability to learn English later in life.

    (C) Such difficulties must be expected in a country as ethnically diverse as America.

    (D) Despite inevitable problems, such programs are important for maintaining cultural diversity.

    (E) Such programs are unnecessary, since families can use other languages at home.

ANSWERS AND EXPLANATIONS

1. E

Getting to the Answer: The word *differ* in the question stem tells you that you need to look for a contrast. Sentence two starts with the phrase *in contrast*. Look for an answer choice that presents or paraphrases this sentence.

(A) is out of the topic's scope. The passage mentions only the Homeric poems, but that doesn't mean that epic similes only occur in Homer's works. (B) is out, too: The *Odyssey* simile singled out by the writer is said to occur at the " climactic moment" of the epic, but nothing in the passage implies that epic similes occur *only* at narrative climaxes. (C) isn't supported in the passage. In (D), the passage states that epic similes also cite peacetime scenes. It is also only about the Iliad. (E) is a good match: It is directly supported by the paragraph's second sentence.

2. B

Getting to the Answer: What is the point of the comparison the author mentions? Odysseus is compared to an epic bard, or poet. The author also states that these similes conveyed major themes, so this comparison must be a major theme.

Nothing in the passage states that the hero triumphs over natural forces, so (A) is out. (C) isn't mentioned. As for (D), Odysseus is a hero, but the passage does not discuss him as godlike. (E) is never discussed. (B) is the answer.

3. D

Getting to the Answer: Examine the key sentence beginning "Yet, however effective and inexpensive email may be …." In the center of the paragraph, the author balances advantages versus disadvantages.

(A) is the opposite of what is written. The author mentions several flaws in the text. (B) is out, too: While the author presents a personal opinion, it is too extreme to say the text is *intensely* subjective. With (C), the author criticizes email as impersonal and mediocre, but he admits that email also has advantages. And (E) is the opposite case. The author is engaged in the subject, and the paragraph does not seem casual or indifferent. (D) is the answer: The author is objectively analytical, presenting both pros and cons.

4. C

Getting to the Answer: The author says that email is impersonal, and lacks the immediacy of a phone call, so immediacy here must have something to do with being personal or intimate.

Quickness is a common meaning of immediacy, but it doesn't fit in a sentence about why email is impersonal. So (A) is out. With (B), email may lack *precision*, but this doesn't follow from the word *immediacy*. (D) makes no sense. (E) means pretty much the same thing as (A), and they can't both be right.

5. D

Getting to the Answer: The question stem refers to questions that remain unanswered today. Look for an answer choice that provides an historical perspective on ecology and its concerns. Watch out for wrong answer choices that confuse the author's perspective with that of someone else.

The passage nowhere mentions funding agencies or the attitudes of the general public, so (A) is wrong. And though many of these regions may indeed be remote or inhospitable, there's no direct evidence to suggest that that's why questions remain, so (B) is out as well. Nothing in the passage indicates a lack of cooperation, so (C) is wrong. (E) is a misused detail. The passage states that the findings of ecology have been helpful to wildlife management, but does not indicate that this is the main concern of ecologists.

6. C

Getting to the Answer: Look for comment of an ecosystem in the passage. In sentence four, ecosystems are described as "collections of communities," with tropical rainforests and coral reefs given as examples. Remember, the question stem says *except*, so your answer must be a *nonecosystem*.

Rainforests are ecosystems, so it's reasonable to infer that temperate forests would also fit the definition of a "collection of communities." (A) is out. (B) and (D) are out because coral reefs and tropical rainforests are mentioned as examples of ecosystems. With (E), the plane is not mentioned, but like a coral reef or a rainforest, it is a "collection of communities."

7. C

Getting to the Answer: This question looks at first like a detail question, but in fact it does ask about the main focus. The opening sentence includes the word *should*. Since that sentence contains an opinion or proposition, look for a choice consistent with the author's outlook.

(A) is out since the author doesn't make this assertion but attributes it instead to critics of bilingual programs, so (A) is out. (B) is too briefly mentioned, and (D) is never discussed. (E) is the opposite case; the programs in these countries are described as successful.

8. D

Getting to the Answer: Recall that many common English words have multiple meanings. They may also be used metaphorically or idiomatically.

Grounds can mean physical grounds, such as soil and earth, or psychological grounds, such as basis or foundation for an argument or action. (D) is correct. With (C), you may be thinking of "from the ground up," but that makes no sense here.

9. E

Getting to the Answer: This question asks you to identify a logical link. Look for a cause-and-effect relationship. The author says that children can learn second languages more easily than adults can. So, she is arguing that childhood (and school) is the best time to learn English as a second language.

If anything, the author is opposed to these programs, so (A) is wrong. (B) cites an irrelevant use of a detail. (C) is not discussed, and with (D), no such prediction is made.

10. A

Getting to the Answer: Author 2 says that many bilingual education programs have "shown mixed results," but author 1 cites successful programs in Belgium, Canada, and India. Look for a choice that captures author 1's point of view.

(B) is the opposite case. Author 1 favors bilingual education, and so wouldn't agree with this statement. With (C), author 1 does describe America as ethnically diverse, but never indicates that this will make bilingual education difficult. (D), like (B), is the opposite case. Author 1 doesn't indicate that problems with bilingual education are inevitable. (E) fits with Passage 2, not Passage 1.

Short Reading Comprehension:
Practice Set Two

Questions 1–2 refer to the following passage.

In Madagascar, the custom of *famadihana,* or "turning of the bones," attests to many cultures' urgent concerns with burial and the spirit world. Practiced by the Merina and the Betsileo, two of
(5) the island's most important ethnic groups, *famadihana* involves temporarily removing the ancestors' remains, cleansing and rewrapping them in new shrouds, and then re-interring them in the existing tomb. Such a ceremony may seem
(10) rather startling to many Americans, but for the Merina and Betsileo it is typically celebrated with great festivity and helps to strengthen familial ties. In fact, many aspects of *famadihana* are reminiscent of an extended family reunion.

1. The author's purpose in the passage is to

   (A) present an argument

   (B) explain a cultural phenomenon

   (C) examine a common misconception

   (D) disprove an outdated theory

   (E) evoke a strong reaction

2. The example of "an extended family reunion" serves to

   (A) argue for the importance of a cultural ritual

   (B) illustrate the author's misgivings about *famadihana*

   (C) question the wisdom of an unusual practice

   (D) convince the reader of the normality of a ceremony

   (E) provide an analogy to a familiar event

Questions 3–4 refer to the following passage.

Until quite recently, hypnosis has been a specialized—and often controversial—technique used only in marginal areas of medicine. However, hypnosis is now increasingly finding mainstream use.
(5) For example, mental health experts have found that the suggestions of a skilled therapist are often remarkably effective in countering anxiety and depression. The benefits of hypnosis, though, are not limited to the emotional and psychological
(10) realm. Hypnosis helps burn center patients to manage excruciating pain, and a recent research study found that hypnosis can dramatically shorten the time required for bone fractures to heal, often by several weeks.

3. The passage indicates that hypnosis

   (A) is the most effective means to manage pain

   (B) was formerly regarded with some suspicion

   (C) is still a controversial means to treat anxiety and depression

   (D) is limited primarily to mental health medicine

   (E) is used in many areas of mainstream medicine

4. The word *manage* in line 11 most nearly means

   (A) direct

   (B) administer

   (C) bring about

   (D) cope with

   (E) remedy

Questions 5–8 refer to the following passages.

Passage 1

The legacy of Eugene O'Neill, a towering figure
in the history of American theater, is best understood as a portfolio of unforgettable families of
characters. Early in his career, O'Neill had derived
(5) a lesson from the ancient Greeks: The family is
one of the most fertile grounds for tragedy.
Indeed, conflicts between family members serve as
the mainspring for O'Neill's greatest plays, such as
Mourning Becomes Electra. And in what is
(10) arguably his greatest work, *Long Day's Journey into
Night*, O'Neill brilliantly portrayed the tortured
relationships of a family suspiciously like his own.

Passage 2

Eugene O'Neill has been the only American
playwright ever to win the Nobel Prize for
(15) literature. Although he created a gallery of memorable characters in his plays, his legacy is most
justly interpreted as that of a technical innovator.
In length, his plays range from the early one-act
dramas to *Strange Interlude*, a stage epic consisting
(20) of nine acts. In the ground-breaking *Mourning
Becomes Electra*, O'Neill appropriated narrative
devices from Greek tragedy. Perhaps most important, in order to reveal the inner thoughts of his
characters on stage, O'Neill experimented with
(25) many devices, including masks, internal monologue, asides, and soliloquies.

5. The word *suspiciously* in line 12 of Passage 1
    implies that O'Neill

    (A) distrusted certain elements of family dynamics

    (B) may not have been the primary author of
    Long Day's Journey into Night

    (C) failed to properly employ some elements of
    Greek drama

    (D) appreciated the tragic nature of most fami-
    lies' relationships

    (E) used elements of his own life as models for
    some features of his work

6. The word *mainspring* in line 8 of Passage 1 most
    nearly means

    (A) source

    (B) driving force

    (C) chronology

    (D) contradiction

    (E) limitation

7. Which item below most accurately describes the
    difference in approach between the two writers?

    (A) Passage 1 praises O'Neill, while Passage 2
    criticizes him.

    (B) The author of Passage 1 is more historically
    oriented than the author of Passage 2.

    (C) Passage 1 focuses on one of O'Neill's main
    themes, while Passage 2 discusses O'Neill as
    a technical innovator.

    (D) The author of Passage 1 feels that O'Neill's
    greatest work is *Long Day's Journey into
    Night*, whereas the author of Passage 2 feels
    that *Strange Interlude* is a better play.

    (E) Passage 1 emphasizes O'Neill's popularity
    during the playwright's lifetime, while
    Passage 2 implies that O'Neill was underes-
    timated by his contemporaries.

8. Which of the following details do both writers
    mention in their discussions of O'Neill?

    (A) family conflicts

    (B) the Nobel Prize

    (C) O'Neill's interest in Greek tragedy

    (D) soliloquies in O'Neill's plays

    (E) the influence of earlier American playwrights
    on O'Neill

Questions 9–10 refer to the following passage.

One of the most enduring American myths has been our image of the West. Two features of Western novels and films justify the use of the term *myth*. First, the Western cowboy is an ideal-
(5) ized figure, far removed from the cowboy in real life. Second, the landscape of the American West is usually a generalized, imaginary locale rather than a real representation. An enormous mural of the West by painter Emanuel Leutze offers a spectacu-
(10) lar illustration of such an imaginary locale. Created in 1861 for the United States Capitol in Washington, D.C., Leutze's mural shows the snow-capped Rockies together with a glowing sunset over San Francisco Bay thousands of miles away.

9. The passage is primarily concerned with

(A) the style of Emanuel Leutze's mural in the U.S. Capitol

(B) the historical relationship of painting and the image the American West

(C) the lifestyle and psychology of the Western cowboy

(D) the mythical features present in the American image of the West

(E) the way 19th-century cowboys are presented in paintings

10. The author uses the example of Leutze's mural in order to illustrate

(A) the inability of painters to capture the true nature of American cowboys

(B) the unfortunate oversimplifications in our images of the cowboy

(C) the American notion of the West as a general-ized, imaginary locale

(D) the beauty of San Francisco Bay

(E) the large distance between San Francisco Bay and the Rockies.

ANSWERS AND EXPLANATIONS

1. B

Getting to the Answer: The author explains *famadihana* and that's about it. There's no argument or point of view beyond this explanation.

(A) is wrong because the author is conveying information, not presenting an argument. In (C), there is nothing in the text that could be described as a *misconception. Outdated theories* aren't mentioned, so (D) is out. And with (E), though the author would like to educate and perhaps entertain us, the passage is too neutral in tone to evoke a strong reaction.

2. E

Getting to the Answer: The author states that Americans may find the process startling, but the practitioners celebrate it much like a family reunion. As readers, this helps us compare the process to a much more familiar event.

(A) is tempting. The author might think that *famadihana* is important, but simply comparing it to a family reunion doesn't prove this. Moreover, even though it is a tempting answer choice, (E) is much more specific and a stronger choice. In (B), though the text mentions that some people might be startled, concrete misgivings are not illustrated. (C) is far too negative: The author never shows an intent to question the wisdom of the practice. (D) is tempting, but doesn't quite fit. We're given an analogy to a familiar event in order to help us understand how the practitioners of *famadihana* feel about the ritual. This doesn't mean that we're expected to feel that the event is normal, only that it is similar in some respects to a familiar event.

3. B

Getting to the Answer: There's no way to predict an answer here, so jump right into the answer choices. But read carefully! Tempting choices like (C) and (E) can be wrong because of a single word.

(A) is too extreme. The passage states that hypnosis is useful for managing pain, but it's never implied that it is the *most* effective means. (C) is wrong because it was controversial, *until recently*. (D) is the opposite case. Hypnosis is also used to speed the healing of bones. (E) is also extreme. Only a few areas are mentioned, and there's nothing to say it is more widespread. (B) is correct. Until recently, hypnosis was "marginal" and "controversial." It makes sense to say that it was regarded with some suspicion.

4. D

Getting to the Answer: Watch out for common meanings that are not appropriate in the sentence. Here, the word *excruciating,* which means "agonizing" or "extremely intense," suggests that patients may live with, but not get rid of, the pain. Your answer should reflect this shade of meaning.

Burn victims are unlikely to be able to *direct* pain, so (A) is out. *Administer*, (B), makes no sense here, even tough it is one meaning of manage. (C) is the opposite case: Patients want to minimize pain, not bring it about. (E) is tempting. You would think that hypnosis might *remedy*, or fix, the pain of burn victims, but in the end, it is too extreme. The pain is not fixed; it is only "coped with," choice (D).

5. E

Getting to the Answer: By including the word *suspiciously* in the sentence, the author is saying that the family in the play is unusually similar to O'Neill's own family. This cannot have been a coincidence. In other words, O'Neill must have based the play on his own family, at least to some extent.

While O'Neill noticed the tragic relationships of families, there's no support for the word *distrust* here, so (A) is wrong. (B) is completely unsubstantiated. With (C), the passage is very positive, and the author thinks that O'Neill learned a lesson from the Greeks. (D) is too extreme. The author doesn't indicate that O'Neill considered *most* families tragic.

6. B

Getting to the Answer: The author uses *mainspring* to describe conflicts, which seem to have been very important in O'Neill's works. Look for an answer choice that means something like *motivation* or *important element*.

(A) is wrong: The conflicts serve as elements of the plays. The conflicts themselves are not the source of the plays. (O'Neill is the source of the plays.) (C) is never discussed. With (D), conflicts can involve contradictions, but that is not the author's point. (E) is far too negative to fit with the positive tone of the passage.

7. C

Getting to the Answer: This question asks you to identify a major contrast between the passages, so avoid elements that are true of both passages. Look for phrases in the answer choices that may repeat or echo the language used in the paragraphs, but watch out for distortions.

In (A), both paragraphs praise O'Neill, though for different achievements. In (B), both writers mention O'Neill's interest in ancient Greek drama, but one writer doesn't seem more historically oriented than the other. In (D), the first part of this statement is in Passage 1, but the writer of Passage 2 does not indicate what play the author thinks is O'Neill's best work. And (E) is out because neither author deals with the playwright's popularity.

8. C

Getting to the Answer: You are asked to identify a similarity between the passages, not a difference, so the detail must be mentioned in both passages.

Family conflicts are mentioned only in Passage 1, so (A) is out. (B) and (D) are mentioned only in Passage 2. And neither author mentions the influence of earlier American playwrights, so (E) is out.

9. D

Getting to the Answer: The first sentence sums this up: Our image of the American west is an enduring myth. Remember, don't be distracted by supporting details when you're searching for the main idea.

Leutze's style is indeed discussed, but it is not the primary focus of the passage, so (A) is out. (B) is wrong because the painting is cited only as support for the main idea. As for (C), the author never discusses the cowboys themselves, only our conception of them. And with (E), the painting is used as an example of the author's major point—that our image of the West constitutes a myth.

10. C

Getting to the Answer: Since half the passage is devoted to a discussion of Leutze's mural, it is reasonable to assume that this example is closely related to the author's purpose or main idea: that our image of the American west is an enduring myth. (A) is tempting, but still a distortion.

The author's point is not that Leutze was *unable* to capture the cowboy's true nature, but that he *chose* to create an unrealistic scene. (A) is out. (B) is out as well; the passage argues that the cowboy has been an idealized figure in our images of the West, but the author doesn't imply that this is *unfortunate*. As for (D), we read of a "glowing sunset" over San Francisco Bay, but this is hardly the main point. And with (E), that the Rockies and San Francisco are thousands of miles apart is brought up only to make a larger point—that the painting is not realistic.

Short Reading Comprehension: Practice Set Three

Questions 1–2 refer to the following passage.

Every morning I turn first to the sports section of the newspaper, but not for the reasons you might imagine. I am not an athlete, and I follow professional and college sports indifferently at
(5) best. What quickens my pulse is not the tightness of a pennant race or a new record in the butterfly, but rather the language of sports writing. Where else can you find such a veritable lexicon of vivid verbs? *Stomp, crush, rob, cream, nip,* and *vaporize*
(10) are among my favorites. The euphemisms of political reporting and the dry objectivity of the finance and obituary sections are not for the sports writer, whose lifeblood is spectacle and hyperbole.

1. The author states that he turns "first to the sports section of the newspaper" (lines 1–2) because it

   (A) contains colorful writing
   (B) focuses on interesting personality profiles of athletes
   (C) functions as a welcome escape from articles on politics and finance
   (D) offers reports about the author's two favorite pastimes, baseball and swimming
   (E) uses many interviews and quotations

2. The author's attitude toward the "lexicon of vivid verbs" can best be described as

   (A) dryly ironic
   (B) calmly objective
   (C) bitterly satirical
   (D) clinically detached
   (E) humorously upbeat

Questions 3–6 refer to the following passages.

Passage 1

To trace the beginnings of collage as a modernist technique is complex. Picasso, Braque, and Matisse all experimented with the method, but the most thorough-going pioneers were the Germans
(5) Max Ernst and Kurt Schwitters in the 1920s. In his works, Ernst combined cut-out photographs of fish, insects, and anatomical drawings, while Schwitters included disparate, everyday items such as train tickets, postage stamps, and lengths of
(10) string in his compositions. For these artists, collage was an ideal technique for expressing the fragmentary, discontinuous aspects of modern life. This approach was not limited to the visual arts but extended to music and literature as well,
(15) such as Igor Stravinsky's discordant harmonies in *The Rite of Spring*, and T. S. Eliot's snippets of interior monologue in "The Love Song of J. Alfred Prufrock."

Passage 2

Collage, which had its beginnings in Europe,
(20) rapidly became one of the most prominent techniques of 20th-century American art. For some time, collage was particularly associated with the use of *objets trouvés**, such items as seashells, newspaper clippings, postage stamps, or playing
(25) cards. In the 1930s, the American artist Joseph Cornell won fame with his carefully juxtaposed selections of such objects, neatly displayed in glass-fronted boxes. The found object became an artistic icon of a world characterized by chance
(30) and fragmentation.

*Objets trouvés: a French phrase meaning *found objects*.

3. In Passage 1, the author is primarily concerned with

  (A) the contributions of Igor Stravinsky to collage
  (B) the beginnings of collage as a modernist technique in the arts
  (C) the influence of Max Ernst and Kurt Schwitters
  (D) the use of found objects in collage
  (E) parallels between collage in the visual arts and other art forms

4. The author of Passage 1 states that the technique of collage

  (A) has an origin that is difficult to determine
  (B) is ignored by artists today
  (C) is less interesting than the techniques of music and poetry
  (D) stems from experimentation by Picasso and Braque
  (E) is closely related to techniques of found objects

5. The author of Passage 2 would likely agree that collage

  (A) originated in America
  (B) often featured found objects as important elements
  (C) reached its peak as an artistic expression in the 1930s
  (D) usually incorporates newspaper clippings
  (E) makes use of icons to represent found objects

6. You can infer that the authors of BOTH passages would agree that

  (A) collage expresses the fragmentation of modern life
  (B) Joseph Cornell's works serve as excellent examples of collage
  (C) collage is an overrated artistic technique
  (D) it is unclear how collage began
  (E) collage stressed the symbolism of found objects

Questions 7–8 refer to the following passage.

One of the most distinctive forms of Roman sculpture was the portrait bust. Developed around 100 B.C., portrait busts were first used to honor important officials. In contrast to Greek portrait
(5) busts which usually depicted the subject in an idealized fashion, Roman portraits were typically realistic, focusing on individual features and characteristics. Experts have remarked that even the carving style in Roman portrait sculpture was
(10) rapid and loose, as though the sculpted image was intended to convey a sense of personality and vigor. In Roman portraits, the head dominated the composition; the figure's draped shoulders are so conventional and unvarying as to seem almost an
(15) afterthought.

7. According to the author, the difference between Greek and Roman busts can best be described by which of the following?

(A) Greek sculptures depict mythical beings while Roman sculptures depict historical ones.

(B) Greek sculptures took much longer to complete than Roman sculptures.

(C) Bronze was the preferred medium for Greek sculptors; Roman sculptors preferred marble.

(D) Greek sculptures idealized their subjects, while Roman sculptures were very realistic portrayals.

(E) Roman sculptors produced amateurish work; Greek sculptors were more professional.

8. The author implies that the head is the dominant feature of a Roman sculpture (line 12) because

(A) the image conveyed a sense of strength

(B) the Romans had few Greek models to imitate

(C) the Romans were interested in individual portrayals

(D) the carving style of Roman sculptors was unsuited to portraying clothing

(E) Roman sculptors didn't consider the draped shoulders until the figure's head was complete

Questions 9–10 refer to the following passage.

In recent years, shark attacks in U.S. waters have received wide attention. Are such attacks a growing threat to swimmers and surfers? Statistics suggest not. The rate of attacks per number of swim-
(5) mers has not increased over time. What *has* increased is the popularity of aquatic sports, such as surfing, sail boarding, and kayaking. More people are in the water these days, and therefore the chances of a shark encounter increase. Still, to
(10) keep the issue in perspective we should remember that there were only six fatal shark attacks in U.S. coastal waters from 1990 to 2000.

9. According to the author, which of the following has NOT increased over time?

(A) the total number of shark attacks in U.S. waters

(B) the popularity of aquatic sports

(C) the number of fatal shark attacks in U.S. coastal waters

(D) the rate of shark attacks per number of people in the water

(E) the estimated shark population in U.S. coastal waters

10. The author most likely provides the statistic in the final sentence in order to

(A) point out that U.S. coastal waters are safer than those of other countries.

(B) illustrate that relatively few fatal shark attacks have occurred in U.S. waters

(C) show that the period 1990–2000 marked a decrease in the number of fatal shark attacks

(D) caution swimmers and surfers against dangers

(E) suggest that the issue of fatal shark attacks may be dismissed as insignificant

ANSWERS AND EXPLANATIONS

1. A

Getting to the Answer: The author is discussing the *language of sports writing,* which he describes as *vivid.* You can predict that the reason he turns to the sports pages has something to do with the writing that he encounters there.

Sports writers may compose personality profiles, but the passage does not mention this type of writing. (B) is out. (C) is a stretch; the author mentions political and financial writing, but he doesn't specifically identify the sports section as an alternative or escape. (D) is out because the author specifically says he's not much of a sports fan. And there's no mention in the text about the points mentioned in (E).

2. E

Getting to the Answer: Ask yourself about the overall atmosphere created here. The passage is pretty positive about sports writing, and the author has a lively approach to his subject matter.

Irony exploits contrasts or reversals, whereas the author here seems to mean what he says on the surface, so (A) is wrong. (B) is true in the sense that the author is calm, but he's clearly enthusiastic about sports writing.

(C) is too negative, and (D) is clearly untrue; the writing is far from clinically detached.

3. B

Getting to the Answer: In Passage 1, the first sentence clues you into the author's purpose: "To trace the beginnings of collage as a modernist technique is complex." Your answer should talk about the beginnings of collage as a modern artistic technique.

(A) is mentioned, but only in the context of a musical analogy to the technique of collage in the visual arts. (B) is a good match, confirmed by the first sentence and your prediction. (C) is wrong because although Ernst and Schwitters are described as "the most thorough-going pioneers," that isn't the author's primary concern. As for (D), this term is mentioned only in Passage 2. (E) is only a detail in Passage 1.

4. A

Getting to the Answer: Don't be afraid of answer choices that quote the passage verbatim or are close paraphrases of information in the passage.

The beginnings of collage are mentioned in the first sentence of Passage 1, (A). Artists today are never mentioned, so (B) is out. Music and poetry, (C), are mentioned at the end of the passage, but their beginnings are not compared to those of collage. (D) is a distortion: The author mentions Picasso and Braque as artists who experimented with collage, but not that the beginnings of collage are the result of this experimentation. (E) is a common trap; you are presented with information from the wrong passage.

5. B

Getting to the Answer: It's difficult to make much of a prediction here, so evaluate each answer choice in turn.

(A) is out, since the passage explicitly locates the beginnings of collage in Europe, not America. With (C), the author cites the work of Cornell from the 1930s as important, but doesn't imply that this was the high point of the technique. (D) is out because newspaper clippings are only one example of objects to be found in collages. And with (E), we're told that the collage became an icon or symbol, not that the artist used icons to create the collage. (B) is correct. The words *objets trouvés, objects,* and *found object* appear in most of the sentences in Passage 2; clearly this is on the author's mind.

6. A

Getting to the Answer: It may be helpful to review the passages for echoes or similarities in phrasing. You can eliminate certain choices rapidly.

Passage 1 never mentions Cornell, so (B) is wrong. With (C), both authors draw attention to the importance and interest of collage. With (D), author 1 implies this, but author 2 seems confident that it began in Europe. He doesn't indicate that the origins are unclear. And with (E), passage 2 refers to this idea, but passage 1 does not. (A) is correct. Note that both authors use the words *fragmentary* or *fragmentation.*

7. D

Getting to the Answer: Since the question stem uses the word *difference*, find a sentence in the text that expresses a contrast or difference. Sentence 2 states: "In contrast to Greek portrait busts, which usually depicted the subject in an idealized fashion, Roman portraits were typically realistic." Look for a choice that reflects the contrast between the ideal and the real.

(A) and (C) are never mentioned. (B) is out as well: While we learn that experts suggest that Roman carving style was "rapid," we don't learn how long it took to complete Greek or Roman sculptures. With (E), the text doesn't take a position on the relative professionalism of Greek and Roman sculptors.

8. C

Getting to the Answer: You have to do some research in the lines preceding the cited lines. Two sentences earlier, you learn that Roman portraits were typically realistic, focusing on individual features and characteristics. Also, the carving style was intended to convey a sense of "personality." So you can infer that Romans concentrated on the head because that's what best conveys a sense of "individual features and characteristics." After all, everyone's head is very different, while shoulders seem quite similar.

(A) is out: While it is stated that the images were intended to convey a sense of vigor, it is mentioned in conjunction with the carving style of the sculptors, not the elements of the sculptures themselves. (B) is never mentioned. With (D), though the Romans did have a rapid, loose carving style, that doesn't mean they couldn't portray clothing. And with (D), though the draped shoulder appeared to be "an afterthought," that doesn't mean literally that the sculptors didn't think about the drapery until after they sculpted the head.

9. D

Getting to the Answer: From the word *NOT* in the question stem, you know to look for something that has either remained constant or decreased. The *rate* of attacks hasn't increased, though the total number *has* increased. That's because the total number of swimmers has increased. Think of it this way: If the number of total swimmers was 5 and there was 1 attack, that would be a rate of 1-in-5. If later, there were 15 swimmers and 3 attacks, the rate would still be 1-in-5, though the total number of attacks increased from 1 to 3.

The rate hasn't increased, but this doesn't mean that the total number hasn't increased. (A) is out. (B) is contradicted in the text. With (C), the text distinguishes between fatal attacks and other attacks only in the last sentence. Since only one period is cited 1990–2000, you don't know if this is an increase or not. (E) is not discussed.

10. B

Getting to the Answer: Before citing the number of fatal attacks, the author says to "keep the issue in perspective." So, the statistic should show that the total number of attacks is fairly small. The correct answer choice should be consistent with this moderate, balanced approach.

(A) and (D) are never mentioned. As for (C), you don't know if this is a decrease, since no other statistics are given for comparison. And (E) is wrong since the issue isn't dismissed as insignificant.

Short Reading Comprehension: Practice Set Four

Questions 1–4 refer to the following passage.

Passage 1

Giuseppe Verdi and Richard Wagner, both born in 1813, were destined to become giants of 19th-century opera, but only Verdi was able to shape this art form so that it had compelling popular
(5) appeal. Verdi coupled an unerring instinct for soaring melodic lines with a sure grasp of the elements of theater. It is no coincidence, perhaps, that his favorite playwright was Shakespeare, and the three Verdi operas based on Shakespearean
(10) plays—*Macbeth, Othello,* and *Falstaff*—serve as examples of the successful transposition of material from one artistic medium to another. While Verdi also had his share of failures—*La Traviata* comes readily to mind—both his tunes and his
(15) plots made him one of the most admired figures of his time.

Passage 2

If Verdi is considered the ultimate practitioner of the operatic tradition, Richard Wagner, Verdi's contemporary, must be considered a pioneer of musi-
(20) cal revolution. From the beginning, Wagner went his own way, seeking patrons who could make his work independent of the public that found the works so challenging. From a theatrical viewpoint, his greatest contributions flowed from his convic-
(25) tion that opera should be a *Gesamtkunstwerk,* a synthesis of all the arts, rather than merely a stage play set to music. In purely musical terms, Wagner's revolutionary experiments with chromaticism and key changes in *Tristan und Isolde* (1865) are often
(30) said to have inaugurated modern music. He powerfully influenced composers as diverse as Anton Bruckner, Giacomo Puccini, and Claude Debussy.

1. In Passage 1, the author's attitude toward Verdi may best be described as

   (A) admiring
   (B) skeptical
   (C) restrained
   (D) critical
   (E) maudlin

2. In Passage 1, one can infer that the author believes that Verdi's operas

   (A) are overly long
   (B) are unimaginative imitations of Shakespearean plays
   (C) were unpopular during the composer's lifetime
   (D) were more appealing than Wagner's
   (E) pioneered a new tradition

3. In Passage 2, one can infer that the author believes that

   (A) Wagner was a greater composer than Verdi
   (B) Wagner had little influence on subsequent composers
   (C) Wagner was more interested in suspenseful stage action than in the orchestra's role
   (D) Wagner's music was so innovative that it was not popular
   (E) Verdi owed a considerable debt to Wagner

4. You can infer from Passage 2 that Wagner sought patrons (line 5) because

   (A) his revolutionary works were quite expensive to stage

   (B) this allowed him create free from pressures of popular tastes

   (C) he wanted to illustrate his independence from the opera-going public

   (D) few composers in Wagner's time could support themselves without such patrons

   (E) such patrons understood his conviction that opera should be a synthesis of all the arts

Questions 5–6 refer to the following passage.

Though many seniors resist technology, embracing high-tech breakthroughs can often help them stay young. My mother's uncle Thomas is a good example. Even though he was in his sev-
(5) enties, he eagerly embraced home-computing and developed a worldwide network of correspondents. As a hospital volunteer, he devised a program through which patients could communicate easily and cheaply by email with their far-flung
(10) relatives. When he turned 83, he moved to a retirement home, and within two months, he knew at least a quarter of the 200 residents. They had all signed up for the biweekly meetings of his new computer club!

5. The author tells the story of his great-uncle Thomas primarily in order to

   (A) entertain the reader

   (B) illustrate the pitfalls of technology

   (C) emphasize the benefits of retirement homes for seniors

   (D) show that learning about technology can keep a person occupied and productive

   (E) recommend the use of computers as a way for seniors to stay in touch with family

6. Which of the following items best describes Thomas's personality, as he is presented in the passage?

   (A) taciturn and reclusive

   (B) egocentric and dull

   (C) industrious and outgoing

   (D) precise and scholarly

   (E) athletic and competitive

Questions 7–8 refer to the following passage.

The history of communications is a chronicle of prophecies as well as of inventions. The appearance of each new medium has provoked the pronouncement that its predecessor is now
(5) obsolete. Yet such forebodings have seldom proved accurate. Television has failed to bury radio, for example, and email has not yet replaced letters or fax. Such a historical perspective should make us wary of the prediction that computers will soon
(10) replace the book. Whole libraries may be available on a single CD-ROM, but there remains the deep-seated sensory pleasure of taking down a volume from the shelves or spreading out on a beach blanket with a page-turner.

7. From the evidence of the passage, what would the author's reaction likely be to the videophone, which combines picture and sound?

    (A) a warm welcome to such a technological breakthrough

    (B) a stern warning about the threat posed by such an instrument

    (C) a philosophical reminder that the days of the conventional telephone aren't yet over

    (D) a puzzled question about the need for such a complex device

    (E) a disgruntled complaint that such high-tech inventions do not address society's needs

8. In line 4, the word *pronouncement* most nearly means

    (A) speech

    (B) prediction

    (C) declaration

    (D) plea

    (E) command

Questions 9–10 refer to the following passage.

In ancient Athens, the term *ostracize* had a very specific legal meaning. At regular yearly meetings, citizens could ostracize a fellow citizen by casting a vote on a pottery shard known as an *ostraka*. If
(5) anyone's name appeared on over half of the *ostraka* and 6,000 total votes were cast, then that unlucky soul had to leave Athens for a period of 10 years. Interestingly, *ostracism* was not as devastating for many Greeks as the modern interpretation of the
(10) word would imply. For example, ostracized citizens could appoint a manager to administer their property, and this manager could forward any profits to the citizen in exile. Some ostracized Athenians were even allowed to return in times
(15) of trouble to serve in the government or military.

9. As used in the passage, the word *soul* (line 7) most nearly means

    (A) power

    (B) ghost

    (C) essence

    (D) spirit

    (E) person

10. The author notes that a "manager could forward any profits to the citizen in exile" (lines 12–13) in order to illustrate

    (A) that ostracism for the Greeks was less severe than modern readers might think

    (B) the importance of monetary property to Athenian citizens

    (C) the devastating effects of ostracism on Athenian citizens

    (D) the Greeks' concern for the legal rights of all citizens

    (E) the importance of the service of ostracized citizens during times of crises

ANSWERS AND EXPLANATIONS

1. A

Getting to the Answer: When asked about tone, look back at the "charge" of the words in the text. Are they mainly negative in connotation? positive? neutral? In Passage 1, the author uses mostly positive words to describe Verdi and his works: "giants of 19th-century opera," "most admired." Look for a choice that reflects this positive tone.

The author is hardly *skeptical* or *restrained*, so (B) and (C) are out. With (D), though it is mentioned that *La Traviata* was a failure, that was amidst many successes. As for (E), *maudlin* means tearfully sentimental. To say that the author is sentimental is an overstatement.

2. D

Getting to the Answer: This is an inference question, asking you to use details in the passage as a basis for a conclusion or generalization. You know that the author of Passage 1 has positive feelings about Verdi, so eliminate any choices that are negative or neutral.

We don't learn about the length of Verdi's operas, so (A) is out. And the author hardly thinks the works are unimaginative imitations, so (B) is out as well. With (C), Passage 1 explicitly mentions the composer's "compelling popular appeal." (E)'s claim is made about Wagner, not Verdi. (D) is a good match. From "only Verdi was able to shape this art form so that it had compelling popular appeal," we know that Verdi made his works more appealing than Wagner did.

3. D

Getting to the Answer: Since the question stem doesn't give you a line reference or point you in a direction, the best approach is to examine each choice and eliminate as you go.

(A) is a distortion; though the composers are compared, one is not described as greater than the other. (B) is contradicted in the last sentence of the passage.

(C) is also a distortion; in fact, the author draws attention to Wagner's belief that opera should be a synthesis of all the arts. With (E), the text doesn't discuss any debt or influence that Verdi owed to Wagner. (D) is correct. The author says that Wagner sought "patrons who could make his work independent of the public that found the works

so challenging." In other words, most people didn't enjoy it and would not support it. Since the author feels that Wagner was so revolutionary, she would agree that this lack of popularity was due to his innovation.

4. B

Getting to the Answer: The author writes that "Wagner went his own way, seeking patrons who could make his work independent of the public that found the works so challenging." So by having patrons, he would be supported, and could "go his own way" and create whatever kind of operas he wanted.

With (A), we don't know that the works were unusually expensive to perform. (C) is wrong because of a single word: Wagner wanted to be free of the need for the public's support, but the text doesn't imply that Wagner wanted to *prove* anything. As for (D), the economic state of other composers isn't discussed, and with (E), though Wagner believed that opera should be a synthesis, we don't know whether his patrons understood this conviction.

5. D

Getting to the Answer: This question addresses the author's purpose; note the phrase *in order to* in the question stem. Sentence 1 provides the information you need. The author then goes on to say that great-uncle Thomas is a good example of his thesis. So, the story illustrates his point. Look for an answer that captures this idea.

The goal of this story is to convey information, so (A) is wrong. (B) is the opposite case: The text focuses on the benefits of technology, not the pitfalls. (C) is completely out of context, and (E) is too much of a stretch.

6. C

Getting to the Answer: Thomas was active and involved with his community, and willing to try new things. Look for a choice that sums this up.

(A) is the opposite case. *Taciturn* means quiet, and Thomas was hardly quiet. And with (B), Thomas could hardly be called egocentric or dull. The traits in (D) and (E) are never discussed. (C) is correct. *Industrious* means active and busy.

7.   C

Getting to the Answer: The writer doesn't seemed opposed to the new, but he would likely warn you not to consign the old to the rubbish heap too quickly. The answer should reflect this balanced philosophy of moderation.

(A) is out; the author doesn't condemn the technological breakthroughs of the past, nor does she praise them just because they represent innovations. And new technologies are neither presented as threats nor questioned for their appeal or utility, so (B) and (D) are out.

8.   C

Getting to the Answer: "The appearance of each new medium has provoked the pronouncement that its predecessor is now obsolete." In other words, each time there's a new invention, people state that what medium it is replacing is no longer useful. Look for a choice that means a *saying*. But beware of common meanings that don't make sense in this context.

(A) is too literal. A speech is something orally spoken, and a pronouncement could also be made in written form. (B) is tempting, but be careful. True, there's an element of prediction in this context, but it is really a formal declaration of opinion. And in this specific sentence, you can't really "predict that its predecessor is now obsolete." You could predict something that is going to happen in the future, but not that it is "now" something. (D), *plea*, implies an emotional element.

9.   E

Getting to the Answer: The "unlucky soul" would have to leave Athens, so *soul* here refers to the person who is ostracized. In fact, *person* is a good prediction.

All of the answer choices except (E) are too abstract. *Soul* here means a real person, not something immaterial. Moreover, (A) and (C) are the wrong meaning of the word, and (B) and (D) are the opposite case.

10. A

Getting to the Answer: Before the cited sentence, the author writes "*ostracism* was not as devastating for many Greeks as the modern interpretation of the word would imply." It might be surprising to learn that an outcast could still collect profits, for one. So ostracism wasn't quite as big a deal for the Greeks as you might think.

(B) ignores the focus of the passage, which is about ostracism. (C) is the opposite: The point is that it was *not* as devastating as you might think. (D) is too broad.

Short Reading Comprehension: Practice Set Five

Questions 1–2 are based on the following passage.

With an estimated 250 million cases and 2 million resulting deaths per year, malaria is the world's number-one public health problem, especially in tropical and subtropical regions. The
(5) struggle with this infection is nothing new—malaria is mentioned in some of the earliest medical records of Western civilization. We know, for example, that the ancient Greek physician Hippocrates identified three types of malarial
(10) fevers in the 5th century BC. By the late 15th century, malaria had spread to the Americas, likely as the result of European explorers. In fact, epidemics in Central America were recorded in 1493, only a year after Columbus's first voyage
(15) there.

1. According to the passage, malaria is

   ✓(A) a disease with a long history that remains a serious public health problem today

   (B) a disease that epidemiologists are steadily bringing under control

   (C) likely to spread from the tropics to temperate regions

   (D) impossible to eradicate from the tropics

   (E) an infection that was probably present in the Americas before the arrival of Europeans

2. Malaria's long history suggests that it has been

   (A) especially well documented in the annals of medicine

   (B) spread primarily from locations in Europe to other parts of the world

   (C) particularly resistant to efforts to eradicate or control the infection

   (D) a disorder whose symptoms were misunderstood for many centuries

   (E) an infection for which there is no known treatment

Questions 3–4 refer to the following passage.

There are three good reasons that schools should restore the study of Latin. First, because Latin is a logically structured language, and knowledge of it helps students to better under-
(5) stand the structure of English. Second, a familiarity with Latin is an incalculable aid in enlarging one's vocabulary in English, since so many words in that language derive from Latin roots. Finally, Latin serves as a gateway to the remarkable civi-
(10) lization of Ancient Rome, whose literature and culture have had a permanent influence on our society. As evidence of this assertion, we need only consider the influence of Republican Rome on the Founding Fathers of the United States.

3. The author's primary purpose in writing the passage was most likely to

    (A) narrate

    (B) describe

    (C) entertain

    (D) analyze

    (E) persuade

4. The author mentions the influence of Republican Rome on the Founding Fathers primarily in order to

    (A) show the lasting influence of Roman culture on our society

    (B) illustrate the benefits of enlarging one's vocabulary

    (C) persuade the reader to re-examine the U.S. Constitution

    (D) provide a link between Latin classes and history and government classes in school

    (E) refute the argument that learning Latin is irrelevant and impractical

Questions 5–8 refer to the following passages.

Paragraph 1

More than 40 years ago, Newton Minow, then head of the Federal Communications Commission, described television as a "vast wasteland." If he were evaluating TV today, his opinion would be
(5) little changed. The amount of violence in television drama series seems to increase every year, while competition for ratings has driven news programs to effectively enter the entertainment business. It is even arguable that sports coverage,
(10) one of the strengths of television in the 1970s and 1980s, has declined in quality. And public-affairs-program producers trot out the same gallery of talking heads—self-proclaimed "experts" who reduce complex arguments to sound bites. In an
(15) industry where programmers search in vain for fresh ideas, it is no wonder that attention spans are short and cliché is king.

Paragraph 2

Critics of television often focus on the preva-lence of violence in today's programming.
(20) However, even after years of study, researchers cannot prove the existence of a link between TV violence and antisocial behavior in real life. One study, for example, studied youngsters in both Michigan and Ontario, Canada who watched the
(25) same programs. No connection between viewing habits and behavior could be established convinc-ingly. Beguiled perhaps by the violence issue, crit-ics of TV regularly fail to acknowledge the medi-um's educational value. With the advent of cable,
(30) many new channels have flourished by focusing on such fields as public affairs, medicine, travel, history, and science.

5. The author of Passage 1 criticizes all the following types of television programming EXCEPT

    (A) news programs

    (B) sports coverage

    (C) dramatic series

    (D) soap operas

    (E) public affairs shows

6. The phrase *cliché is king* in line 17 of Passage 1 implies that the author regards television programming as

   (A) stimulating and thought-provoking

   (B) violent and demeaning

   (C) exciting and suspenseful

   (D) unoriginal and stale

   (E) difficult to understand

7. In Passage 2, which of the following does the author mention in order to defend television programming?

   (A) Studies that established links between viewing habits and behavior

   (B) The quality of sports coverage during the 1970s and 1980s

   (C) The educational potential of the medium

   (D) Public affairs experts who help viewers to understand complex arguments

   (E) The superiority of American television programming compared to that of Canada

8. Both passages address

   (A) news coverage on television

   (B) violence on television

   (C) the variety of cable television channels

   (D) differences between Canadian and American television

   (E) regulation by the Federal Communications Commission

Questions 9–10 refer to the following passage.

Alfred Stieglitz was a key figure in the development of American Modernism. A superbly talented photographer, Stieglitz tirelessly campaigned for the recognition of photography as an art form.
(5) His influence, however, transcended his contributions to photography. As both critic and patron, he promoted Modernist painting on both sides of the Atlantic. The first American showings of Pablo Picasso's and Henri Matisse's work occurred at
(10) Stieglitz's art gallery in New York City. American painters indebted to Stieglitz included John Marin, Marsden Hartley, and Georgia O'Keeffe, who was married to the photographer from 1924 until his death in 1946.

9. The word *patron* in line 6 most nearly means

   (A) customer

   (B) fan

   (C) sponsor

   (D) saint

   (E) reviewer

10. The author of this passage would most likely agree that

   (A) innovative photography can have a profound influence on other art forms

   (B) without the contributions of Stieglitz, many Modernist painters would not have found success

   (C) Stieglitz was largely responsible for the widespread recognition of photography as a legitimate art

   (D) artists can make important contributions to the art world beyond the creation of works of art

   (E) Modernism was a tremendously important movement in the history of American painting

ANSWERS AND EXPLANATIONS

1. A

Getting to the Answer: Reread the paragraph to acquire an overview, and pay special attention to the opening sentences, which introduce the topic.

With (B), we have no idea whether scientists are bringing the disease under control. (C) is not discussed. (D) is too extreme; the author doesn't claim that malaria *cannot* be eradicated. And with (E), malaria spread to the Americas only after Columbus arrived.

2. C

Getting to the Answer: Note the use of the word *suggests*. Draw a reasonable conclusion from the evidence offered in the passage.

(A) is tempting. The author refers to two examples of historically documented incidents of the disease, but that is not the same thing as a *well-documented disease*. We have no way of knowing whether the disease is well-documented. With (B), we know only that malaria was spread to the Americas from Europe. (D) is out since there's nothing about misunderstanding the symptoms of the disease. (C) is correct. A long history, significant spread, and 250 million cases annually all support this conclusion.

3. E

Getting to the Answer: The key word is *should* in the first sentence. The passage opens with an assertion, which the author then argues in favor of.

(A) is out. Since there is no story here. So is (B), since the study of Latin is described only to make an argument. (C) is completely incorrect, and (D) is incomplete: The passage is somewhat analytical, but this is done in order to present an argument.

4. A

Getting to the Answer: The key phrase in the mention of Republican Rome and the description of the Founding Fathers is "as evidence of this assertion." This "assertion" is the assertion that Roman culture has had a permanent influence on modern society.

With (B), enlarging one's vocabulary is identified as a benefit of learning Latin, but it has nothing to do with the Founding Fathers. (C) is out of scope. (D) is close, but not entirely correct. Latin is discussed, but not other classes. And with (E), while the author plainly considers Latin relevant and practical, the influence of Republican Rome on the Founding Fathers does not specifically relate to this view.

5. D

Getting to the Answer: Keep in mind that you're not asked for a program the author *might* criticize, you're asked for a program she hasn't *explicitly* criticized. Also, since this is an elimination question, your answer needs to be the one that is *not* mentioned in the passage.

The only answer choice that isn't criticized in the text is (D). This is a little tricky: Though soap operas are a type of program we'd expect the author to criticize, soap operas are not actually mentioned, so this is the correct answer.

6. D

Getting to the Answer: Locate the phrase in paragraph 1 and examine the context for clues. A *cliché* is a trite expression or idea; look for an answer choice that captures this sense.

With (A), the author doesn't think television programming is thought-provoking, she thinks it lacks originality. As for (B), it is consistent with the author's point-of-view, but it doesn't address the question. The author does believe that TV is excessively violent, but this isn't implied by the phrase *cliché is king*. (E) isn't the point. (D) makes sense, since the "programmers search in vain for fresh ideas."

7. C

Getting to the Answer: Examine the structure of Passage 2. How does the author support the argument? The final two sentences in the paragraph are great clues.

(A) is the opposite case: No links were established. (B) is a detail that appears in Passage 1, not in Passage 2. (D) is out of scope. As for (E), while there is mention of a study of Michigan and Canadian children, there is no description of either area as producing superior programming.

8. B

Getting to the Answer: Compare the passages for common ground. Eliminate answer choices that appear in just one passage (or in neither passage).

(A) and (E) are mentioned only in Passage 1. (C) and (D) are mentioned only in Passage 2.

9. C

Getting to the Answer: The answer must reflect what we learn about Stieglitz in the passage—that he promoted Modernist painting and that his art gallery held pioneering exhibitions of the Modernists.

(A) is the wrong context. Patron can mean *customer*, as in the patron of a store. But it also means *one that supports or champions something*, such as a cause. The passage here takes on this meaning of the word, as in a patron of the arts. (B) is out because Stieglitz wasn't just a fan, he was also an active advocate. A fan doesn't necessarily take action, while a patron actively shows support. (D) is the wrong context, and (E) doesn't capture the full meaning of patron. (C) captures the full meaning of patron.

10. D

Getting to the Answer: The author feels that Stieglitz made important contributions to Modernism, because he was such a strong supporter.

(A) is too far a stretch: Stieglitz himself was influential in the art world, but we don't know that his photographs would necessarily influence painters or sculptors. (B) is also a stretch. With (C), though "Stieglitz tirelessly campaigned for the recognition of photography as an art form," we don't know that he was *largely responsible* for the success of this effort. Others may have also been involved in the campaign. And with (E), we don't know how important Modernism was to American painting in general.

Short Reading Comprehension: Practice Set Six

Questions 1–4 refer the following passages.

Passage 1

In the United States, we should make it an urgent priority to reform the process of campaigning for elective office. The vast sums necessary to mount credible Presidential and
(5) Congressional campaigns are especially detrimental. They threaten to limit the pool of candidates to the very wealthy and also give disproportionate influence to lobbyists and other special interests. We should also change the length of such cam-
(10) paigns. In the United Kingdom, campaigns for Parliamentary elections last for weeks; in the United States, the process lasts for well over a year. Finally, the two major parties should establish norms for campaign advertising, with the goal of
(15) sharply curtailing "attack ads."

Paragraph 2

American elections would be more democratic if candidates were required to debate and if everyone eligible to vote was required to do so. Under the present system, a candidate with the advan-
(20) tages of incumbency or widespread name recognition is free to sidestep an opponent's challenge to debate. This puts the opponent at a disadvantage and compromises the goals of our two-party system. Debates needn't play the determining role in
(25) elections, but they should be an important factor as the public evaluates candidates' positions on issues. Of course, a well-informed public is irrelevant if people don't vote. Many foreign countries have a far higher election turnout than we do in
(30) the United States. We should consider legislation requiring people to vote in national elections. Citizenship has its privileges, but it also involves responsibilities.

1. According to Author 1, which aspect of American campaigns for elective office most urgently needs reform?

    (A) The length of campaigns

    (B) The procedures used in candidates' debates

    (C) The use of attack ads

    (D) The expense of campaigns

    (E) Poor voter turnout

2. Author 1 refers to U.K. campaigns for Parliamentary elections in order to

    (A) provide a contrast

    (B) refute a theory

    (C) quote an expert

    (D) create a metaphor

    (E) emphasize a parallel

3. Author 2 would most likely agree with which of the following?

    (A) Televised debates always help the incumbent.

    (B) Campaigns for public office in the United States have become too expensive.

    (C) Debates should help voters to choose candidates.

    (D) Attack ads, while unfortunate, have proven to be effective.

    (E) Debates should be conducted at the national level but are not necessary at the state or local level.

4. Which statement below best expresses the primary difference between the passages?

(A) Passage 1 is primarily persuasive while Passage 2 is mainly informative.

(B) Passage 1 focuses on campaign reform while Passage 2 stresses debates and voter participation.

(C) Passage 1 concentrates on the differences between U.S. and U.K. campaigns, while Passage 2 discusses campaigns for office in the U.S. alone.

(D) Passage 1 argues for the importance of campaign reform, while Passage 2 argues against such a proposal.

(E) Passage 1 expresses a personal opinion, while Passage 2 is highly objective.

Questions 5–6 refer to the following passage.

With the rise of the Internet, computer manufacturers and users confronted a new problem: how to create an international standard for computer code to represent languages that do not use
(5) the Roman alphabet. Without a shared, worldwide standard, many users could not create email, develop websites, or search databases in their own tongues. During the 1990s, a solution emerged: Unicode. Now in its fourth version, Unicode con-
(10) tains unique encodings for 96,000 letters and symbols that appear in 55 writing systems. (Interestingly, more than 70 percent of these encodings represent Chinese characters.) Notwithstanding this progress, the project is far
(15) from complete. Nearly 100 additional writing systems remain to be encoded.

5. As used in the passage, *tongues* (line 8) most nearly means

(A) organs

(B) tastes

(C) flavors

(D) languages

(E) programs

6. Which of the following statements best expresses the main idea of the paragraph?

(A) Chinese characters account for more than 70 percent of the encoding in Unicode.

(B) Converting the text of languages with non-Roman alphabets has been an expensive but worthwhile project.

(C) It is useless to hope that the Unicode project will ever achieve completion.

(D) Many people who could not use email before Unicode can now do so.

(E) Although Unicode has made substantial progress, challenges remain.

Questions 7–8 refer to the following passage.

Kente, a strip-woven cloth woven by the Asante peoples of Ghana and the Ewe of Ghana and Togo is the best known African textile. The original purpose of kente was to serve as festive attire for
(5) special occasions. Men wore the cloth in the fashion of a Roman toga, while women used multiple kentes as wraps. The cloth was once closely associated with kings and queens, but its much broader dispersal is clearly evident today, in both West
(10) Africa and the United States. Kente patterns have been adapted for a wide range of products, including greeting cards, balloons, even Band-Aids.

7. According to the passage, in the past, kente was

(A) worn only by men
(B) broadly dispersed
(C) woven primarily by the Asante people
(D) a symbol of royalty
(E) commonly found in the United States

8. The passage suggests that, over time, kente patterns have

(A) deteriorated in quality
(B) gained in popularity in Europe
(C) been highly adaptable
(D) become more expensive to produce
(E) been widely imitated

Questions 9–10 refer to the following passage.

The all-boys' school I attended, St. Bartolph's, was known for its strict discipline, its devotion to academic standards, and a slightly offbeat eccentricity. At the faculty's apex stood the headmaster,
(5) the redoubtable R. I. W. Westfield. Tall and slim, Mr. Westfield was born in Kenya, won a Rhodes Scholarship, and studied classics at Oxford. During the three years he taught us Latin, woe to the boy whose attention to conjugations and
(10) declensions slackened. I can still hear Mr. Westfield's voice as he meted out punishment for excessive noise at school lunches: In fair weather and foul, the offender was sentenced to run five times around the schoolyard, a book balanced on
(15) his head.

9. The passage is primarily concerned with

(A) St. Bartolph's academic standards
(B) student morale at St. Bartolph's
(C) the impression made on the writer by Mr. Westfield
(D) the atmosphere at school lunches
(E) the value of studying Latin

10. The author would most likely describe Mr. Westfield as

(A) cruel
(B) brilliant
(C) mild
(D) angry
(E) stern

ANSWERS AND EXPLANATIONS

1. D

Getting to the Answer: The author mentions a number of aspects of the campaign process that need reform, but comments that "the vast sums … are especially detrimental." The phrase "especially detrimental" tells you that the author feels that the cost of campaigns is the most important issue.

(A) is included, but it isn't described as urgent. (B) and (E) are mentioned in Paragraph 2. (C) is a detail that appears in Passage 1 but isn't highlighted.

2. A

Getting to the Answer: Locate the reference to Parliamentary campaigns and examine it in context. The author thinks that U.S. elections are too long. By contrast, in the United Kingdom, they are short.

The author doesn't refute a theory. In fact, no theory is mentioned, so (B) is wrong. Neither quotes nor metaphors are mentioned, so (C) and (D) are also out. With (E), be careful to distinguish between a *parallel*, or similarity, and a *contrast*, or difference.

3. C

Getting to the Answer: Some of the answer choices refer to Passage 1 rather than Passage 2. Be sure you discard these choices.

(A) is wrong because while debates are mentioned, televised debates are not. Also, be skeptical of the word *always*—extreme answer choices tend not to be correct on the SAT. (B) and (D) are contained in Passage 1. (C)'s point is certainly made in Passage 2. "Debates … should be an important factor as the public evaluates candidates' positions on issues."

4. B

Getting to the Answer: You need to locate a *difference* between the paragraphs. It's tough to make a prediction here, but you can briefly summarize the focus of each author. Author 1 writes about reforming the financing and length of campaigns, while author 2 discusses the importance of debates and voter turnout.

Both paragraphs attempt to persuade, so (A) is out. Passage 1 does cite the United Kingdom during the dis-cussion of the lengths of campaigns, but not during the discussion of campaign costs or attack ads. So the word *concentrates* in this answer choice makes (C) wrong. With (D), Author 2 argues for some types of campaign reform, though she doesn't concentrate on the same issues as author 1. As for (E), neither passage is more objective. Both express an argument for a proposal. (B) is the answer.

5. D

Getting to the Answer: The passage emphasizes the importance of Unicode to allow computers to handle different languages. In fact, *languages* is a good prediction here.

(A) is a common meaning of *tongue*, but it doesn't work here. With (B), you might associate *tastes* with your *tongue*, but it doesn't make sense to say that people were trying to search databases in their own *tastes*. (C) is also related to tongue, but doesn't work here. And with (D), you might associate *programs* with all these computer tasks, but this doesn't fit with the word *tongue*.

6. E

Getting to the Answer: Eliminate answer choices that concentrate on details.

(A) is stated, though not as the main idea. (B) is not stated. (C) is too pessimistic a prediction given the author's neutral tone. (D) might be something you would infer from the text. But something that must be inferred cannot be the main point of a passage. (E) is a good match, supported by the concluding sentences, "Notwithstanding this progress, the project is far from complete. Nearly 100 additional writing systems remain to be encoded."

7. D

Getting to the Answer: The question stem asks about the past. Look for an answer choice that contains a historical fact that is no longer true. Be wary of vague or partial matches.

(A) is too extreme. The passage provides evidence that kente was worn by both men and women. (B) is out because the text says that kente has become "commercialized … today," not that it was once so. With (E), Kente in the United States is only mentioned in the context of the present.

8. C

Getting to the Answer: Once again, your task is to match each answer choice with specific details in the passage. The phrase *over time* should alert you to look for a detail involving development or change.

The passage mentions nothing about changes in quality or expense, so (A) and (D) are out. And Europe is not mentioned, so (B) is out as well. With (E), Kente patterns have been *adapted*, but we don't know that they have been *imitated*.

9. C

Getting to the Answer: The phrase *primarily concerned with* tells you to look for the main idea. After the opening sentence, the author devotes the entire paragraph to a description of the headmaster. So you might predict that the text's primary concern is Mr. Westfield.

Academics standards are not the main focus, so (A) is wrong. (B) isn't mentioned. The "excessive noise at school lunches" in (D) is a detail used only to describe something that Mr. Westfield did. And with (E), we don't how the author feels about Mr. Westfield's having taught the boys Latin.

10. E

Getting to the Answer: Use every detail available to form a complete picture. Mr. Westfield was quite tough, so look for an answer choice that captures this sense.

Cruel, (A), doesn't fit, since the school is described in positive terms. There is no sense of negativity or disapproval of the teacher. (B), *brilliant*, is a stretch. The author mentions that Mr. Westfield went to Oxford, so he might consider the headmaster *brilliant*, but he never says that he was unusually intelligent. With (C), the headmaster seems to be anything but *mild*. And *angry*, (D), is also a stretch. Mr. Westfield is tough, but that doesn't mean he is angry. He might have had a very cool demeanor.

Short Reading Comprehension: Practice Set Seven

Questions 1–2 refer to the following passage.

Proverbs are hard to define, but one could do worse than the pithy definition offered by an 18th-century British statesman, Lord John Russell. A proverb, Russell is said to have remarked at

(5) breakfast, is "one man's wit and all men's wisdom." Proverbs have been identified in all the world's spoken languages, and—unlike Lord Russell's adage—they are almost always anonymous. Interestingly, similar sayings seem to have devel-

(10) oped independently in many parts of the world. For example, the English saying, "A bird in the hand is worth two in the bush," has counterparts in Romania, Spain, and Iceland.

1. Which of the following best expresses the author's attitude toward Lord Russell's definition of a proverb?

(A) dismissive

(B) skeptical

(C) loyal

(D) favorable

(E) exuberant

2. Based on the passage, the author would most likely agree that

(A) proverbs are passed down in writing from one generation to the next

(B) proverbs that have originated in English often spread to other languages

(C) it is very difficult to analyze a proverb's meaning

(D) it is not uncommon for different cultures to hold similar views

(E) Lord John Russell was mistaken in his view of the nature of proverbs

Questions 3–4 refer to the following passage.

On a stormy June day in 1752, Benjamin Franklin carried out the famous experiment in which he channeled lightning down a kite string and stored the electric charge in a Leyden jar, the
(5) precursor to the modern capacitor. The consequences could not have been more pronounced. Franklin proved that electricity was a force of nature, like Newton's gravity, and the subsequent invention of the lightning rod (based on
(10) Franklin's theories) sharply reduced risk of fire to tall buildings. Franklin's experiment had cultural repercussions as well. It showed that scientific research could have practical benefits, and it impugned the superstitious belief—widespread at
(15) the time—that lightning resulted from divine displeasure.

3. The sentence, "The consequences could not have been more pronounced," conveys

   (A) that it was difficult to describe the results of the experiment
   (B) that Franklin became famous because of the experiment
   (C) the importance of Franklin's findings to the scientific understanding of electricity
   (D) that Franklin's experiment had far-reaching effects
   (E) the degree to which lightning was misunderstood before the experiment

4. Based on the passage, Franklin's kite experiment played a part in

   (A) promoting superstitious beliefs
   (B) explaining the force of gravity
   (C) the development of the Leyden jar
   (D) illustrating the utility of scientific research
   (E) repairing damage done by lightning strikes

Questions 5–6 refer to the following passage.

The Saturday morning recitals at the Daniels School of Music were part of my weekend routine as a child. After a two-hour class on music theory, we would adjourn to the auditorium to hone our
(5) performance skills before a beaming audience: our parents. One Saturday, I was scheduled to play two brief piano pieces. We were required to play from memory, and I had practiced hard. The opening notes of the first piece, however, just wouldn't
(10) come to my fingers. After four false starts, I rose, bowed to the audience, and told them, "Since I can't remember the first selection, I will be happy to play you the second."

5. The word "routine" in line 2 most nearly means

   (A) boring regimen
   (B) customary schedule
   (C) theatrical skit
   (D) series of dance steps
   (E) set of computer instructions

6. The author would most likely agree with which of the following statements about the events described in the passage?

   (A) He learned that parents are a warmly appreciative audience.
   (B) He learned to recover gracefully from an embarrassing moment.
   (C) He learned not to rely on memory to perform piano pieces.
   (D) He concluded that his piano performances would be more effective if he played more spontaneously.
   (E) He learned that performers can get away without practicing.

Questions 7–10 refer to the following passages.

Passage 1

Our school administration should seriously consider giving students more responsibility and empowering the student council to play more than a symbolic role. Over the past year, the coun-
(5) cil has recommended several times that a conflict resolution board be set up, where students and faculty would arbitrate student disputes. Yet the administration has responded with little interest, despite the evidence that other schools in our
(10) region have experimented successfully with such a project. Adults regularly emphasize to us the goals of responsibility and accountability. Isn't it time that students at Chatham High were entrusted with a stake in these goals?

Passage 2

(15) Although it is fashionable these days to tout the notions of *partnership* and *participation* in schools, most schools work best when adults are clearly in charge. Professional studies have shown that students learn and behave best in a structured
(20) atmosphere. The fact is that students look to adults as role models and guides. Our school's faculty and administration should not sacrifice high standards and sound regulations in order to make students temporarily happy. Schools are not
(25) democracies, and students depend—often unwittingly—on the guidance and wisdom of teachers and administrators in order to develop into healthy productive adults.

7. Based on the phrase "a symbolic role" in Passage 1 (line 4), we can assume the author feels that

   (A) the ineffective student council symbolizes the widespread powerlessness of students at the writer's school

   (B) the student council now has little power in decision-making

   (C) the school administration should establish a conflict resolution board

   (D) a more active role in decision making would foster responsibility in students

   (E) the school's administration should establish a student council as a symbol of trust in the student body

8. The author of Passage 1 is most likely

   (A) a conflict resolution board member

   (B) a faculty member

   (C) a member of the school administration

   (D) a parent

   (E) a student

9. The author of Passage 2 would most likely agree that

   (A) the student council of a school should take an active role in policy making

   (B) parents should defer to decisions and policies made by teachers and administrators

   (C) the establishment of a conflict resolution board at most schools might have disastrous consequences

   (D) students may not realize the extent to which they rely on adult supervision

   (E) teachers and administrators provide the primary means of guidance and support for their students

10. The authors of Passage 1 and Passage 2 disagree about

   (A) the wisdom of establishing a conflict resolution board

   (B) the role of a school's student council

   (C) the importance of the guidance of teachers and administrators

   (D) the extent to which students should participate in decisions about school policies

   (E) the wisdom of establishing a structured atmosphere for school life

ANSWERS AND EXPLANATIONS

1. D

Getting to the Answer: The simple fact that the author cites Russell's definition is a clue that she considers it a good one. She also writes, "but one could do worse than…," which is an indirect way of showing her approval. In other words, she is saying that there are worse definitions than this [out there in the world]. *Pithy* means concise, to-the-point.

(A) and (B) are the opposite case. The writer is not dismissive or skeptical. (C) is out-of-scope; loyalty is irrelevant to the discussion. And (E) is extreme. The writer seems positive, but *exuberant* implies high spirits that aren't consistent with the paragraph's tone.

2. D

Getting to the Answer: (A) might be a true statement, but it is completely off-topic. And the passage never says that the proverbs originated in English; in fact, it says that similar proverbs have developed *independently* in many parts of the world. That means (B) is out as well. (C) is out of scope. (D) is correct: The author agrees that proverbs express "all men's wisdom." Since the proverbs express the wisdom of a culture, and similar proverbs can be found in different cultures, the author would probably agree that different cultures often hold similar views.

3. D

Getting to the Answer: After the cited sentence, the author describes many effects that Franklin's experiment had. The sentence sets up this idea, conveying that the experiment was important.

(A) assumes that *pronounced* takes on the meaning of *declared* or *stated*, but that isn't appropriate for the text. There's nothing in the text to indicate that the experiment was *stated*. (B) is out-of-scope. The experiment itself was famous, but we don't know that Franklin was. (Be careful here; even though we know from history that Benjamin Franklin was quite famous indeed, there is nothing in the text that tells us that. On the SAT, you should not use your previous knowledge of a topic; you should use only the information presented on the test. That is all that will be necessary to answer the question.) (C) is tempting. It's close, but it's not entirely complete. The effects of Franklin's experiment also included practical and cultural effects—lightning rods, and dispelling a misunderstanding of lightning. True, it had a large impact in the scientific world, but those were not the only consequences. As for (E), watch out. It hints at an idea expressed in the text, but it doesn't truly address the function of the sentence. Though lightning seems to have been misunderstood before the experiment, this fact isn't conveyed by the sentence in question.

4. D

Getting to the Answer: You can't make a prediction, so jump into the answer choices.

(A) is the opposite case: The experiment helped to *dispel* a superstitious belief, not promote it, (B) and (C) are misused details. The text doesn't say that Franklin studied gravity; gravity is simply mentioned as an example of another natural force. And though Franklin used a Leyden jar, we don't know he helped to develop it. (E) is a distortion: The lightning rod could reduce the risk of fire damage, not repair the damage after the fact. (D) makes sense. The experiment had a cultural effect in "show[ing] that scientific research could have practical benefits."

5. B

Getting to the Answer: Here, "routine" means that the narrator did the same thing every weekend.

The passage offers no evidence that the narrator found the recitals boring, so (A) is out. (C) is also wrong because the students performed music, not drama. As for (D), a *routine* can refer to a series of dance steps, but such a reference is irrelevant in this context.

6. B

Getting to the Answer: What is the point of the story? The author says that the students "honed their performance skills," and dealing with mistakes would qualify as one of these skills.

Don't be tempted by (A): While the parents were an appreciative audience, they were probably appreciate of their son's talents *before* the recital took place. So to say that he *learned* this isn't likely. (C) is a distortion: Students were required to play from memory, but it would be a stretch to say the author learned not to rely on memory after that event. (D) is out-of-scope, and (E) is way too far a stretch.

7. B

Getting to the Answer: Don't fall for statements that the author would agree with but that don't answer the question. The author believes that the council now has a symbolic role, and that this should change. The phrase *symbolic role* shows that the council is only a symbol, and has no real power.

(A) is tempting but it's a distortion. It suggests that the council is ineffective, but that is not exactly what the text suggests. The text says that the council is unempowered. That is, it isn't given the "power" to do anything on its own. (C) and (D) are tricky. They are true, but they don't have much to do with the phrase "symbolic role," and that's what the question asks. As for (E), a student council already exists, so there's no need to establish one.

8. E

Getting to the Answer: Consider the author's tone, as well as the word choice in the text. The phrase *Adults regularly emphasize to us* indicates that the author doesn't consider herself an adult, and is likely a student of the school.

(A) is a distortion. The school never established the conflict resolution board. (B) can't be right, since the author doesn't consider herself an adult. As for (C), the author is quite critical of the administration, and sets herself apart from it. (D) is wrong since the writer isn't an adult.

9. D

Getting to the Answer: Author 2 definitely favors the supervision of adults, so look for a choice that captures this.

Parents are never mentioned, so (B) is out-of-scope. (C) is too extreme an idea, given the information in the text. (E) is extreme: Teachers and administrators are important, but the word *primary* makes this too extreme. It leaves out parents, who play a major role in the area of guidance and support. (D) makes sense. The text says that "students depend—often unwittingly—on the guidance and wisdom of teachers and administrators…." In other words, students may not realize how much they rely on adults.

10. D

Getting to the Answer: Author 1 feels that students should have more responsibility, while Author 2 believes students are better off when adults are firmly in charge.

(A) and (B) are out-of-scope. Author 2 mentions neither a conflict resolution board nor a student council. (C) is the reverse: Teacher and administrator guidance isn't mentioned by Author 1. Author 1 feels that students should participate in decision, but never denies that teachers and administrators provide important guidance. (E) is a distortion: Author 2 stresses the importance of this, but Author 1 never argues that structure is unimportant, only that the structure should included mechanisms for students to make their voices heard. (D) fits. Both authors directly address this; Author 1 thinks students should have a voice, and Author 2 says that schools run better when adults are in charge.

Short Reading Comprehension: Practice Set Eight

Questions 1–2 refer to the following passage.

What will be "cool" next year? Though it's impossible to predict with certainty, profit-minded fashion designers, music industry executives, and television producers would very much like to
(5) have a leg up on their competition. In fact, this ever-accelerating quest to spot trends and trend-setters has spawned a new industry. Trend-analysis experts specialize in predicting what will be in and what will be out. Some firms hire legions of young
(10) people to track the interests and fads of their contemporaries. One especially innovative trend-spotting firm uses the Internet to compile massive amounts of data from its informants, known as "field correspondents."

1. As used in the passage, *spawned* most nearly means

   (A) paved the way for
   (B) illustrated the wisdom of
   (C) questioned the necessity of
   (D) given rise to
   (E) shown the need for

2. Based on the passage, the author would most likely agree that

   (A) those who pursue information about future trends will likely be frustrated in this attempt
   (B) the predictions of trend-analysis experts should be regarded with at least some skepticism
   (C) young people are a vital resource for those who would predict future trends
   (D) the increasing pressure to predict trends has had a negative effect on the fashion, music, and television industries
   (E) the Internet is a valuable tool in the process of analyzing data about future trends

Questions 3–4 refer to the following passage.

The first African American painter to achieve an international reputation was Henry Ossawa Tanner. Born in 1859, Tanner spent much of his childhood sketching animals at the Philadelphia
(5) Zoo, displaying at an early age the talent and inclination necessary to become an artist. After studying with Thomas Eakins, America's premier realist painter of the late 19th century, Tanner traveled to Paris, where he remained for 40 years.
(10) It was there that he created some of his most impressive canvases, many of them on Biblical themes, such as *Daniel in the Lions' Den* and *The Raising of Lazarus*. In Tanner's last years during the 1930s, his Paris studio was a pilgrimage desti-
(15) nation for admiring younger African American artists, including Aaron Douglas and Palmer Hayden.

3. As used in the passage, *inclination* most nearly means

   (A) angle
   (B) capacity
   (C) skill
   (D) slant
   (E) desire

4. The passage suggests that younger African American artists visited Tanner in Paris because they

   (A) looked to Tanner as a role model
   (B) wanted to emulate the painting style of Tanner
   (C) admired the Biblical themes in Tanner's work
   (D) felt they would find success in Paris as Tanner had
   (E) hoped to study with Tanner

Questions 5–8 refer to the following passages.

Passage 1

I am at a loss to explain the passion for collecting that has descended on our neighborhood. If you take a walk on a Saturday morning, you'll find that more than one house in three is holding a
(5) garage sale. No matter what hours are advertised in our local paper, shoppers invariably arrive an hour or two early to churn through the stuff. Many of them charge from sale to sale, attending half a dozen or more in a morning. Some of them
(10) have turned what began as a hobby into a business: one professional shopper I know, for example, recycles the goods at her own store, marking them up and making a tidy profit. Most garage sale fans, though, are habitual collectors. When
(15) they've acquired enough stuff, they in turn will hold their own sales.

Passage 2

Although stamp collecting was a popular hobby in my childhood, it seems to be going out of fashion. Perhaps it has lost ground these days because
(20) so many people prefer email to "snail mail." Whatever the explanation, I think it's a pity. Stamps almost always reflect key facts about a country's history, geography, and culture, and often also possess an intrinsic aesthetic value:
(25) many of them exhibit ingenious designs and color combinations. The process of collecting the stamps also has much to recommend it. There is the challenge of locating rare items and building an impressive collection, and trading stamps
(30) brings friends together as they share the pleasure of indulging in the same hobby.

5. The author's tone in Passage 1 might best be described as

   (A) highly passionate
   (B) bitterly satirical
   (C) coldly objective
   (D) avidly pleading
   (E) gently amused

6. According to Author 2, stamp collecting may be declining in popularity because

   (A) few people now have groups of stamp-collecting friends with whom to trade stamps

   (B) the use of email has compromised many of the benefits of stamp collecting

   (C) of fundamental changes in our country's history, geography, and culture

   (D) changes in communications methods have made stamps partially obsolete

   (E) collecting hobbies in general have declined in popularity

7. Author 2 mentions all the following as reasons to collect stamps EXCEPT

   (A) discovering key facts about geography and history

   (B) aesthetic appeal

   (C) the increase in value of vintage stamps

   (D) the challenge of building a collection

   (E) sharing the same hobby with friends

8. How would Author 2 most likely respond to the concept of reselling objects originally purchased at garage sales cited in Passage 1?

   (A) Such sales illustrate that the original purchase was ill-advised.

   (B) Exchanging objects in this manner is a valuable way to meet other collectors with similar interests.

   (C) Though somewhat humorous, the image is also regrettable, since the seller will likely lose money in the resale.

   (D) Such actions illustrate the futility of collecting objects that do not have practical value, as stamps do.

   (E) "Garage sale reselling" is unlikely to occur among stamp collectors, who place a high value on building up an impressive collection.

Questions 9–10 refer to the following passage.

We think of Thanksgiving as a distinctively American holiday, and it is true that the celebration can be traced back to December 13, 1621 to the Puritan settlers of Plymouth Colony. Harvest
(5) and festivity, however, have gone together for thousands of years. In ancient Greece, the festival of Thesmophoria honored Demeter, the goddess of grain and the crops, and in ancient Israel, the Feast of Tabernacles, called Sukkoth, celebrated
(10) the earth's bounty. Today, customs are similar: in Germany, Oktoberfest marks the end of the harvest, and in China, lanterns are lit by partygoers celebrating the Harvest Moon.

9. Which of the following best summarizes the purpose the passage?

   (A) Thanksgiving is a distinctively American holiday.

   (B) The ancient Greek Thesmophoria anticipated the American celebration of Thanksgiving by thousands of years.

   (C) Little is known about the origins of the German festival of Oktoberfest.

   (D) Harvest celebrations have been common in all eras throughout the world.

   (E) Today's harvest celebrations are outdated remnants of ancient rituals.

10. The author cites Greek and Israeli harvest festivals in order to illustrate that

   (A) harvest celebrations occur in many parts of the world

   (B) these were the first harvest celebrations

   (C) Thanksgiving is not truly an American holiday

   (D) harvest celebrations occurred long ago

   (E) such celebrations were once more relevant than they are today

ANSWERS AND EXPLANATIONS

1. D

Getting to the Answer: The passage suggests that an entire industry has been *created* by the drive to predict trends.

The specific sentence says, "In fact, this ever-accelerating quest to spot trends and trendsetters has spawned a new industry." In other words, a new industry has been *triggered*. (A) is wrong because the quest didn't just *pave the way* for an industry, it actually helped create an industry. As for (B), it isn't complete enough: It doesn't convey the full idea that an industry was actually created. (C) is totally wrong—it didn't question the need at all. And (E) means much the same thing as (B).

2. B

Getting to the Answer: Compare each choice against what you know from the passage.

(A) is extreme. Though the text says it's impossible to predict trends with certainty, it doesn't suggest that everyone who pursues knowledge about trends will be frustrated. (C) is a misused detail. We know that "some" companies hire young people, not that most companies do—or even that this is vital or particularly effective. (D) is out-of-scope. These industries are interested in trends, but we don't know what kind of effect this is having. (E) is an overstatement, as only one firm is described as using the Internet, and there's no indication as to its value. (B) is correct: The author says that it is impossible to predict what will be cool next year, so it makes sense to regard the predictions about trends with skepticism.

3. E

Getting to the Answer: Don't be distracted by nearby words. Tanner had the "talent and inclination to become an artist." Several of the wrong choices here are synonyms for *talent*, not for *inclination*. Inclination means that Tanner had an *interest* in becoming an artist.

(A) and (D) are other meanings of inclination, but don't fit here. With (B), *capacity* indicates that Tanner had the ability to become an artist. This is different from having an interest in becoming an artist. (C), too, doesn't capture the meaning of *inclination* because it doesn't show that Tanner had an interest.

4. A

Getting to the Answer: The passage describes Tanner's studio as a "pilgrimage destination," and describes the younger artists as "admiring." They looked up to him as a successful African American painter, and wanted to meet him. Review the context in which the visits by other artists to Tanner in Paris are mentioned.

(B) and (E) are distortions. The younger painters admired Tanner, but that doesn't mean they wanted to paint like him or study with him. (C) is a misused detail: We don't know that the younger artists admired the Biblical themes. (D) is also a distortion; it doesn't capture the sense expressed in the words *admiring* and *pilgrimage destination*.

5. E

Getting to the Answer: The author finds collecting amusing and somewhat silly.

The author thinks that collecting is silly, but (A) is too extreme. And the author seems amused, not bitter, so (B) is wrong. (C) is clearly wrong, as there's definitely a personal opinion here. (E) is correct: The author is mildly amused.

6. D

Getting to the Answer: The author writes that "perhaps it has lost ground these days because so many people prefer email to "'snail mail.'" Why would the increase of email cause stamp collecting to decrease in popularity? Well, if people are mailing fewer letters, then there are fewer stamps in use. That would mean that people are exposed to fewer stamps on a day-to-day basis.

(A) is a distortion: Groups of friends are mentioned to explain the benefits of stamp collecting, not the decline of its popularity. (B) is tricky, but notice something: It's not the *benefits* that have been compromised by email—it's the *exposure* to stamps that has been compromised. Stamps are still a gateway to foreign cultures, pleasing aesthetic objects, a good way to meet friends, and so forth. (C) just lifts a few words from the text and hopes you'll think they're correct. In fact, they make a total misstatement here. (E) is out-of-scope. Author 2 discusses only stamp collecting, not other hobbies. (D) fits. People use fewer stamps because of email, so stamps have become partially obsolete.

7. C

Getting to the Answer: Only one answer choice can be correct. Look for a detail that is *absent* from the passage.

(C) is the only detail that is not mentioned in the passage. Although this might indeed be a reason to collect stamps, it is not included here. As for (D), though the challenge of building a stamp collection might seem like an obstacle, that's precisely why the author thinks it appealing.

8. B

Getting to the Answer: Author 1 thinks that the image of reselling objects is amusing, since it illustrates that people value the *process* of collecting the objects more than they value the objects themselves. Author 2 would probably have a different view, however, since he approves of collecting.

(A) is a complete overstatement. (C) is out-of-Scope; Author 2 never discusses money, so you don't know his thoughts on the subject. (D) is out of-scope as well. Author 2 doesn't discuss the practical value of stamps. Instead he concentrates on their beauty, and the way they can teach you about other cultures and help you to meet friends. (E) is too much of a stretch. (B) makes sense. Author 2 believes that trading stamps with other collectors is a good way to meet friends, and re-circulating garage sale items might well serve a similar purpose.

9. D

Getting to the Answer: Look for an answer choice that concisely expresses the writer's main idea.

(A) is the opposite case: Thanksgiving is American, but it is cited as an example of a larger point—that harvest festivals are very common. (B) is a detail in the passage, not its main thrust. As for (C), though the passage mentions Oktoberfest, the festival's origins aren't discussed. (E) is a distortion: Harvest festivals have been around for a long time, but there's no evidence that they're *outdated*.

10. D

Getting to the Answer: Before citing the Greek and Israeli festivals, the author writes, "Harvest and festivity, however, have gone together for thousands of years." Since both the Greek and Israeli festivals are described as *ancient*, you know they have been cited to help prove that harvest festivals have been around for a long time.

(A) is challenging. The example comes right after the sentence about the harvest festivals being ancient. The point of these two examples is that the festivals have occurred for a long time, not that they occur all over the world. (B) is out-of-scope. Though they occurred a long time ago, the author never implies that these were the first such festivals. (C) is the opposite case: The author doesn't debate that Thanksgiving is American, only that the idea of a harvest festival is not uniquely American. With (E), the author doesn't suggest that the festivals are now less relevant.

Long Reading Comprehension: Practice Set One

Directions: Answer the questions below based on the information in the accompanying passage.

The following passage analyzes one of Willa Cather's (1873–1947) novels.

Sapphira and the Slave Girl was the last novel of Willa Cather's illustrious literary career. Begun in the late summer of 1937 and finally completed in 1941, it is often regarded by critics as one of her
(5) most personal works. Although the story takes place in 1856, well before her own birth, she drew heavily on both vivid childhood memories and tales handed down by older relatives to describe life in rural northern Virginia in the middle of the
(10) 19th century. She even went on an extended journey to the area to give the story a further ring of authenticity.

Of all of Cather's many novels, *Sapphira and the Slave Girl* is the one most concerned with provid-
(15) ing an overall picture of day-to-day life in a specific era. A number of the novel's characters, it would seem, are included in the story only because they are representative of the types of people to be found in 19th-century rural Virginia;
(20) indeed, a few of them play no part whatsoever in the unfolding of the plot. For instance, we are introduced to a poor white woman, Mandy Ringer, who is portrayed as intelligent and content, despite the fact that she has no formal educa-
(25) tion and must toil constantly in the fields. And we meet Dr. Clevenger, a country doctor who, with his patrician manners, evokes a strong image of the pre-Civil War South.

The title, however, accurately suggests that the
(30) novel is mainly about slavery. Cather's attitude toward this institution may best be summed up as somewhat ambiguous. On the one hand, she displays almost total indifference to the legal and political aspects of slavery when she misidentifies
(35) certain crucial dates in its growth and development. Nor does she ever really offer a direct condemnation of slavery. Yet, on the other hand, the evil that was slavery gets through to us, albeit in typically subtle ways. Those characters, like Mrs.
(40) Blake, who oppose the institution are portrayed in a sympathetic light. Furthermore, the suffering of the slaves themselves and the petty, nasty, often cruel, behavior of the slaveowners are painted in stark terms.

(45) Although *Sapphira and the Slave Girl* was certainly not meant to be a political tract, the novel is sometimes considered to be a denunciation of bygone days. Nothing could be further from the truth. In spite of her willingness to acknowledge
(50) that particular aspects of the past were far from ideal, Willa Cather was, if anything, a bit of a romantic. Especially in the final years of her life, an increasing note of anger about the emptiness of the present crept into her writings. Earlier genera-
(55) tions, she concluded, had been the real heroes, the real creators of all that was good in America.

1. The word *extended* in line 10 most nearly means

   (A) enlarged
   (B) increased
   (C) postponed
   (D) stretched
   ✓(E) prolonged

2. In the discussion of Willa Cather's *Sapphira and the Slave Girl*, the author refers to the book primarily as a

   (A) heroic tale of the Civil War

   (B) sweeping epic of the old South

   ✓(C) story based on personal material

   (D) political treatise on slavery

   (E) veiled condemnation of 1930s America

3. In paragraph 2, Mandy Ringer and Dr. Clevenger are mentioned in order to emphasize which point about *Sapphira and the Slave Girl*?

   (A) A number of the characters in the novel are based on people Cather knew in her childhood.

   (B) The novel displays Cather's mixed feelings about slavery.

   (C) Cather took four years to complete the novel because she carefully researched her characters.

   (D) One of Cather's purposes in writing the novel was to paint a full portrait of life in rural Virginia in the years before the Civil War.

   (E) The characters in the novel are portrayed in a positive light since Cather was a great admirer of the old South.

4. According to the author, why is Willa Cather's attitude toward slavery "somewhat ambiguous" (line 32)?

   (A) She was ignorant of the legal and political aspects of slavery even though she was a keen observer of history.

   (B) She did not denounce slavery directly but criticized it in more roundabout ways.

   (C) She sympathized equally with both slaves and slave owners.

   (D) She was an enemy of slavery but refrained from getting involved in political issues.

   ✓(E) She disliked the treatment of slaves yet never tried to help improve their lot in life.

5. In context, "a bit of a romantic" (lines 51–52) suggests that Willa Cather

   (A) condemned the evils of slavery

   ✓(B) favored the past over the present

   (C) disliked writing about life in the 1930s

   (D) denounced certain aspects of 19th-century life

   (E) exaggerated the evils of earlier generations

ANSWERS AND EXPLANATIONS

After your first reading, you should know roughly what the passage as a whole is about, and what each paragraph is about. Paragraph 1 tells us that *Sapphira and the Slave Girl* is one of Cather's most authentic and personal works. Paragraph 2 tells us that the novel sets out to provide a picture of everyday life in the pre-Civil War South. Paragraph 3 explains that while the novel is mainly about slavery, Cather's attitude toward slavery is ambiguous. The final paragraph says that although some consider *Sapphira* a denunciation of the past, the author feels the opposite is true.

1. E

Getting to the Answer: If an answer choice has already grabbed your eye, try it in context. If not, check out each choice.

(A) *enlarged* might seem related to a long trip, but it doesn't sound right. (B) *increased* doesn't make sense; increased from what? (C) *postponed* is easy to eliminate; Cather's trip was not put off until a future time. (D) *stretched* is a definition of extended, but not one that works here. (E) is a good match. *Prolonged* makes sense. The line "She went on an extended journey," keeps its meaning if you substituted *prolonged* for *extended*. Both words give the idea of an extensive trip, one where Cather could get a real feel for the places she would later describe in her novel.

2. C

Getting to the Answer: Paragraph 1 holds the answer. It tells us that *Sapphira* is one of Cather's most personal works and drew heavily on her childhood memories. The answer is almost certainly (C).

With (A), paragraph 2 tells us that the novel is largely a portrait of the pre-Civil War South, and paragraph 3 tells us that *Sapphira* is mainly about slavery. With (B), there is nothing in the text to suggest that *Sapphira* is a sweeping epic. If anything, it's the opposite, a very personal novel. As for (D), this can't be right, because the first line in paragraph 4 says *Sapphira* is "not meant to be a political tract." And though (E) is less obviously wrong, it is still wrong. Also in paragraph 4, the author tells us Cather was dissatisfied with the present, but this is not the focus of her novel. (C) is the right answer.

3. D

Getting to the Answer: Go back to paragraph 2 and see what's going on. The author mentions two characters who are included mainly to help complete Cather's portrait of rural Virginia.

(A) and (C) are discussed in paragraph 1. (B) is discussed in paragraph 3. (E) is an overstatement of the content in paragraph 4. (D) is a good match. Other answer choices might agree with points the author makes elsewhere in the passage, but this question asks specifically about paragraph 2.

4. B

Getting to the Answer: Paragraph 3 says that Cather's attitude toward slavery is "somewhat ambiguous," and offers several bits of evidence. On the one hand, Cather never comes out and directly condemns slavery, and she displays ignorance of and indifference to its legal and political aspects. On the other hand, she sympathetically portrays characters opposed to slavery and clearly portrays the suffering of slaves and the cruelty of slave owners.

(A) captures only part of this evidence. And the text never says that Cather sympathizes with slave owners, so (C) is wrong. As for (D), the passage says Cather's attitude toward slavery was "ambiguous," not that she was an enemy of slavery. With (E), the author is talking about Cather's attitude toward slavery as expressed in *Sapphira*, not in terms of what she did or did not do in her life.

5. B

Getting to the Answer: The last paragraph refers to Cather as "a bit of a romantic" who cherished past creativity over the present emptiness.

(A) can't be right, because the passage says Cather's views of slavery are "ambiguous." *Ambiguous* means "not clear; capable of being understood in two or more ways." With (C), nothing suggests Cather disliked writing about the 1930s. As for (D), Cather did dislike certain aspects of mid-19th-century life, but that's the opposite of romanticizing those times. And with (E), Cather didn't exaggerate the evils of the past; if anything, she underestimated them.

Long Reading Comprehension: Practice Set Two

The following passage is excerpted from a popular journal of archeology.

About 50 miles west of Stonehenge, buried in the peat bogs of the Somerset flatlands in southwestern England, lies the oldest road known to humanity. Dubbed the "Sweet Track" after its dis-
(5) coverer, Raymond Sweet, this painstakingly constructed 1,800-meter road dates back to the early Neolithic period, some 6,000 years ago. Thanks primarily to the overlying layer of acidic peat, which has kept the wood moist, inhibited the
(10) growth of decay bacteria, and discouraged the curiosity of animal life, the road is remarkably well preserved. Examination of its remains has provided extensive information about the people who constructed it.

(15) The design of the Sweet Track indicates that its builders possessed extraordinary engineering skills. In constructing the road, they first hammered pegs into the soil in the form of upright X's. Single rails were slid beneath the pegs, so that
(20) the rails rested firmly on the soft surface of the bog. Then planks were placed in the V-shaped space formed by the upper arms of the pegs. This method of construction—allowing the underlying rail to distribute the weight of the plank above
(25) and thereby prevent the pegs from sinking into the marsh—is remarkably sophisticated, testifying to a surprisingly advanced level of technology.

Furthermore, in order to procure the materials for the road, several different species of tree had to
(30) be felled, debarked, and split. This suggests that the builders possessed high quality tools, and that they knew the differing properties of various roundwoods. It appears also that the builders were privy to the finer points of lumbering, maximizing
(35) the amount of wood extracted from a given tree by slicing logs of large diameter radially and logs of small diameter tangentially.

Studies of the Sweet Track further indicate a high level of social organization among its
(40) builders. This is supported by the observation that the road seems to have been completed in a very short time; tree-ring analysis confirms that the components of the Sweet Track were probably all felled within a single year. Moreover, the fact that
(45) such an involved engineering effort could be orchestrated in the first place hints at a complex social structure.

Finally, excavation of the Sweet Track has provided evidence that the people who built it com-
(50) prised a community devoted to land cultivation. It appears that the road was built to serve as a footpath linking two islands—islands that provided a source of timber, cropland, and pastures for the community that settled the hills to the south.
(55) Furthermore, the quality of the pegs indicates that the workers knew enough to fell trees in such a way as to encourage the rapid growth of long, straight, rodlike shoots from the remaining stumps, to be used as pegs. This method is called
(60) coppicing and its practice by the settlers is the earliest known example of woodland management.

Undoubtedly, the discovery of the Sweet Track in 1970 added much to our knowledge of Neolithic technology. But while study of the
(65) remains has revealed unexpectedly high levels of engineering and social organization, it must be remembered that the Sweet Track represents the work of a single isolated community. One must be careful not to extrapolate sweeping generalizations
(70) from the achievements of such a small sample of Neolithic humanity.

1. In paragraph 1, the author claims that which of the following was primarily responsible for the preservation of the Sweet Track until modern times?

   (A) It was located in an area containing very few animals.

   (B) Its components were buried beneath the peat bog.

   (C) It was only lightly traveled during its period of use.

   (D) Local authorities prohibited development in the surrounding area.

   (E) It was protected from excessive humidity.

2. The author's reference to the peat bog as "acidic" (line 8) primarily serves to

   (A) indicate the importance of protecting ancient ruins from the effects of modern pollution

   (B) emphasize that the Sweet Track was constructed of noncorrosive materials

   (C) distinguish between the effects of acidic and basic conditions on ancient ruins

   (D) suggest that acidic conditions were important in inhibiting decay

   (E) prove the relevance of knowledge of chemical properties to archaeological concerns

3. In paragraph 2, the author describes the construction of the Sweet Track primarily in order to

   (A) explain the unusual strength of the structure

   (B) show how it could withstand 6,000 years buried underground

   (C) prove that its builders cooperated efficiently

   (D) indicate its builders' advanced level of technological expertise

   (E) emphasize the importance of careful construction techniques

4. The primary focus of the passage is on

   (A) the high degree of social organization exhibited by earlier cultures

   (B) the complex construction and composition of the Sweet Track

   (C) an explanation for the survival of the Sweet Track over 6,000 years

   (D) ways in which the Sweet Track reveals aspects of a particular Neolithic society

   (E) the innovative methods of woodland management practiced by early builders

5. In line 34, the phrase *privy to* means

   (A) close to

   (B) expert at

   (C) concealed from

   (D) likely to

   (E) familiar with

6. In her discussion of social organization in paragraph 4, the author mentions ring analysis primarily as evidence that

   (A) the road is at least 6,000 years old

   (B) the Sweet Track was constructed quickly

   (C) the techniques used in building the road were quite sophisticated

   (D) the builders knew enough to split thick trees radially and thin trees tangentially

   (E) the builders felled a large variety of trees

7. The cited example of "woodland management" (line 61) is best described as a system in which trees are

   (A) lumbered in controlled quantities

   (B) planted only among trees of their own species

   (C) cultivated in specialized ways for specific purposes

   (D) felled only as they are needed

   (E) harvested for use in construction only

8. In the last paragraph, the author cautions that the Sweet Track

   (A) is not as technologically advanced as is generally believed

   (B) should not necessarily be regarded as representative of its time

   (C) has not been studied extensively enough to support generalized conclusions

   (D) is probably not the earliest road in existence

   (E) will force historians to reevaluate their assumptions about the Neolithic technology

ANSWERS AND EXPLANATIONS

This passage, which comes from a popular journal of archeology, is about the "oldest road known to humanity," also known as the Sweet Track after its discoverer. The last sentence paragraph 1 makes the main point: that examination of the remains of the Sweet Track has revealed lots of information about the people who built it. The next four paragraphs provide examples and insights about the builders, revealed by studying the remains. Do you have to sweat the details of each example? No way. Don't waste time trying to understand the specific construction techniques, materials, tools, etcetera.

In the second paragraph, for instance, we hope you skimmed over all that description about wooden X-Shaped pegs and the upper and lower rails. All you need to know is that the builders of the Sweet Track had a "surprisingly advanced level of technology."

The passage concludes with a little warning: Although the Sweet Track shows X, Y, and Z about the builders, this small group of people does not represent Neolithic peoples in general. You can't assume that all people in those long-ago days were as advanced as the builders of the Sweet Track.

1. B

Getting to the Answer: This question sends you back to the first paragraph. What accounts for the road's being so well preserved? The remains were buried under a layer of acidic peat, which kept the wood moist, prevented decay from bacteria, and kept nosy animals away.

(A) may have given you pause, since a lack of interfering animals is mentioned in paragraph 1. But it wasn't the location of the road that kept animals away; it was the fact that the road was buried, so the animals couldn't get to it. (C) and (D) might seem to offer reasonable explanations for the road's good condition, but the passage never mentions light travel patterns or development prohibitions. Finally, (E) gets it dead wrong; the road was kept "moist," according to the author, so it was hardly protected from excessive humidity.

2. D

Getting to the Answer: Reread the sentence in which *acidic* is mentioned. It says that the "acidic peat" allowed for three conditions that caused the road to be preserved: It kept it moist, relatively free of bacteria, and free from animal interference. So the fact that the bog was "acidic" must have something to do with causing those conditions. Only (D) mentions one of these three conditions, so it's the answer.

(A) and (C) bring in unmentioned issues, and (B) is wrong because the author never mentions noncorrosive materials as a factor that kept the road in such good shape. (E) is too general; the author is not making a big point about chemicals and archeology.

3. D

Getting to the Answer: You're asked why the author describes the construction of the Sweet Track. In the last sentence, it says that method of construction "is remarkably sophisticated, testifying to a surprisingly advanced level of technology"—(D).

(B) and (C) point to conclusions the author makes elsewhere in the passage, not in the lines specified in this question. (A) talks about the *unusual strength* of the road, which the author never discusses. (E)'s sweeping reference to the importance of careful construction techniques is too general, since the author is only drawing conclusions about this one specific culture.

4. D

Getting to the Answer: The key to this question is in the last sentence of the paragraph 1. The author says she's going to discuss how Sweet Track's remains tell us a great deal about the Neolithic people who built it—a focus best summed up by (D).

(B) is probably the closest wrong choice, but it's only half of the main focus. The author does focus on the complex construction and composition of the road, but for a purpose—to discuss what that construction and composition tells us about the builders of the road. (A) is too broad. (C) and (E) are too narrow. The survival of the road over 6,000 years (C) is the purpose of just the end of the first paragraph. And (E) is too narrow because woodland management is the topic of paragraph 5 only.

5. E

Getting to the Answer: Go back and examine how *privy to* is used in the sentence *before* you try to answer. The sentence says, "the builders were *privy to* the finer points of lumbering" because they knew how to maximize the amount of wood extracted from a log by slicing it in different ways. That shows they were (E) *familiar with* the finer points of lumbering.

(A), (C), and (D) don't make sense. How can somebody be close to, concealed from, or likely to the finer points of lumbering? (B) sounds possible, but *familiar with* is a more moderate choice. Remember, you're looking for the "best" answer.

6. B

Getting to the Answer: To find out why the author brings up *ring analysis,* reread paragraph 4. The road "seems to have been completed in a very short time." How do we know? Because "tree-ring analysis," the topic of this question, confirms that the trees used to build the road were all felled within a single year. So tree-ring analysis offers evidence to support the claim that the Sweet Track was built quickly; choice (B).

(A) may seem plausible, because we usually count tree-rings to find out how old trees are. But in paragraph 4, tree-ring analysis was used for another purpose. The other choices raise issues discussed elsewhere. Those *sophisticated building techniques*, (C), were the subject of paragraph 2, while the fancy lumbering technique mentioned in (D), as well as the *large variety of felled trees* mentioned in (E), were brought up in paragraph 3 and have nothing to do with the tree-ring analysis mentioned in paragraph 4.

7. C

Getting to the Answer: What is the cited example of "woodland management" that the question refers to? When you go to the line reference given, you'll find it's called "coppicing." Coppicing is described as the process of felling trees "in such a way as to encourage the rapid growth of long, straight, rodlike shoots from the remaining stumps, to be used as pegs." In other words, trees are grown in a special way in order to yield *special* materials—that is, the rodlike shoots.

(A) and (D) have nothing to do with the paragraph. (B) may sound plausible, but the process described here focuses not on the *kind* of trees being planted, but rather the *way* they are planted. And (E) may seem tempting, because the lumber in question *was* harvested for use in construction, but again, the point is how the trees were planted, not what they were used for.

8. B

Getting to the Answer: This question directs you to that interesting last paragraph we discussed above—the one that cautions not to generalize too much from the Sweet Track. The author says the Sweet Track represents "the work of a single isolated community," and that therefore we shouldn't use it to make conclusions about all Neolithic communities.

(A) and (D) are not the subject of the last paragraph; besides, they're just plain wrong. (C) is a distortion. The reason we shouldn't draw generalized conclusions from the Sweet Track is because it's the work of just one small community, not because the road has been studied too little. And (E) implies that the study of the Sweet Track will bring about a fundamental revolution in historical thought about the whole Neolithic period—just the kind of general conclusions that the author explicitly warns against.

Long Reading Comprehension: Practice Set Three

Directions: Answer the questions below based on the information in the accompanying passage.

The following passage is excerpted from a study of modern architecture.

Fallingwater, a small country house constructed in 1936, stands as perhaps the greatest residential building achievement of the American architect Frank Lloyd Wright. In designing the dwelling for
(5) the Pittsburgh millionaire Edgar J. Kaufmann, Wright was confronted with an unusually challenging site, beside a waterfall deep in a Pennsylvania ravine. However, Wright viewed this difficult location not as an obstacle, but as a
(10) unique opportunity to put his architectural ideals into concrete form. In the end, Wright was able to turn Fallingwater into an artistic link between untamed nature and domestic tranquility, and a masterpiece in his brilliant career.
(15) Edgar J. Kaufmann had originally planned for his house to sit at the bottom of the waterfall, where there was ample flat land on which to build. But Wright proposed a more daring response to the site. The architect convinced Kaufmann to
(20) build his house at the top of the waterfall on a small stone precipice. Further, Wright proposed extending the living room of the house out over the rushing water, and making use of modern building techniques so that no vertical supports
(25) would be needed to hold up the room. Rather than allowing the environment to determine the placement and shape of the house, Wright sought to construct a home that actually confronted and interacted with the landscape.

(30) In one sense, Fallingwater can be viewed as a showcase for unconventional building tactics. In designing the living room, for example, Wright made brilliant use of a technique called the cantilever, in which steel rods are laid inside a shelf of
(35) concrete, eliminating the need for external supports. But Fallingwater also contains a great many traditional and natural building materials. The boulders which form the foundation for the house also extend up through the floor and form part of
(40) the fireplace. A staircase in the living room extends down to an enclosed bathing pool at the top of the waterfall. To Wright, the ideal dwelling in this spot was not simply a modern extravaganza or a direct extension of natural surroundings;
(45) rather, it was a little of both.
Critics have taken a wide range of approaches to understanding this unique building. Some have postulated that the house exalts the artist's triumph over untamed nature. Others have compared
(50) Wright's building to a cave, providing a psychological and physical safe haven from a harsh, violent world. Edgar Kaufmann Jr., the patron's son, may have summed up Fallingwater best when he said, "Wright understood that people were creatures of
(55) nature; hence an architecture which conformed to nature would conform to what was basic in people . . . . Sociability and privacy are both available, as are the comforts of home and the adventures of the seasons." This, then, is Frank Lloyd Wright's
(60) achievement in Fallingwater, a home which connects the human and the natural, for the invigoration and exaltation of both.

KAPLAN

1. The primary purpose of the passage is to

   (A) showcase Wright's use of unconventional building tactics and techniques

   (B) describe the relationship between Wright and Edgar J. Kaufmann

   (C) judge the place of Fallingwater in the history of architecture

   (D) describe Fallingwater as Wright's response to a challenging building site

   (E) evaluate various critical responses to Fallingwater

2. The word *concrete* in line 11 could best be replaced by

   (A) dense

   (B) hard

   (C) substantial

   (D) durable

   (E) reinforced

3. The passage suggests that Edgar J. Kaufmann's original plans for the site were

   (A) conservative

   (B) inexpensive

   (C) daring

   (D) idealistic

   (E) architecturally unsound

4. The author includes a description of a cantilever (lines 33–36) in order to explain

   (A) the technique used to create the fireplace in Fallingwater

   (B) the use of traditional engineering techniques in Fallingwater

   (C) an unusual design feature of Fallingwater

   (D) modern technological advances in the use of concrete

   (E) how Fallingwater conforms to nature

5. The end of paragraph 3 indicates that, above all else, Wright wanted Kaufmann's home to be

   (A) representative of its owner's wealth and position

   (B) as durable as current construction techniques would allow

   (C) a landmark in 20th century American architecture

   (D) impressive yet in harmony with its surroundings

   (E) a symbol of man's triumph over the natural landscape

6. Critics' comparison of Fallingwater to a cave (line 50) suggests that the house conveys a sense of

   (A) warmth

   (B) darkness

   (C) simplicity

   (D) claustrophobia

   (E) security

7. In context, the phrase *for the invigoration and exaltation of both* (line 62) suggests that Fallingwater

   (A) encourages visitors to appreciate the change of seasons

   (B) benefits the environment as well as its occupants

   (C) stands out as the most beautiful feature in the local landscape

   (D) enables its owners to entertain in an impressive setting

   (E) typifies Wright's efforts to infuse modern architecture with spirituality

ANSWERS AND EXPLANATIONS

Fallingwater, a house designed by the famous American architect Frank Lloyd Wright, is regarded by most as a bold architectural statement, both because of its dramatic location atop a waterfall and because of various unconventional building techniques used in the design. One running theme is the relationship of the house to the natural setting around it. Throughout the passage, the author comments on that relationship, indicating that Fallingwater "confronted and interacted with the landscape," so that it was an extension of nature and also an impressive "modern extravaganza."

1.   D

Getting to the Answer: Your initial response to this question might have been to describe the design of the Fallingwater house. But the answer should incorporate the running theme mentioned above—the relationship of the house to the natural setting. That's why (D) is correct.

(A) is too broad. The author discusses Wright's *tactics and techniques* only in the design of one specific building, Fallingwater, which this choice does not specify. (B) is a distortion; although Kaufmann and Wright had different ideas about the ideal location for the house, *describing their relationship* is not the purpose of the passage. In (C), though the author says Fallingwater is unique, she never discusses its place in *architectural history*. And finally, (E) is the focus of the last paragraph only, where *critical responses* are discussed.

2.   C

Getting to the Answer: To find a synonym for *concrete* that fits the context, go back to the actual sentence. You'll see *concrete* is used figuratively. Wright, the author says, regarded Fallingwater's site as an "opportunity to put his architectural ideals into concrete form"—out of the realm of ideals, in other words, and into the realm of real, tangible things. So (C) *substantial* is the best replacement word: Wright wanted to give substance to his ideals by incorporating them in an actual building.

Choices (A), (B), and (E) are all too literal. We talk about *reinforced* concrete, about something being hard or dense as concrete, but that's not the meaning of concrete here. (D) *durable* doesn't work either; though concrete is a durable substance, durable isn't a synonym for this figurative sense of the word.

3.   A

Getting to the Answer: Kaufmann's original plans for the house are discussed only at the beginning of paragraph 2. Kaufmann had originally planned to put the house on a flat place near the bottom of the waterfall, but Wright convinced him to accept the "more daring" response of building the house right over the waterfall. While she doesn't say so directly, the author implies that Kaufmann's original plans were less daring, less risky, or, as (A) has it, more *conservative*.

(C) is the opposite case here, since it was Wright who had the daring plan for the house. Similarly, (D) better describes Wright's plan than Kaufmann's, since the author claims that Wright's plan "put his architectural ideals into concrete form." (B) may be true, but the cost of the two plans are never discussed. And nowhere is Kaufmann's plan criticized as (E) *architecturally unsound*; in fact, it was almost certainly regarded as *more* sound than Wright's daring idea.

4.   C

Getting to the Answer: Don't worry if you can't tell a cantilever from a cantaloupe. You just have to know *why* the technique is described. In the spot where the cantilever process is explained, we're told that it's an example of the "unconventional building tactics" mentioned in the sentence before. *Unconventional* translates nicely to unusual, (C).

The construction of the *fireplace*, choice (A), is mentioned as an example of the traditional elements used in the house; it has nothing to do with cantilevers. (B) is the opposite of what you want, since *unconventional* and *traditional* are virtual antonyms. (D) might seem logical, but it's not in the paragraph; the author isn't talking broadly about modern technological advances in concrete; she only describes the advances used in the Fallingwater house. Finally, (E) is off base since there's nothing particularly natural about a cantilever; the discussion about nature comes later in the same paragraph and is not directly related.

5. D

Getting to the Answer: At the end of paragraph 3, we learn that Wright's ideal dwelling for the waterfall site "was not simply a modern extravaganza or a direct extension of natural surroundings, [but] a little bit of both." So your answer has to incorporate both elements. And that makes (D) correct; Wright wanted the house to be impressive but still harmonious.

(A) is wrong because the passage offers no evidence that Kaufmann's money and position influenced Wright's thinking. (B)'s focus on *durability* makes it inappropriate; the end of paragraph 3 doesn't deal with Fallingwater's ability to survive over time. Nor does it deal with Wright's desire for the house to be considered an architectural *landmark*, so (C) is wrong. And (E) is a distortion; Wright wanted Fallingwater to be an "extension of [the] natural surroundings" —not a *triumph* over them.

6. E

Getting to the Answer: The absolutely wrong way to approach this question is to use your own impression of "cave[s]" as your guide. It's the critics' idea of a "cave" that's important here. According to the cited sentence, critics compared Fallingwater to a "cave" because the house provided "a psychological and physical safe haven from a harsh, violent world." So it's the quality of safety that's being equated here, leading you to (E) *security*.

(A) seems possible, since *warmth* conveys a sense of refuge from the cold, but compare it with (E). Since security is more directly related to the mention of "safe haven," (A) is only second-best. (B) *darkness* and (D) *claustrophobia* are qualities that you personally may associate with "cave[s]," but they're not the qualities these "critics" had in mind. Finally, (C) *simplicity* is way off base; first, there's nothing particularly simple about a cave, and second, the "safe haven" is not from a complex world, but a "harsh, violent" world.

7. B

Getting to the Answer: The line reference refers you to the very end of the passage. To answer correctly, you need to see that "both" refers to both "the human and the natural." This underlines the running theme we mentioned earlier—the interaction between the human, as represented by the house, and the natural, as represented by the natural setting. Wright wants to do justice to both, and so (B) best answers the question.

(A) and (D) miss half the message; they show how humans are "invigorated and exalted" by the natural setting, but not how nature benefits. (C) does the opposite, emphasizing how the house beautifies the setting but failing to mention how the setting beautifies the house. And (E) is an inference that goes too far. (B) is a better answer.

Long Reading Comprehension:
Practice Set Four

The following passages present two views of the city. Passage 1 focuses on the decline of the city park system. Passage 2 describes the decline of the city as a work of art.

Passage 1

City parks were originally created to provide the local populace with a convenient refuge from the crowding and chaos of its surroundings. Until quite recently, these parks served their purpose
(5) admirably. Whether city dwellers wanted to sit under a shady tree to think or take a vigorous stroll to get some exercise, they looked forward to visiting these nearby oases. Filled with trees, shrubs, flowers, meadows, and ponds, city parks
(10) were a tranquil spot in which to unwind from the daily pressures of urban life. They were places where people met their friends for picnics or sporting events. And they were also places to get some sun and fresh air in the midst of an often
(15) dark and dreary environment, with its seemingly endless rows of steel, glass, and concrete buildings.

For more than a century, the importance of these parks to the quality of life in cities has been recognized by urban planners. Yet city parks
(20) around the world have been allowed to deteriorate to an alarming extent in recent decades. In many cases, they have become centers of crime; some city parks are now so dangerous that local residents are afraid even to enter them. And the great
(25) natural beauty which was once their hallmark has been severely damaged. Trees, shrubs, flowers, and meadows have withered under the impact of intense air pollution and littering, and ponds have been fouled by untreated sewage.

(30) This process of decline, however, is not inevitable. A few changes can turn the situation around. First, special police units, whose only responsibility would be to patrol city parks, should be created to ensure that they remain safe
(35) for those who wish to enjoy them. Second, more caretakers should be hired to care for the grounds and, in particular, to collect trash. Beyond the increased staffing requirements, it will also be necessary to insulate city parks from their surround-
(40) ings. Total isolation is, of course, impossible; but many beneficial measures in that direction could be implemented without too much trouble. Vehicles, for instance, should be banned from city parks to cut down on air pollution. And sewage
(45) pipes should be rerouted away from park areas to prevent the contamination of land and water. If urban planners are willing to make these changes, city parks can be restored to their former glory for the benefit of all.

Passage 2

(50) With the rise of the great metropolis in the industrial era, city planning in the West passed out of the hands of the architect and into the hands of the technocrat.* Unlike the architect who thought of the city as a work of art to be built up with an
(55) eye toward beauty, the technocrat has always taken a purely functional approach to city planning; the city exists for the sole purpose of serving the needs of its inhabitants. Its outward appearance has no intrinsic value.

(60) Over the span of a few centuries, this new breed of urban planner has succeeded in forever changing the face of the Western city. A brief visit to any large metropolis is enough to confirm this grim

fact. Even a casual observer could not fail to notice
(65) that the typical urban landscape is arranged along
the lines of the tedious chessboard pattern, with
its four-cornered intersections and long, straight
and dull streets. Strict building codes have resulted
in an overabundance of unsightly neighborhoods
(70) in which there is only slight variation among
structures. Rows of squat concrete apartment
houses and files of gigantic steel and glass skyscrapers have almost completely replaced older,
more personal buildings. Moreover, the lovely nat-
(75) ural surroundings of many cities are no longer a
part of the urban landscape. For the most part,
the hills and rivers which were once so much a
part of so many metropolitan settings have now
been blotted out by thoughtless construction.
(80)   The lone bright spot amidst all of this urban
blight has been the local park system, which is to
be found in most Western cities. Large, centrally-
located parks— for example, New York's Central
Park or London's Hyde Park—and smaller, outly-
(85) ing parks bring a measure of beauty to Western
cities by breaking up the man-made monotony.
With their green pastures, dense woods, and pleas-
ant ponds, streams and waterfalls, local park systems also offer a vast array of opportunities for
(90) city dwellers to rest or recreate, free of the intense
burdens of urban life. If they have understood
nothing else about the quality of life in urban
areas, technocrats have at least had the good sense
to recognize that people need a quiet refuge from
(95) the chaotic bustle of the city.

*technocrat: technical expert

1. The author of Passage 1 uses the phrase *convenient refuge* in line 2 to suggest that parks were

    (A) built in order to preserve plant life in cities

    (B) designed with the needs of city residents in mind

    (C) meant to end the unpleasantness of city life

    (D) supposed to help people make new friends

    (E) intended to allow natural light to filter into cities

2. By mentioning crime and pollution (lines 22–29), the author of Passage 1 primarily emphasizes

    (A) how rapidly the city parks have deteriorated

    (B) how city parks can once again be made safe and clean

    (C) why people can no longer rest and relax in city parks

    (D) why urban planners should not be in charge of city parks

    (E) who is responsible for damaging the quality of life in cities

3. In line 28 of Passage 1, the word *intense* most nearly means

    (A) severe

    (B) fervent

    (C) piercing

    (D) strenuous

    (E) meticulous

4. In the last paragraph of Passage 1, the author acknowledges which problem in restoring city parks?

    (A) the constant need to collect trash

    (B) the difficulty in rerouting sewage pipes

    (C) the congestion caused by banning vehicular traffic

    (D) the lack of total separation from the surrounding city

    (E) the expense of creating additional police patrol units

5. In Passage 2, the reference to "a purely functional approach to city planning" (line 56) serves to

   (A) demonstrate that architects and technocrats should cooperate

   (B) imply that architects are unconcerned about human comfort

   (C) indicate that architects are obsolete in an industrial era

   (D) stress that architects and technocrats have different priorities

   (E) show that technocrats have destroyed the natural beauty of cities

6. The word *face* in line 62 means

   (A) reputation

   (B) expression

   (C) value

   (D) dignity

   (E) appearance

7. In lines 60–71, the author's description of cities is

   (A) tolerant

   (B) surprised

   (C) derogatory

   (D) nostalgic

   (E) bewildered

8. In context, "the good sense to recognize" (lines 93–94) suggests that technocrats

   (A) want to get rid of urban blight

   (B) are aware of the stress of city life

   (C) support nature conservation programs

   (D) favor large city parks over smaller ones

   (E) think that greenery makes cities more attractive

9. Both passages focus primarily on

   (A) criticizing certain aspects of the city

   (B) romanticizing city life in a bygone era

   (C) exploring the origins of urban decay

   (D) blaming urban problems on city residents

   (E) pointing out how city life could be improved

10. Author 1 would most likely react to the characterization of city parks presented in lines 84–91 (Passage 2) by pointing out that

    (A) this characterization is confirmed by the evidence

    (B) future reforms will render this characterization false

    (C) urban planners would reject this characterization

    (D) this characterization is in bad taste

    (E) recent developments have made this characterization obsolete

11. How would Author 1 respond to the way Author 2 uses the phrase "urban blight" (lines 80–81) to describe the current state of cities?

    (A) This phrase is not supported by the facts.

    (B) It is being used to denounce what is best about cities.

    (C) It is an accurate description of the situation.

    (D) Choosing this phrase demonstrates very poor taste.

    (E) New studies show that this phrase will soon be outdated.

ANSWERS AND EXPLANATIONS

With paired passages, always read the brief introduction first, because it will indicate how the two passages relate. Do the questions keyed to Passage 1 after you read it. Then read Passage 2 and answer the rest of the questions. That way, the appropriate text will be fresh in your mind. Passage 1, on the decline of the city park system, is not wholly pessimistic. After depicting the parks as a once ideal place for people to escape from the city, the text describes city parks around the world as ruined by crime and pollution. But the final paragraph expresses hope that the parks can be restored.

In contrast, Passage 2 sees parks as the "lone bright spot" amid cities marred by technocrats' "purely functional approach" to city planning. Technocrats get blamed for the ugly, unnatural, and impersonal look of the urban landscape of Western cities. The only good thing the technocrats have done is recognize that people need a park system as a refuge from city life.

1. B

Getting to the Answer: The author says parks were created to give people a "refuge" from the city. Scanning quickly through the answer choices, (B) jumps out because it fits the opening statement: Parks were designed with the needs of city residents in mind.

(A), (D), and (E) are misleading bits of information from the rest of the first paragraph. Though parks may house plant life, allow natural light into cities, and provide a place to meet or make friends, that's not what "convenient refuge" means. As for (C), the author never suggests that parks are supposed to end the unpleasantness of city life. They merely provide a refuge.

2. C

Getting to the Answer: To answer this question, you have to understand the context in which crime and pollution are mentioned in the second paragraph. The author describes the deterioration of parks, including the effects of crime and pollution, to show that people can no longer use the parks as they were meant to be used. In other words, why people can no longer rest and relax in the parks, (C).

Parks have deteriorated in recent decades, but the information on *crime and pollution* doesn't emphasize how

rapidly, so (A) is out. Making parks *safer and cleaner* is the topic of the third paragraph, not the second, so (B) is wrong. And there's nothing negative about urban planners or those responsible for damaging the quality of life in cities, so eliminate (D) and (E).

3. A

Getting to the Answer: Since all the answer choices except (E) *meticulous* are possible synonyms for *intense*, you have to figure out how the word is used in the sentence.

We learn that greenery in the parks has been destroyed by *intense* pollution and littering. Pollution and littering clearly can't be (B) *fervent*, (C) *piercing*, or (D) *strenuous*, so (A) *severe* is the right choice.

4. D

Getting to the Answer: The last paragraph of Passage 1 offers suggestions for reversing the decline of the parks: adding more police units and caretakers, banning vehicles, and rerouting sewage pipes. It is also necessary, the author says, to "insulate city parks from their surroundings," but the problem here is that "total isolation" is "impossible." This is paraphrased in (D).

(A), (B), (C), and (E) twist information from the author's suggestions. Trash does need to be collected, but the text never says that (A) the *constant need* to collect trash would be a problem. Nor does it say that (B) *rerouting sewage pipes* will be difficult, (C) *banning traffic* will cause congestion, or (E) *additional police* units will be expensive.

5. D

Getting to the Answer: This is the first question about Passage 2. Look again at the sentence that describes "a purely functional approach to city planning." The author contrasts architects, who view building a city as an artistic endeavor, to technocrats, who focus only on "serving the needs of . . . inhabitants." In other words, the author is (D) stressing that architects and technocrats have different priorities.

The author does not imply here that (A) architects and technocrats should cooperate or that architects do not care (B) about human comfort. Certainly, the author does not think (C) architects are obsolete; if anything, he regrets they no longer do city planning. As for (E), the author does think technocrats have destroyed the natural beauty of the cities, but this point comes up in paragraphs 2 and 3, not the first. In keyed questions like this, concentrate on the few sentences around the quoted phrase.

6. E

Getting to the Answer: Reread the sentence in question. If you don't, several answer choices may look tempting.

The author is talking about how the *face,* or appearance, of the Western city has been changed forever, so (E) is the only choice that fits.

7. C

Getting to the Answer: Skim over the sentence referred to in the second paragraph of Passage 2. You'll see phrases like "tedious chessboard pattern," "straight and dull streets," and "an overabundance of unsightly neighborhoods." Clearly, the author has a low opinion of modern cities; the tone is disparaging, or (C) derogatory.

(A) *tolerant*, (B) *surprised*, and (E) *bewildered* are clearly wrong. Nor are the comments *nostalgic*, so (D) is out. Although the author states that older, more personal buildings and lovely natural surroundings can no longer be found in cities, the tone is critical, rather than yearning.

8. B

Getting to the Answer: Passage 2 concludes by saying that technocrats "have at least had the good sense to recognize that people need a quiet refuge" from the chaos of the city. The inference is that technocrats (B) are *aware* of the stress of city life.

The author certainly doesn't believe technocrats (A) want to *get rid of urban blight*; according to him, the technocrats caused it all. Nor does the final sentence indicate that technocrats (C) *support nature conservation programs*, or (D) *favor large city parks over smaller ones*, or (E) *think that greenery makes cities more attractive*.

9. A

Getting to the Answer: The last three questions ask you to compare and contrast the two passages. For this one, look for the choice that accurately covers the subject matter of *both* passages, not just one. Both passages certainly criticize aspects of the city, so (A) seems right, but check out the other choices.

(B) is wrong because it doesn't fit *both* passages: Although Passage 1 may romanticize parks of a bygone era, Passage 2 focuses on the present. (C) can be eliminated because it's not the primary focus of either passage; besides, only Passage 2 discusses the origins of urban decay; Passage 1 talks about the decline of parks. Passage 2 blames urban problems on technocrats, not *city residents*, so (D) is out. Finally, (E) doesn't fit because only Passage 1 points out how city life can be improved.

10. E

Getting to the Answer: The final paragraph of Passage 2 offers a vision of a beautiful park system, very similar to the description in Passage 1 of the way parks used to be. But Passage 1 says parks have deteriorated considerably in recent decades. So Author 1 would probably point out that (E) *recent developments have made this [idealized] characterization obsolete*.

(A) is contrary to the evidence of Passage 1. (B) is wrong because reforms would improve parks, so the characterization in Passage 2 might be true, not false. Finally, since the parks in Passage 2 are presented as delightful places, the author of Passage 1 would be foolish to think that (C) or (D) would be true.

11. C

Getting to the Answer: The phrase *this urban blight* refers back to the bleak landscape described in the paragraph just above: "rows of squat concrete apartments" and "files of gigantic steel and glass skyscrapers." The author of Passage 1 portrays cities, aside from the parks, as "dark and dreary" environments, with "seemingly endless rows of steel, glass, and concrete buildings."

The two pictures are very similar, so the author of Passage 1 would probably find *urban blight* to be an accurate description of the situation. Since the two authors agree on this point, (A), (B), and (D) can be eliminated.

Long Reading Comprehension:
Practice Set Five

The following passage discusses the possibility that there is life on Mars. Interest in the subject reached a peak when NASA sent two unmanned spacecraft to Mars in 1975. After 10 months, Vikings 1 and 2 entered orbits around the red planet and released landers.

When the first of the two Viking landers touched down on Martian soil on July 20, 1976, and began to send camera images back to Earth, the scientists at the Jet Propulsion Laboratory
(5) could not suppress a certain nervous anticipation, like people who hold a ticket to a lottery they have a one-in-a-million chance of winning. The first photographs that arrived, however, did not contain any evidence of life. What revealed itself to
(10) them was merely a barren landscape littered with rocks and boulders. The view resembled nothing so much as a flat section of desert—in fact, the winning entry in a contest at J.P.L. for the photograph most accurately predicting what Mars
(15) would look like was a snapshot taken in a particularly arid section of the Mojave Desert.

The scientists were soon ready to turn their attention from visible life to microorganisms. The twin Viking landers carried three experiments
(20) designed to detect current biological activity and one to detect organic compounds, because researchers thought it possible that life had developed on early Mars just as it is thought to have developed on Earth, through the gradual chemical
(25) evolution of complex organic molecules. To detect biological activity, Martian soil samples were treated with various nutrients that would produce

characteristic by-products if life forms were active in the soil. The results from all three experiments
(30) were inconclusive. The fourth experiment heated a soil sample to look for signs of organic material but found none, an unexpected result because at least organic compounds from the steadybombardment of the Martian surface by meteorites
(35) were thought to have been present.

The absence of organic materials, some scientists speculated, was the result of intense ultraviolet radiation penetrating the atmosphere of Mars and destroying organic compounds in the soil.
(40) Although Mars' atmosphere was at one time rich in carbon dioxide and thus thick enough to protect its surface from the harmful rays of the Sun, the carbon dioxide had gradually left the atmosphere and been converted into rocks. This means
(45) that even if life had gotten a start on early Mars, it could not have survived the exposure to ultraviolet radiation when the atmosphere thinned. Mars never developed a protective layer of ozone as Earth did.
(50) Despite the disappointing Viking results, there are those who still keep open the possibility of life on Mars. They point out that the Viking data cannot be considered the final word on Martian life because the two landers only sampled two limit-
(55) ed—and uninteresting—sites. The Viking landing sites were not chosen for what they might tell of the planet's biology. They were chosen primarily because they appeared to be safe for landing a spacecraft. The landing sites were on parts of the
(60) Martian plains that appeared relatively featureless from orbital photographs.

The type of Martian terrain that these researchers suggest may be a possible hiding place for active life has an Earthly parallel: the ice-free

(65) region of southern Victoria Land, Antarctica,
where the temperatures in some dry valleys aver-
age below zero. Organisms known as endoliths, a
form of blue-green algae that has adapted to this
harsh environment, were found living inside cer-
(70) tain translucent, porous rocks in these Antarctic
valleys. The argument based on this discovery is
that if life did exist on early Mars, it is possible
that it escaped worsening conditions by similarly
seeking refuge in rocks. Skeptics object, however,
(75) that Mars in its present state is simply too dry,
even compared with Antarctic valleys, to sustain
any life whatsoever.

    Should Mars eventually prove to be completely
barren of life, as some suspect, then this would
(80) have a significant impact on the current view of
the chemical origin of life. It could be much more
difficult to get life started on a planet than scientists thought before the Viking landings.

1. The major purpose of the passage is to

   (A) relate an account of an extraordinary scientif-
       ic achievement

   (B) undermine the prevailing belief that life may
       exist on Mars

   (C) discuss the efforts of scientists to determine
       whether Martian life exists

   (D) show the limitations of the scientific investi-
       gation of other planets

   (E) examine the relationship between theories
       about Martian life and evolutionary theory

2. In line 5, the word *suppress* most nearly means

   (A) oppose

   (B) vanquish

   (C) prohibit

   (D) stifle

   (E) disguise

3. The reference to "people who hold a ticket to a
   lottery" (line 6) serves to

   (A) point out the human facet of a scientific
       enterprise

   (B) indicate the expected likelihood of visible
       Martian life

   (C) show that there was doubt as to whether the
       camera would function

   (D) imply that any mission to another planet is a
       risky venture

   (E) reveal how the success of the Viking mission
       depended largely on chance

4. The author uses the evidence from the four Viking
   experiments (lines 18–35) to establish that

   (A) meteorites do not strike the surface of Mars
       as often as scientists had thought

   (B) current theory as to how life developed on
       Earth is probably flawed

   (C) there was no experimental confirmation of
       the theory that life exists on Mars

   (D) biological activity has been shown to be
       absent from the surface of Mars

   (E) the experiments were more fruitful than was
       examination of camera images

5. The third paragraph (lines 36–49) of the passage
   provides

   (A) an analysis of a theory proposed earlier

   (B) evidence supporting a statement made earlier

   (C) a theory about findings presented earlier

   (D) criticism of experiments discussed earlier

   (E) a synthesis of facts reviewed earlier

6. The author suggests that an important difference between Mars and Earth is that, unlike Earth, Mars

    (A) accumulated organic compounds from the steady bombardment of meteorites

    (B) possessed at one time an atmosphere rich in carbon dioxide

    (C) is in the path of the harmful rays of ultraviolet radiation

    (D) has an atmospheric layer that protects organic compounds

    (E) could not have sustained any life that developed

7. The author mentions the Viking landing sites (lines 55–59) in order to emphasize which point?

    (A) Although evidence of life was not found by the landers, this does not mean that Mars is devoid of life.

    (B) Although the landing sites were uninteresting, they could have harbored Martian life.

    (C) The Viking mission was unsuccessful largely due to poor selection of the landing sites.

    (D) The detection of life on Mars was not a primary objective of the scientists who sent the Viking landers.

    (E) Scientists were not expecting to discover life on the Martian plains.

8. In lines 62–74, the researchers' argument that life may exist in Martian rocks rests on the idea that

    (A) organisms may adopt identical survival strategies in comparable environments

    (B) life developed in the form of blue-green algae on Mars

    (C) life evolved in the same way on two different planets

    (D) endoliths are capable of living in the harsh environment of Mars

    (E) organisms that have survived in Antarctica could survive the Martian environment

ANSWERS AND EXPLANATIONS

The subject of this science passage is the possibility that life exists, or has existed, on Mars. Paragraph 1 begins with a description of the scene at the Jet Propulsion Lab when pictures first arrived from the Viking landers on Mars. Paragraph 2 discusses the Viking experiments designed to detect microscopic signs of life on Mars, and the inconclusive or negative results of these experiments.

Paragraph 3 disccues the theory that some scientists have advanced to explain the negative results: Organic materials on Mars might have been destroyed by the lack of protection from ultraviolet radiation. Paragraph 4 addresses the possibility that there is life on Mars, and the two landers simply missed it, while the fifth discusses the suggestion that if life can survive in Antarctica by living inside rocks, maybe life does the same thing on Mars. The author concludes the passage in paragraph 6 by remarking that the evidence we have from Mars influences scientific theory regarding the chemical origin of life on Earth.

Some of this may have seemed difficult to wade through if you tried to get all of it the first time around, but remember, it isn't necessary to do that. The questions tell you where to go back to get the information you need.

1.   C

Getting to the Answer: The answer here has to be broad enough to cover the entire passage. We just reviewed the topics of the individual paragraphs; scientists get pictures, scientists run experiments, scientists propose theories and make suggestions throughout the passage. Clearly, the author is *discussing* the (C) efforts of scientists.

Though the Viking mission may have been an extraordinary scientific achievement, there's much more than a simple *account* of it here, (A). (B) is out, because the passage presents a balanced view on the question of life on Mars. (D) is wrong because the only time the author discusses *limitations of the scientific investigation* of Mars is in the fourth paragraph. (E) is wrong for a similar reason: The relationship between life on Mars and evolutionary theory is mentioned only in paragraphs 2 and 6.

2.   D

Getting to the Answer: The scientists are trying in vain to *suppress,* or (D) *stifle*, their nervous anticipation.

(A), (B), and (C) can all be synonyms of *suppress,* but none of them works in the context of the sentence. (E) *disguise* is not a synonym for *suppress.*

3.   B

Getting to the Answer: The word *however* in the sentence right after the cited sentence indicates that what the scientists hardly dared to hope for (and didn't get) was some visible sign of Martian life. So the reference to "people who hold a ticket to the lottery" is there to show how likely it was that the photographs would show Martian life (B).

(C) is a misreading of the first two sentences; there is nothing there to suggest that the scientists thought the camera might not *function*. (D) and (E) miss the mark completely by being far too broad.

4.   C

Getting to the Answer: You know by the end of the second paragraph that the experiments designed to detect biological life were inconclusive, and that no organic materials were found either. (C) is the answer.

Several of the other choices may have tempted you, but they all involve making unsupported inferences. Just because there weren't organic materials from meteorites on Mars doesn't mean that (A) *meteorites do not strike the surface of Mars* as often as scientists thought. The author never implies (B), and (D) is too sweeping. These four experiments were not the evidence to prove or disprove the existence of life on Mars. Finally, (E) can be eliminated because the experiments certainly didn't tell scientists much more than the photographs did.

5.   C

Getting to the Answer: Here you need to understand the role of paragraph 3. Reread it, starting from the end of paragraph 2. The author states that a Viking experiment turned up no trace of organic material on the Martian surface. We are then presented with a theory that UV radiation may have destroyed any organic materials once present in the Martian soil. So the third paragraph provides (C) a *theory* about findings presented earlier.

The theory is not *proposed* earlier in the passage, so (A) is out. And there's no *evidence supporting a statement made earlier*, so (B) is out. Nor is there *criticism* (D). Finally, there are no earlier facts reviewed, so (E) is out.

6.   E

Getting to the Answer: The author mentions Earth in the passage at the end of the third paragraph, where he says that Mars "never developed a protective layer of ozone as Earth did." Since it is life that the ozone layer protected on Earth, you can infer that Mars was not able to support life, (E), as Earth was.

(A) contradicts information from the passage that says that no organic compounds were found on Mars. (B) is out, because although Mars possessed at one time an atmosphere rich in carbon dioxide, the author never suggests that Earth *didn't*. Mars and Earth are both in the path of the ultraviolet radiation of the Sun, so (C) is out. Finally, (D) reverses Mars and Earth: Earth is the planet with an atmospheric layer that protects organic compounds from UV radiation, not Mars.

7.   A

Getting to the Answer: Reread the sentences surrounding the reference to Viking landing sites, and look for a paraphrase among the answer choices. Those who still think that there might be life on Mars point out that there were only two Viking landers, that the experimental sites were limited and uninteresting, and that scientists were not concerned about finding life when they chose the landing spots. In other words, they are saying that although evidence of life was not found by the landers, this does not mean that Mars is devoid of life, choice (A).

Though (B) is a true statement, this isn't why the author mentions the landing sites. The author never says that the Viking mission was unsuccessful or that the selection of landing sites was poor, so (C) is wrong. (D) and (E) focus on the intentions and expectations of the scientists. All you know is that they wanted to land the spacecrafts safely, not whether they thought *detection of life was a primary objective* (D) or whether they *expected to discover life* on the Martian plains (E).

8.   A

Getting to the Answer: The argument of the researchers in paragraph 5 is that, if endoliths could adapt to the harsh conditions of Antarctica by living in rocks, maybe some form of life did the same thing to survive on early Mars. The idea here is that Mars and Antarctica are (A) comparable environments and that life may adapt in the same way, or adopt identical strategies, to survive.

All of the wrong choices are based on distortions of the argument. (B) and (D) are out because the argument never states that *blue-green algae* or *endoliths* have anything to do with Mars; they were found in Antarctica and merely became the subject of speculation for the researchers. (C) is too broad. As for (E), the author never suggests that the endoliths or any other type of organism that has survived in Antarctica *could survive on Mars*.

Long Reading Comprehension: Practice Set Six

The role of television in the courtroom has been debated by members of the judicial system for the last two decades. Those who favor its presence feel that broadcasting courtroom proceedings is fully consistent with the ideal of the "public's right to know." Others believe that television distorts the judicial process by creating a theatrical atmosphere in the courtroom.

The following is an excerpt from a speech about this issue given by a retired Chief Judge of New York State at a Pre-law Association meeting.

Justice is the most profound aspiration of men and women on Earth; it is the allotment to each person of that to which he or she is entitled; it exists only when there has been adherence to prin-
(5) ciples of honesty and fairness and disregard of other considerations.

Down through the centuries, the character of a particular government or civilization could be measured best by the sort of justice meted out to
(10) its citizens. In the more advanced and more humane governances, trials have taken place in courtrooms to which the public has been admitted. On the other hand, secret trials have almost invariably been the telltale sign of oppressive and
(15) autocratic regimes. Indeed, the grant of a fair trial is the greatest contribution of any jurisprudence.

The difference in openness is not without significance. It is not a matter of mere entertainment. It is far more serious than that. First, and
(20) foremost, unobstructed courtrooms are a guarantee of fairness and justice. Furthermore, the public officials functioning therein can be observed so that those performing well may be retained and those not may be replaced.

(25) Courtrooms with "open doors" have always been a fetish for me. I stood here in this city sixteen years ago and in an interview announced that I favored cameras in the courts. Broadcasting from courtrooms was unpopular then and there were
(30) only four states in the Union permitting television of judicial proceedings. My response shocked many in this state. When the Chief Judgeship came my way, a rule was adopted permitting television and still cameras in the appellate courts of
(35) our jurisdiction and it was a success. I worked long and hard in favor of an amendment of the Civil Rights Law to allow photography in the trial courts. I am pleased that that is now reality.

However, I am worried. I am worried about
(40) what seems to be an increasing antipathy toward the media and concurrent attempts to narrow the doors leading into courtrooms by distinguishing ancillary or supplemental proceedings from trials themselves. Freedom of the press and open court-
(45) rooms go together.

I believe in the First Amendment. I believe with might and main in the constitutional guarantee of freedom of the press, not merely to curry favor with those of the "Fourth Estate," not merely as an
(50) aid to the media in its varied shapes and forms, but more as a benefit for all the people. A broadly defined freedom of the press assures the maintenance of our political system of democracy, social equality, and public exposure. Indeed, the strength
(55) of America, different from any nation in the world, lies in its openness.

1. In line 17, the word *openness* most probably means

   (A) candor
   (B) tolerance
   (C) receptivity
   (D) friendliness
   ✓(E) accessibility

2. The information in lines 39–45 suggests that the judge is very concerned about

   (A) restrictions being placed upon people opposed to media participation in the judicial process
   (B) undermining the rights of the accused by giving the media too much access to the judicial process
   (C) media abuse of the First Amendment to distort the judicial process
   (D) harm being caused to the judicial process by a distaste for the media
   (E) encouraging those who favor a narrow definition of civil rights by allowing the media to participate in the judicial process

3. The judge's point about the role of the media in the judicial process is made mainly through

   ✓(A) general statements
   (B) specific examples
   (C) statistical data
   (D) long citations
   (E) scientific evidence

4. In lines 46–56, the judge reflects on the

   (A) strengths and weaknesses of the judicial system
   (B) attitude of the judicial system toward the media
   ✓(C) role of a free press in maintaining a democratic society
   (D) ability of the media to function effectively in the courtroom
   (E) connection between the First Amendment and the Civil Rights Law

5. Which best describes the judge's view of cameras in the courtroom?

   (A) Cameras do not play a useful part in determining which members of the judicial system are competent and which members are incompetent.
   (B) While the First Amendment gives the media the right to bring cameras into the courtroom, their use has impaired the proper functioning of the judicial system.
   (C) Judicial systems that allow cameras into the courtroom are no more likely to be fair than judicial systems which do not admit them.
   ✓(D) Regardless of the fact that many members of the judicial system do not approve of their presence, cameras should be permitted in every courtroom.
   (E) Oppressive and autocratic regimes are likely to place cameras in the courtroom to deter their subjects from committing criminal acts.

ANSWERS AND EXPLANATIONS

This is a strong statement of an individual point of view. You may naturally respond by taking a stand yourself, for or against the author. But the questions never ask for your personal point of view. They ask only about the author's opinion. In reading, skim over the first few paragraphs. Look for a definite statement of the author's opinion, which you get in paragraph 4—the author favors cameras in court. This puts the rest of the passage in perspective.

1. E

Getting to the Answer: *Openness* here refers to the discussion in paragraph 2 about whether the public can be admitted to the courtroom. (E) *accessibility* best defines this sense of *openness*.

The other choices are all possible meanings of *openness*, but none fits the context. (A) *candor*, or frankness, refers to openness of one's own opinions; (B) *tolerance* is openness to other people or their views; (C) *receptivity* implies a willingness to be convinced. (D) *friendliness* suggests an outgoing nature, which doesn't match what the author is saying here.

2. D

Getting to the Answer: In paragraph 5, the author worries over "antipathy," or dislike, toward the media. This is paraphrased as *distaste* in (D). The harm . . . to the judicial process in this answer choice arises from the author's strong belief that media access is good for the judicial process, as expressed earlier.

If you know the author favors cameras, or *media participation*, you're likely to pick the right answer. The other choices, in different ways, say the author worries about too *much* media participation; they contradict the author's point of view.

3. A

Getting to the Answer: Paragraphs 1, 3, and 6 all contain broad arguments about the nature of justice, the need for public trials, and the importance of freedom of the press—(A) *general statements*.

The author gives no (B) *specific examples* of how courtroom openness works, though there is one example of the author's own activity (paragraph 4). (C), (D), and (E) are not in the text.

4. C

Getting to the Answer: This question asks about the last paragraph of the passage, which discusses freedom of the press and its importance in upholding *democracy*, equality, and other American values (C).

Since the passage as a whole discusses the *attitude of the judicial system toward the media*, you might be tempted to choose (B). But you're being asked to focus on only certain lines from the paragraph. Similarly, (A) *strengths and weaknesses of the judicial system*—or strong and weak judicial systems—are discussed only in paragraph 2. And while the *First Amendment* is mentioned in the last paragraph, the *Civil Rights Law* isn't (E). Finally, (D) is never discussed.

5. D

Getting to the Answer: You need to describes the overall point of view here. Since the author strongly supports cameras in the courts (paragraph 4) and the whole passage defends this view, your answer must be (D), the only pro-camera choice. It acknowledges the opposition to cameras that the author notes in paragraph 5, but says this opposition should be disregarded—as the author implies, too (paragraph 6).

(A) contradicts a minor point the author raises in the last part of paragraph 3. (B) distorts what paragraph 6 says about the First Amendment, as well as the author's pro-media position. (C) contradicts the general sense of paragraph 2, though cameras are not specifically discussed there. (E) refers to the discussion of *oppressive regimes* in this same paragraph, but the author never raises this point.

Long Reading Comprehension: Practice Set Seven

In the following excerpt from a novella, Rosemary, an elderly woman, reminisces about her childhood as she waits for her grandson to wake up.

Rosemary sat at her kitchen table, working a crossword puzzle. Crosswords were nice; they filled the time, and kept the mind active. She needed just one word to complete this morning's

(5) puzzle; the clue was "a Swiss river," and the first of its three letters was "A." Unfortunately, Rosemary had no idea what the name of the river was, and could not look it up. Her atlas was on her desk, and the desk was in the guest room, currently

(10) being occupied by her grandson Victor. Looking up over the tops of her bifocals, Rosemary glanced at the kitchen clock: It was almost 10 A.M. *Land sakes!* Did the boy intend to sleep all day? She noticed that the arthritis in her wrist was throb-

(15) bing, and put down her pen. At 87 years of age, she was glad she could still write at all. She had decided long ago that growing old was like slowly turning to stone; you couldn't take anything for granted. She stood up slowly, painfully, and start-

(20) ed walking to the guest room.

The trip, though only a distance of about 25 feet, seemed to take a long while. Late in her ninth decade now, Rosemary often experienced an expanded sense of time, with present and past

(25) tense intermingling in her mind. One minute she was padding in her slippers across the living room carpet, the next she was back on the farm where she'd grown up, a sturdy little girl treading the path behind the barn just before dawn. In her

(30) mind's eye, she could still pick her way among the stones in the darkness, more than 70 years later . . . . Rosemary arrived at the door to the guest room. It stood slightly ajar, and she peered through the opening. Victor lay sleeping on his

(35) side, his arms bent, his expression slightly pained. *Get up, lazy bones,* she wanted to say. Even in childhood, Rosemary had never slept past 4 A.M.; there were too many chores to do. How different things were for Victor's generation! Her youngest

(40) grandson behaved as if he had never done a chore in his life. Twenty-one years old, he had driven down to Florida to visit Rosemary in his shiny new car, a gift from his doting parents. Victor would finish college soon, and his future appeared

(45) bright—if he ever got out of bed, that is.

Something Victor had said last night over dinner had disturbed her. Now what was it? Oh yes; he had been talking about one of his college courses—a "gut," he had called it. When she had

(50) asked him to explain the term, Victor had said it was a course that you took simply because it was easy to pass. Rosemary, who had not even had a high school education, found the term repellent. If she had been allowed to continue her studies, she

(55) would never have taken a "gut" . . . The memory flooded back then, still painful as an open wound all these years later. It was the first day of high school. She had graduated from grammar school the previous year, but her father had forbidden

(60) her to go on to high school that fall, saying she was needed on the farm. After much tearful plead-ing, she had gotten him to promise that next year, she could start high school. She had endured a whole year of chores instead of books, with ani-

(65) mals and rough farmhands for company instead of people her own age. Now, at last, the glorious

day was at hand. She had put on her best dress
(she owned two), her heart racing in anticipation.
But her father was waiting for her as she came
(70) downstairs.

"Where do you think you're going?" he asked.

"To high school, Papa."

"No you're not. Take that thing off and get back
to work."

(75) "But Papa, you promised!"

"*Do as I say!*" he thundered.

There was no arguing with Papa when he spoke
that way. Tearfully, she had trudged upstairs to
change clothes. Rosemary still wondered what her
(80) life would have been like if her father had not
been waiting at the bottom of the stairs that day,
or if somehow she had found the strength to defy
him . . . .

Suddenly, Victor stirred, without waking, and
(85) mumbled something unintelligible. Jarred from
her reverie, Rosemary stared at Victor. She wondered if he were having a nightmare.

1. Rosemary's attitude toward the physical afflictions
of old age can best be described as one of

(A) acceptance

(B) sadness

(C) resentment

(D) anxiety

(E) optimism

2. Rosemary's walk to the guest room (lines 20–31)
reveals that she

(A) feels nostalgia for her family

(B) is anxious about Victor

(C) is determined to conquer her ailments

(D) has an elastic perception of time

(E) suffers from severe disorientation

3. In context, "if he ever got out of bed" (line 45)
suggests that Rosemary thinks Victor

(A) lacks a sense of humor

(B) is ashamed of what he said last night

(C) is promising but undisciplined

(D) works himself to exhaustion

(E) has failed to plan for the future

4. The reason Rosemary finds Victor's use of the
term *gut* (line 49) repellent is because it

(A) has unpleasant digestive associations

(B) is typical of Victor's disregard for traditional
values

(C) signifies a disrespect for education

(D) reminds Rosemary of her grammar school
classes

(E) implies that Rosemary is lacking in education

5. Lines 63–65 indicate that, for Rosemary, the year
after she graduated from grammar school was

(A) marred by illness and hardship

(B) filled with travel and adventure

(C) a year of reading and study

(D) spent isolated from her peers

(E) difficult because of her father's temper

6. Rosemary's memory of the day she finally prepared to start high school indicates that she had

(A) anticipated her father's command to stay
home

(B) hesitated over her choice of clothes

(C) done especially well in grammar school

(D) already decided to pursue a career

(E) strongly desired to continue her education

7. The passage as a whole is most concerned with

   (A) Rosemary's affectionate concern for Victor

   (B) Rosemary's struggle to suppress painful memories

   (C) the abusive treatment Rosemary suffered at the hands of her father

   (D) the interplay in Rosemary's mind between present and past

   (E) whether Rosemary will wake Victor up

ANSWERS AND EXPLANATIONS

Next up is a fiction passage about Rosemary, an elderly woman, who recalls parts of her childhood as she waits for her grandson Victor to wake up. There's nothing too difficult here. The most interesting thing about this passage is the way it jumps between the present and the past, by way of Rosemary's wandering mind. Notice the contrast between Victor's cavalier attitude toward his schooling and Rosemary's painful memories of being denied an education—that's sure to generate some questions.

1.   A

Getting to the Answer: The last four sentences of paragraph 1 discuss Rosemary's attitude toward old age. Thankful that she could write at all, she decided that growing old was like turning to stone: "You couldn't take anything for granted." The attitude that best sums this up is (A) *acceptance*.

She doesn't talk about things she can't do or misses, so (B) *sadness* is incorrect. And since she's not complaining or worrying, (C) and (D) are wrong. (E) *optimism* is too positive. There's no sense that she believes her life is going to improve.

2.   D

Getting to the Answer: When we read the lines around the lines cited, we see that the trip, though short, "seemed to take a long while," and that Rosemary "often experienced an expanded sense of time." (D) restates this perfectly, since *elastic* means to be able to expand and contract.

(A) is wrong because at this point in the passage, she's just thinking about her life on the farm, not her family. Though Rosemary may be anxious about Victor, he isn't mentioned in the lines cited in the stem, so (B) is also wrong. (C) is tricky: It picks up on the gist of the last question, but she's not thinking about her physical problems. Finally, (E) is too strong, even though it's related to (D). Rosemary's mind is flooded with memories, but she's not severely disoriented.

3.   C

Getting to the Answer: Rosemary refers to Victor as a "lazy bones" who's been given every advantage by his "doting parents . . . his future appeared bright—*if he ever got out of bed,* that is." (C) sums up that idea.

There's nothing in the passage about Victor's *sense of humor*, so (A) is unsupported. (B) is out of context and remember, this is a context question. Victor's remark isn't discussed until paragraph 3. (D) is almost the exact opposite of what the cited lines say about Rosemary's feelings toward Victor. (E) sounds right, but it makes an assumption that's not supported in the passage. Rosemary says his "future appeared bright." Victor may be lazy, but the only things we know about his future are positive.

4.   C

Getting to the Answer: The line reference points you to the start of paragraph 3. Notice the definition of the term *gut*—"a course you took simply because it was easy to pass." Rosemary thinks the word is *repellent*, a very strong word, and believes that "if she had been allowed to continue her studies, she would never had taken a 'gut.'" Obviously, Rosemary has different feelings about education than did Victor. Given her respect for education, you can infer that she is reacting to what she feels is Victor's lack of respect.

(A) is just silly. (B) feels close, but since the passage is concerned only with education and not things like family, religious beliefs, and society, it's too vague to be correct. (D) suggests that Rosemary didn't enjoy her own schooling, which we know is false. It's true that the word upsets her because it makes her think about her experiences, but the experiences were good ones. She's not repelled by thinking about them. Finally, while Rosemary may not have a broad education, Victor was only referring to his own classes, (E).

5.   D

Getting to the Answer: Go straight to the lines cited: "She had endured a whole year of chores instead of books, with animals and rough farmhands for company instead of people her own age."

Working on the farm may have been hard, but *illness* is never mentioned, so (A) is out. In fact, Rosemary is referred to as "a sturdy little girl." Since she was on the farm the whole time, she could not have been *traveling and having adventures*, as (B) claims. (C) directly contradicts the question stem, as the phrase says that she spent the year with "chores instead of books." (E) may be tempting, because it's true that her father had a *temper*. This isn't mentioned, however, as a reason the year is so difficult, so ultimately it is wrong.

6. E

Getting to the Answer: This is a relatively easy question. The question refers to Rosemary on that "glorious" day when she was going to high school, which is found near the end of paragraph 3. She gets up, puts on her "best dress, her heart racing in anticipation." These facts point to (E).

Though you may have expected that Rosemary's father would stop her from going to school, there's no evidence that Rosemary anticipated it, so (A) is wrong. Remember that Rosemary had only two dresses, which makes it unlikely that she *hesitated* in her choice, (B). Again, as with (A), you may be tempted to make an assumption with (C) that's not supported. The passage makes it clear that Rosemary enjoyed grammar school, but nowhere does it says she did especially well. Same with (D).

7. D

Getting to the Answer: What is the primary concern of the passage? Though Victor is important in this passage, his real role is to awaken thoughts in Rosemary about her past. Most of the passage is about Rosemary and her life. (D) is really the only one that addresses this in a wide enough way.

(A) is too narrow. (B) feels close, but we never get the sense that she's trying to suppress the unhappy memories. (C) is a distortion; we're told that Rosemary was forbidden from attending school, but there's no suggestion she was *abused* by her father. (E) is too trivial.

Long Reading Comprehension: Practice Set Eight

Directions: Answer the questions below based on the information in the accompanying passage.

This pair of passages presents contrasting views of the music of jazz trumpeter Miles Davis, who died in 1993. Author 1 argues that Davis's artistry reached its peak in the 1950s. Author 2 claims that Davis remained an important creative force in jazz to the end of his life.

Passage 1

The recent death of trumpeter Miles Davis brought an end to one of the most celebrated careers in the history of jazz. Few musicians have ever enjoyed such popularity for so long. Much

(5) has been made of Davis's influence on the historical development of jazz, his ability to "show the way" to other musicians. Yet it must be said that Miles reached the artistic high point of his career in the 1950s.

(10)   Davis came to New York City from the Midwest in the mid-1940s while still a teenager. Studying at the Juilliard School of Music by day, he haunted the city's jazz clubs by night, receiving another education entirely. Bebop, the hot, frantic new

(15) sound in jazz, was being played by such musical revolutionaries as Charlie Parker, Dizzy Gillespie, and Thelonious Monk, and Davis was sometimes invited up on the bandstand to play with them. Though obviously talented, Davis had to struggle

(20) to keep up with these musicians, and he worked tirelessly to perfect his technique.

Even at this early stage, Davis's sound and style on trumpet set him apart. Rather than filling the air with a headlong rush of musical notes, as other

(25) bebop musicians did, Davis played sparingly. He seemed more interested in the silences between the notes than in the notes themselves. This less-is-more approach became the basis of "Cool" jazz, the counterrevolution Davis led which dominated

(30) West Coast jazz in the 1950s. The Miles Davis quintet set the standard for all other jazz combos of the era, and produced a series of recordings culminating in the classic *Kind of Blue*.

Although *Kind of Blue* represents the high-water

(35) mark of Davis's career, his artistic decline was not immediately apparent. In the early 1960s, playing with a different set of musicians, he produced some excellent albums. But the end was near. His last pure jazz album is named, fittingly enough, *In*

(40) *a Silent Way*. After issuing this recording in 1969, Davis turned his back on traditional jazz, disappointingly opting for an electronic "fusion" sound that blurred the lines between jazz and rock. Yes, he continued to enjoy a lucrative recording career

(45) and public adulation. But for all those who learned to love jazz by listening to the plaintive sounds of the Miles Davis of the 1950s, it was as if he had already fallen silent.

Passage 2

Miles Davis was a protean* figure in jazz; like

(50) some musical Picasso, he mastered and then shed a series of styles throughout the course of his career. This is rare in any artist, but almost unheard of in the world of jazz, where a musician's style is usually formed extremely early, and

(55) then refined and repeated for the remainder of his or her life. Although Davis could have earned millions by continuing to play the music that had first made him famous in the 1950s, he refused to

repeat himself. He consistently sought to expand
(60) his musical horizons, working with young, emerg-
ing musicians, restlessly searching for new sounds.
    After cutting his teeth on the bebop jazz of the
1940s, Davis developed a "cooler" style and made
his name in the 1950s with a five-man combo. The
(65) so-called "purists" have often claimed that this
period represents the zenith of Davis's achievement. But this argument reveals more about the
narrow tastes of certain critics than it does about
the supposed limitations of Miles Davis. The
(70) groups Davis led in the 1960s featured a new generation of superb musicians such as Wayne
Shorter and Herbie Hancock, and produced music
that explored new and complex rhythmic textures.
    Yet critics continued to complain. And when
(75) Davis released *Bitches Brew* in 1970, the jazz
"purists" were horrified: His band was using electronic instruments, and its music borrowed heavily from rock rhythms and the psychedelic sound
of "acid" rock. Typically, Davis ignored the storm
(80) of protest, secure in his artistic vision.
    Throughout the early 1970s, he continued to
attract the best new players to his side. They benefited from his vast experience and mastery, and he
from their youthful energy and fresh approach to
(85) the music.
    After a six-year retirement brought on by ill-
ness, Davis re-emerged in 1981. Ever willing to
court controversy, he wore outrageous clothes,
grew his hair long, and even did a television com-
(90) mercial. But musically, Davis was as exciting as
ever. Once again, he sought out some of the finest
young musicians, and played to great acclaim. A
restless innovator to the end of his life, Miles
Davis deserves his place as the dominant figure in
(95) jazz in the second half of the 20th century.

*protean: able to assume different shapes or roles

1. In paragraph 1, the phrase *show the way* most
    nearly means

    (A) lead a band
    (B) bring publicity to
    (C) teach novice musicians
    (D) affect the creative development of
    (E) compose music of high quality

2. The author suggests that "Cool" jazz was a "count-
    er-revolution" (lines 28–30) because it

    (A) reflected Davis's unique sound on trumpet
    (B) improved the quality of jazz on the West
         Coast
    (C) marked Davis's emergence as the premier
         trumpeter of his generation
    (D) represented a stylistic alternative to bebop
         jazz
    (E) grew out of Davis's disagreements with
         Parker, Gillespie, and Monk

3. In lines 35–38, when discussing the Davis group of
    the early 1960s, the author of Passage 1 suggests
    that

    (A) critics persuaded Davis that he should reject
         the "Cool" sound of the 1950s
    (B) Davis's individual style of play became even
         more spare and economical
    (C) Davis continued to produce music of high
         quality even though past his prime
    (D) musicians and audiences alike began treating
         Davis with increased respect
    (E) Davis gave up electronic instruments and
         returned to playing traditional jazz

4. The author of Passage 1 suggests that the music
    Miles Davis played after *In a Silent Way*

    (A) ignored current musical trends
    (B) alienated most of his listeners
    (C) revived bebop jazz
    (D) disappointed influential music critics
    (E) remained highly profitable

5. By saying that "it was as if he had already fallen silent" (lines 47–48), the author of Passage 1 suggests that

(A) it would have been preferable if Davis had not played at all, rather than play "fusion" jazz

(B) by 1970, Davis no longer had the ability to play in the plaintive style that had made him famous

(C) people who loved traditional jazz stopped buying recordings after the use of electronic instruments became popular

(D) Davis lost most of his popular following when he began to blur the lines between jazz and rock music

(E) younger listeners learned about jazz in a completely different way than those who had first heard it in the 1950s

6. The author of Passage 2 suggests that, unlike Miles Davis, most jazz musicians

(A) find it difficult to earn a living playing music

(B) know very little about the tradition of jazz

(C) solidify their playing style early in life

(D) refuse to work with musicians younger than themselves

(E) prefer to play a "hot" style of jazz

7. The phrase *cutting his teeth* (line 62) most nearly means

(A) getting excited about

(B) acquiring skill

(C) becoming injured by

(D) memorizing fully

(E) criticizing sharply

8. The references in Passage 2 to "purists" (line 65) and "supposed limitations" (line 69) serve to

(A) emphasize the shortcomings of Miles Davis as a bebop player

(B) show what Davis might have accomplished had he continued to play "cool" jazz

(C) give an assessment of Davis's reaction to his critics

(D) criticize those who would say negative things about Miles Davis

(E) prove that Davis entered a period of artistic decline in the 1960s

9. According to the author of Passage 2, the relationship between Davis and the musicians he played with in the early 1970s can best be summarized as which of the following?

(A) It was similar to that of teacher and pupil.

(B) It was filled with dissension and conflict.

(C) It was the focus of critical acclaim.

(D) It lacked the "chemistry" of Davis's earlier groups.

(E) It was mutually beneficial.

10. The author of Passage 1 would most likely react to the characterization of Miles Davis as a "restless innovator" (line 93) by arguing that

(A) Davis was no longer the dominant figure in jazz after 1950

(B) only a critic can properly judge the extent of a musician's artistic achievement

(C) Davis should have concentrated less on innovation and more on perfecting his technique

(D) the artistic quality of any musical innovation depends largely on the caliber of the musicians involved

(E) Davis should have realized that change for change's sake is not always a positive thing

11. Both passages are concerned primarily with

   (A) describing the evolution of jazz from the
       1940s onward
   (B) explaining why Miles Davis continually
       played with new groups of musicians
   (C) showing how the music of Miles Davis was
       heavily influenced by bebop jazz
   (D) evaluating the career and achievements of
       Miles Davis
   (E) indicating the high point of Miles Davis's
       career

ANSWERS AND EXPLANATIONS

Each of these two authors has a different take on the life of jazz trumpet player Miles Davis. Author 1 says Davis played his best music in the 1950s and then went off in the wrong direction—eventually switching to electronic instruments and borrowing from rock music. Author 2 celebrates the very thing Passage 1 criticizes: Davis's ability to change styles over the course of his career. You don't need to be a musical expert to do well here. The paragraphs of each passage are organized chronologically, which makes it doubly easy to go back and relocate material pertinent to the questions.

1. D

Getting to the Answer: Look at the entire sentence in which the keyed phrase occurs: "Much has been made of Davis's influence on the historical development of jazz, his ability to 'show the way' to other musicians." *Show the way* means to influence or affect the historical development of jazz. Davis was able to affect the creative development of other musicians, even his peers, which is one reason he was so influential.

(A) *lead a band*, (B) *bring publicity to jazz*, and even (E) *compose excellent music* can all be done without necessarily being historically influential. Likewise, (C) *teach novice musicians* influences *their* personal development, but not necessarily the historical development of jazz.

2. D

Getting to the Answer: Paragraph 3 of Passage 1 says Davis played differently from other bebop players. Earlier, paragraph 2 describes bebop jazz as "the hot, frantic new sound" being played by "revolutionaries." So the "Cool" sound Davis developed was "counter-revolutionary" because stylistically it differed dramatically from bebop.

(A) and (B) touch on other details mentioned in paragraph 3, but neither creates the direct opposition of "revolution" and "counter-revolution." (C) distorts the final sentence of paragraph 3, which says that Davis's quintet "set the standard" for all other jazz combos of the era. That's different from saying Davis was the premier trumpeter of his generation. Finally, (E) is plausible but unsupported. We don't know whether Davis *disagreed with Parker, Gillespie, and Monk* or simply followed his own instincts.

3. C

Getting to the Answer: This inference question is keyed to the top of the last paragraph of Passage 1. It says that, after the "high-water mark" of *Kind of Blue,* Davis's "artistic decline was not immediately apparent"; that in the early 1960s he played with another group and "produced some excellent albums." So (C) is correct: In the 1960s Davis still made high-quality music, although he was past his prime.

Critics are not mentioned in Passage 1, so (A) is a poor guess. Nor does the author say Davis's playing became (B) *more economical*. (D) distorts the assertion, near the end of Passage 1, that Davis "continued to enjoy . . . public adulation." This suggests that his popularity remained high, not that it increased. And (E) gets it backwards: Davis gave up traditional jazz and turned to electronic instruments.

4. E

Getting to the Answer: This is a question about Davis's music after 1969. In Passage 1, the second half of the last paragraph says that after *In a Silent Way,* Davis "turned his back on traditional jazz," so you can eliminate C). (A) is wrong because Davis *was* influenced during this time by current trends—i.e., by rock music.

(B) is wrong because Davis "continued to enjoy . . . public adulation." (D) is tempting, but we don't know that Passage 1 was written by a critic, and the author never suggests that influential music critics were *disappointed.* That leaves (E) as correct. It's based on the reference to Davis continuing to enjoy a "lucrative recording career."

5. A

Getting to the Answer: The phrase *fallen silent* intentionally echoes the title of *In a Silent Way,* the album that marked the end of Davis's traditional jazz playing. The suggestion is that Davis *should have* fallen silent, rather than make music the author disliked. (A) restates this.

(B) is wrong because there's no suggestion that Davis was *unable* to play traditional jazz. Rather, he *chose* to play a different style. (C) is completely unwarranted; we know nothing about the record-buying habits of people who love traditional jazz. (D) is contradicted by the reference to Davis continuing to enjoy public adulation. And (E) has nothing to do with the issue of Davis falling silent.

6. C

Getting to the Answer: Now you're into Passage 2. The first paragraph says Davis "mastered and then shed a variety of styles" during his career. It goes on to say that this is rare in the jazz world, "where a musician's style is usually formed extremely early, and then refined and repeated for the remainder of his or her life." So (C) is correct.

(A) is wrong; We're told Davis earned "millions," but the passage never mentions whether most jazz musicians find it hard to earn a living. There's no evidence for (B) or (D). And (E) refers only to bebop players, not *most jazz musicians.*

7. B

Getting to the Answer: We talk about babies teething or cutting their first teeth. The figurative use of the phrase conveys the image of a beginner learning and improving, which points to (B) *acquiring skill.* If you aren't familiar with this expression, information in Passage 1 can help you answer correctly. Davis "cut his teeth" on the bebop in the 1940s, at the earliest phase of his career.

(A) has nothing to do with "cutting one's teeth." (C) and (E) try to distract you by playing off the use of the verb *cut,* (C) literally and (E) figuratively. *Memorization* (D) is related to learning, but doesn't fit the cliché; you don't always need to memorize in order to acquire skill.

8. D

Getting to the Answer: The question stem quotes from two successive sentences in paragraph 2 of Passage 2, and a careful reading of context helps here. Responding to critics who think Davis's 1950s music was the "zenith," or highest point, of his career, the author argues that this "reveals more about the narrow tastes of . . . critics than it does about the supposed limitations of Miles Davis." In other words, the author is attacking Davis's critics.

(A), (B), and (E) incorrectly focus on Davis's music instead of his detractors, and (C) wrongly puts the author's words in Davis's mouth.

9. E

Getting to the Answer: Always check the context. In this case, the last two sentences of paragraph 3. During the early '70s, Davis played with the best young jazz musicians, who "benefited from his vast experience and mas-

tery," as he did from their "youthful energy and fresh approach." In other words, both sides got something good; the relationship was mutually beneficial, so (E) is correct.

(A) fails on two counts: First, Davis was playing with the younger musicians as peers, and second, teacher-pupil relationships are not necessarily mutually beneficial. The passage suggests neither (B) *conflict* between Davis and the young players, nor a drop-off in (D) *"chemistry."* Finally, in (C), the critics did not *praise* the work of Davis and the musicians he played with; on the contrary, in 1970, purists complained when his band was using electronic instruments.

10. E

Getting to the Answer: Here you're asked to compare the viewpoints in Authors 1 and 2. An "innovator" introduces something new, or changes the way things are done. While Author 2 praises Davis for restlessly changing musical styles, Author 1 wishes Davis had continued playing traditional jazz. So Author 1 would argue that Davis's "innovations" were a mistake, and this suggests (E).

(A) doesn't address whether Davis's innovations were a good thing; in addition, Author 1 thought Davis reached his peak after 1950. (B) is a poor guess, since the Author 1 never takes this position. The first half of (C) is accurate, but the second half is untrue: Author 1 thinks Davis's decline stemmed from the kind of music that he chose to play, *not* from imperfect technique. Nor does Author 1 suggest that Davis's mistake was playing with inferior musicians, (D).

11. D

Getting to the Answer: This question asks about the main point of *both* passages. The wording suggests they share the same primary purpose. Though each author has a different opinion of Davis, both evaluate his music and trace the arc of his career, so (D) is correct.

(A) is too broad; it doesn't even mention Davis. (B) reflects Passage 2, but not Passage 1, which argues that Davis should have stayed with his '50s music. (C) relates only to a minor point in each passage—how Davis got started. And (E) accurately describes Passage 1, but not Passage 2, which argues that Davis's career was a succession of high points.

Practice Tests and Explanations

SAT Practice Test A
Answer Sheet

Remove (or photcopy) this answer sheet and use it to complete the practice test. See the answer key following the test when finished. The "Compute Your Score" section at the back of the book will show you how to find your score.

Start with number 1 for each section. If a section has fewer questions than answer spaces, leave the extra spaces blank.

SECTION 1

1. Ⓐ Ⓑ Ⓒ Ⓓ Ⓔ	11. Ⓐ Ⓑ Ⓒ Ⓓ Ⓔ	21. Ⓐ Ⓑ Ⓒ Ⓓ Ⓔ	31. Ⓐ Ⓑ Ⓒ Ⓓ Ⓔ
2. Ⓐ Ⓑ Ⓒ Ⓓ Ⓔ	12. Ⓐ Ⓑ Ⓒ Ⓓ Ⓔ	22. Ⓐ Ⓑ Ⓒ Ⓓ Ⓔ	32. Ⓐ Ⓑ Ⓒ Ⓓ Ⓔ
3. Ⓐ Ⓑ Ⓒ Ⓓ Ⓔ	13. Ⓐ Ⓑ Ⓒ Ⓓ Ⓔ	23. Ⓐ Ⓑ Ⓒ Ⓓ Ⓔ	33. Ⓐ Ⓑ Ⓒ Ⓓ Ⓔ
4. Ⓐ Ⓑ Ⓒ Ⓓ Ⓔ	14. Ⓐ Ⓑ Ⓒ Ⓓ Ⓔ	24. Ⓐ Ⓑ Ⓒ Ⓓ Ⓔ	34. Ⓐ Ⓑ Ⓒ Ⓓ Ⓔ
5. Ⓐ Ⓑ Ⓒ Ⓓ Ⓔ	15. Ⓐ Ⓑ Ⓒ Ⓓ Ⓔ	25. Ⓐ Ⓑ Ⓒ Ⓓ Ⓔ	35. Ⓐ Ⓑ Ⓒ Ⓓ Ⓔ
6. Ⓐ Ⓑ Ⓒ Ⓓ Ⓔ	16. Ⓐ Ⓑ Ⓒ Ⓓ Ⓔ	26. Ⓐ Ⓑ Ⓒ Ⓓ Ⓔ	36. Ⓐ Ⓑ Ⓒ Ⓓ Ⓔ
7. Ⓐ Ⓑ Ⓒ Ⓓ Ⓔ	17. Ⓐ Ⓑ Ⓒ Ⓓ Ⓔ	27. Ⓐ Ⓑ Ⓒ Ⓓ Ⓔ	37. Ⓐ Ⓑ Ⓒ Ⓓ Ⓔ
8. Ⓐ Ⓑ Ⓒ Ⓓ Ⓔ	18. Ⓐ Ⓑ Ⓒ Ⓓ Ⓔ	28. Ⓐ Ⓑ Ⓒ Ⓓ Ⓔ	38. Ⓐ Ⓑ Ⓒ Ⓓ Ⓔ
9. Ⓐ Ⓑ Ⓒ Ⓓ Ⓔ	19. Ⓐ Ⓑ Ⓒ Ⓓ Ⓔ	29. Ⓐ Ⓑ Ⓒ Ⓓ Ⓔ	39. Ⓐ Ⓑ Ⓒ Ⓓ Ⓔ
10. Ⓐ Ⓑ Ⓒ Ⓓ Ⓔ	20. Ⓐ Ⓑ Ⓒ Ⓓ Ⓔ	30. Ⓐ Ⓑ Ⓒ Ⓓ Ⓔ	40. Ⓐ Ⓑ Ⓒ Ⓓ Ⓔ

☐ # right

☐ # wrong

SECTION 2

1. Ⓐ Ⓑ Ⓒ Ⓓ Ⓔ	11. Ⓐ Ⓑ Ⓒ Ⓓ Ⓔ	21. Ⓐ Ⓑ Ⓒ Ⓓ Ⓔ	31. Ⓐ Ⓑ Ⓒ Ⓓ Ⓔ
2. Ⓐ Ⓑ Ⓒ Ⓓ Ⓔ	12. Ⓐ Ⓑ Ⓒ Ⓓ Ⓔ	22. Ⓐ Ⓑ Ⓒ Ⓓ Ⓔ	32. Ⓐ Ⓑ Ⓒ Ⓓ Ⓔ
3. Ⓐ Ⓑ Ⓒ Ⓓ Ⓔ	13. Ⓐ Ⓑ Ⓒ Ⓓ Ⓔ	23. Ⓐ Ⓑ Ⓒ Ⓓ Ⓔ	33. Ⓐ Ⓑ Ⓒ Ⓓ Ⓔ
4. Ⓐ Ⓑ Ⓒ Ⓓ Ⓔ	14. Ⓐ Ⓑ Ⓒ Ⓓ Ⓔ	24. Ⓐ Ⓑ Ⓒ Ⓓ Ⓔ	34. Ⓐ Ⓑ Ⓒ Ⓓ Ⓔ
5. Ⓐ Ⓑ Ⓒ Ⓓ Ⓔ	15. Ⓐ Ⓑ Ⓒ Ⓓ Ⓔ	25. Ⓐ Ⓑ Ⓒ Ⓓ Ⓔ	35. Ⓐ Ⓑ Ⓒ Ⓓ Ⓔ
6. Ⓐ Ⓑ Ⓒ Ⓓ Ⓔ	16. Ⓐ Ⓑ Ⓒ Ⓓ Ⓔ	26. Ⓐ Ⓑ Ⓒ Ⓓ Ⓔ	36. Ⓐ Ⓑ Ⓒ Ⓓ Ⓔ
7. Ⓐ Ⓑ Ⓒ Ⓓ Ⓔ	17. Ⓐ Ⓑ Ⓒ Ⓓ Ⓔ	27. Ⓐ Ⓑ Ⓒ Ⓓ Ⓔ	37. Ⓐ Ⓑ Ⓒ Ⓓ Ⓔ
8. Ⓐ Ⓑ Ⓒ Ⓓ Ⓔ	18. Ⓐ Ⓑ Ⓒ Ⓓ Ⓔ	28. Ⓐ Ⓑ Ⓒ Ⓓ Ⓔ	38. Ⓐ Ⓑ Ⓒ Ⓓ Ⓔ
9. Ⓐ Ⓑ Ⓒ Ⓓ Ⓔ	19. Ⓐ Ⓑ Ⓒ Ⓓ Ⓔ	29. Ⓐ Ⓑ Ⓒ Ⓓ Ⓔ	39. Ⓐ Ⓑ Ⓒ Ⓓ Ⓔ
10. Ⓐ Ⓑ Ⓒ Ⓓ Ⓔ	20. Ⓐ Ⓑ Ⓒ Ⓓ Ⓔ	30. Ⓐ Ⓑ Ⓒ Ⓓ Ⓔ	40. Ⓐ Ⓑ Ⓒ Ⓓ Ⓔ

☐ # right

☐ # wrong

SECTION 3

1. Ⓐ Ⓑ Ⓒ Ⓓ Ⓔ	11. Ⓐ Ⓑ Ⓒ Ⓓ Ⓔ	21. Ⓐ Ⓑ Ⓒ Ⓓ Ⓔ	31. Ⓐ Ⓑ Ⓒ Ⓓ Ⓔ
2. Ⓐ Ⓑ Ⓒ Ⓓ Ⓔ	12. Ⓐ Ⓑ Ⓒ Ⓓ Ⓔ	22. Ⓐ Ⓑ Ⓒ Ⓓ Ⓔ	32. Ⓐ Ⓑ Ⓒ Ⓓ Ⓔ
3. Ⓐ Ⓑ Ⓒ Ⓓ Ⓔ	13. Ⓐ Ⓑ Ⓒ Ⓓ Ⓔ	23. Ⓐ Ⓑ Ⓒ Ⓓ Ⓔ	33. Ⓐ Ⓑ Ⓒ Ⓓ Ⓔ
4. Ⓐ Ⓑ Ⓒ Ⓓ Ⓔ	14. Ⓐ Ⓑ Ⓒ Ⓓ Ⓔ	24. Ⓐ Ⓑ Ⓒ Ⓓ Ⓔ	34. Ⓐ Ⓑ Ⓒ Ⓓ Ⓔ
5. Ⓐ Ⓑ Ⓒ Ⓓ Ⓔ	15. Ⓐ Ⓑ Ⓒ Ⓓ Ⓔ	25. Ⓐ Ⓑ Ⓒ Ⓓ Ⓔ	35. Ⓐ Ⓑ Ⓒ Ⓓ Ⓔ
6. Ⓐ Ⓑ Ⓒ Ⓓ Ⓔ	16. Ⓐ Ⓑ Ⓒ Ⓓ Ⓔ	26. Ⓐ Ⓑ Ⓒ Ⓓ Ⓔ	36. Ⓐ Ⓑ Ⓒ Ⓓ Ⓔ
7. Ⓐ Ⓑ Ⓒ Ⓓ Ⓔ	17. Ⓐ Ⓑ Ⓒ Ⓓ Ⓔ	27. Ⓐ Ⓑ Ⓒ Ⓓ Ⓔ	37. Ⓐ Ⓑ Ⓒ Ⓓ Ⓔ
8. Ⓐ Ⓑ Ⓒ Ⓓ Ⓔ	18. Ⓐ Ⓑ Ⓒ Ⓓ Ⓔ	28. Ⓐ Ⓑ Ⓒ Ⓓ Ⓔ	38. Ⓐ Ⓑ Ⓒ Ⓓ Ⓔ
9. Ⓐ Ⓑ Ⓒ Ⓓ Ⓔ	19. Ⓐ Ⓑ Ⓒ Ⓓ Ⓔ	29. Ⓐ Ⓑ Ⓒ Ⓓ Ⓔ	39. Ⓐ Ⓑ Ⓒ Ⓓ Ⓔ
10. Ⓐ Ⓑ Ⓒ Ⓓ Ⓔ	20. Ⓐ Ⓑ Ⓒ Ⓓ Ⓔ	30. Ⓐ Ⓑ Ⓒ Ⓓ Ⓔ	40. Ⓐ Ⓑ Ⓒ Ⓓ Ⓔ

☐ # right

☐ # wrong

Before taking these practice tests, find a quiet room where you can work uninterrupted for 70 minutes. Make sure you have a comfortable desk and several No. 2 pencils. Use the answer sheets provided to to record your answers. (You can tear them out or photocopy them.)

Once you start each practice test, do not stop until you have finished. Remember, you may review any questions within a section, but you may not go back or forward a section.

When you have finished taking a practice test, go on to the Compute Your Score section to see how you did.

Good luck.

Practice Test A

SECTION ONE

Time—25 Minutes
27 Questions

For each of the following questions, choose the best answer and darken the corresponding oval on the answer sheet.

1. Most of those polled stated that they would vote to reelect their legislators; this response showed the public was ---- a change in leadership.

    (A) partial to
    √(B) wary of
    (C) inured to
    (D) confident of
    (E) receptive to

2. Mountain lions are very ---- creatures, able to run at high speed and capable of climbing any tree.

    √(A) agile
    (B) passive
    (C) capricious
    (D) attentive
    (E) dominant

3. Although organic farming is more labor intensive and thus initially quite ----, it may be less expensive in the long term than conventional farming.

    (A) nutritious
    (B) tasteful
    (C) restrained
    √(D) costly
    (E) arduous

4. Diego Rivera was one of the most ---- painters of the modern Mexican mural movement, ---- a generation of young artists with his bold, dramatic forms.

    (A) famous . . . displacing
    (B) convoluted . . . attracting
    (C) antagonistic . . . prompting
    √(D) influential . . . inspiring
    (E) observant . . . thwarting

5. Although the Druids, an ancient Celtic priestly class, were ----, they preferred to use ---- teaching methods to educate the young.

    (A) uneducated . . . illegible
    (B) enduring . . . intelligent
    (C) earnest . . . unexceptional
    (D) religious . . . haphazard
    √(E) literate . . . oral

GO ON TO THE NEXT PAGE

KAPLAN

6. Emphysema, a chronic lung disease, can occur in either a localized or ---- form.

   (A) a contained
   (B) an acute
   (C) a restricted
   (D) a diffuse
   (E) a fatal

7. Even though her friends described Veronica as amiable and frank, she was really a very ---- and ---- woman.

   (A) dependable ... unfriendly
   (B) rude ... calculating
   (C) gregarious ... insignificant
   (D) entertaining ... antagonistic
   (E) frugal ... mysterious

8. Despite much educated ----, there remains no ---- relationship between sunspot cycles and the earth's weather.

   (A) argument ... decisive
   (B) confusion ... clear
   (C) conjecture ... proven
   (D) evidence ... tenuous
   (E) disagreement ... systematic

GO ON TO THE NEXT PAGE

KAPLAN

Questions 9–12 refer to the following passage.

Passage 1

Captive breeding programs now demand a sizable portion of the annual budget and research efforts at many major zoological gardens. Originally, these programs were designed to keep
(5) zoos stocked while causing as little disruption to nature as possible; every animal bred in a zoo represented an animal that needn't be taken from the wild. Now, however, zoos often consider captive breeding programs an insurance policy for severe-
(10) ly endangered species. If a species is on the brink of extinction, the thinking goes, animals bred in captivity may, with careful research and planning, be introduced into the wild.

Passage 2

Zoos have oversold captive breeding programs
(15) as a method of reversing the tide of extinctions that threatens to engulf the much of the planet, but such action ignore the true cause of species extinction. Advocates of these programs often single out the recent examples of the reintroduction
(20) of the golden lion tamarin, a small primate native to the tropical forests of Brazil, and the Arabian oryx, an antelope in the deserts of Oman. These programs were remarkably expensive, however, and produced mixed results at best. Instead, we
(25) should concentrate our efforts on conserving the habitats that host a diversity of life forms. Only thus can we guarantee lasting safety for endangered species.

9. According to Passage 1, zoos now regard captive breeding programs as

(A) primarily a means to provide animals for zoo exhibits
(B) a method to assure the survival of endangered species
(C) a distraction from the true mission of wildlife preservation
(D) a means to expand their collections of animals
(E) an important effort largely without drawbacks

10. In line 11 of Passage 1, the phrase *the thinking goes* serves primarily to convey that

(A) the viewpoint may not be shared by the author
(B) considerable research goes into such an effort
(C) the author disagrees strongly with the policy
(D) such a policy is now only theoretical, and has not been put into practice
(E) this course of action is unlikely to actually succeed

11. In passage 2, the writer's outlook on captive breeding programs may best be described as

(A) enthusiastic
(B) critical
(C) cautiously positive
(D) impartial
(E) unique

12. In reaction to the term "insurance policy" (line 9) as used in Passage 1, Author 2 would most likely state that such a policy

(A) may have harmful effects that cannot be known in advance.
(B) is likely to fail because it misunderstands the cause of species extinction.
(C) is an important component of a larger, more comprehensive effort at wildlife preservation.
(D) is ill-advised because it distorts the healthy mechanism of natural evolution.
(E) is unlikely to succeed since it requires unrealistic levels of funding.

GO ON TO THE NEXT PAGE

Questions 13–21 are based on the following passage.

The following passage was written in 1992 by France Bequette, a writer who specializes in environmental issues.

The ozone layer, the fragile layer of gas surrounding our planet between 7 and 30 miles above the earth's surface, is being rapidly depleted. Seasonally occurring holes have appeared in it
(5) over the Poles and, recently, over densely populated temperate regions of the northern hemisphere. The threat is serious because the ozone layer protects the earth from the sun's ultraviolet radiation, which is harmful to all living organisms.
(10) Even though the layer is many miles thick, the atmosphere in it is tenuous and the total amount of ozone, compared with other atmospheric gases, is small. Ozone is highly reactive to chlorine, hydrogen, and nitrogen. Of these chlorine is the
(15) most dangerous since it is very stable and long-lived. When chlorine compounds reach the stratosphere, they bond with and destroy ozone molecules, with consequent repercussions for life on Earth.
(20) In 1958, researchers began noticing seasonal variations in the ozone layer above the South Pole. Between June and October the ozone content steadily fell, followed by a sudden increase in November. These fluctuations appeared to result
(25) from the natural effects of wind and temperature. But while the low October levels remained constant until 1979, the total ozone content over the Pole was steadily diminishing. In 1985, public opinion was finally roused by reports of a "hole"
(30) in the layer.
The culprits responsible for the hole were identified as compounds known as chlorofluorocarbons, or CFCs. CFCs are compounds of chlorine and fluorine. Nonflammable, nontoxic and non-
(35) corrosive, they have been widely used in industry since the 1950s, mostly as refrigerants and propellants and in making plastic foam and insulation.
In 1989 CFCs represented a sizeable market valued at over $1.5 billion and a labor force of 1.6
(40) million. But with CFCs implicated in ozone depletion, the question arose as to whether we were willing to risk an increase in cases of skin cancer,

eye ailments, even a lowering of the human immune defense system—all effects of further loss
(45) of the ozone layer. And not only humans would suffer. So would plant life. Phytoplankton, the first link in the ocean food chain and vital to the survival of most marine species, would not be able to survive near the ocean surface, which is where
(50) these organisms grow.
In 1990, 70 countries agreed to stop producing CFCs by the year 2000. In late 1991, however, scientists noticed a depletion of the ozone layer over the Arctic. In 1992 it was announced that the layer
(55) was depleting faster than expected and that it was also declining over the northern hemisphere. Scientists believe that natural events are making the problem worse. The Pinatubo volcano in the Philippines, which erupted in June 1991, released
(60) 12 million tons of damaging volcanic gases into the atmosphere.
Even if the whole world agreed today to stop all production and use of CFCs, this would not solve the problem. A single chlorine molecule can
(65) destroy 10,000–100,000 molecules of ozone. Furthermore, CFCs have a lifespan of 75–400 years and they take ten years to reach the ozone layer. In other words, what we are experiencing today results from CFCs emitted ten years ago.
(70) Researchers are working hard to find substitute products. Some are too dangerous because they are highly flammable; others may prove to be toxic and to contribute to the greenhouse effect—to the process of global warming. Nevertheless, even if
(75) there is no denying that the atmosphere is in a state of disturbance, nobody can say that the situation will not improve, either in the short or the long term, especially if we ourselves lend a hand.

GO ON TO THE NEXT PAGE

13. As it is described in the passage, the major function of the ozone layer is closest to that of

    (A) an emergency evacuation plan for a skyscraper

    (B) a central information desk at a convention center

    (C) a traffic light at a busy intersection

    (D) the structural support for a suspension bridge

    (E) the filtering system for a city water supply

14. The word *tenuous* in line 11 most nearly means

    (A) doubtful

    (B) tense

    (C) clear

    (D) thin

    (E) hazy

15. The passage implies which of the following about the "seasonal variations in the ozone layer" (lines 20–21) observed by scientists in 1958?

    (A) They were caused by industrial substances other than CFCs.

    (B) They created alarm among scientists but not the public.

    (C) They were least stable in the months between June and November.

    (D) They opened the public's eye to the threat of ozone depletion.

    (E) They focused attention on the dangers posed by CFCs.

16. In context, the word *constant* in line 27 means

    (A) gentle

    (B) steady

    (C) pestering

    (D) unerring

    (E) considerable

17. The author mentions market and workforce figures related to CFC production in lines 38–40 in order to point out that

    (A) responsibility for the problem of ozone depletion lies primarily with industry

    (B) the disadvantages of CFCs are obvious while the benefits are not

    (C) the magnitude of profits from CFCs has turned public opinion against the industry's practices

    (D) while the economic stakes are large, they are overshadowed by the effects of CFCs

    (E) curbing the use of CFCs will lead to a crippling loss of jobs worldwide

18. In paragraph 6, the author cites the evidence of changes in the ozone layer over the northern hemisphere to indicate that

    (A) the dangers of ozone depletion appear to be intensifying

    (B) ozone depletion is posing an immediate threat to many marine species

    (C) scientists are unsure about the ultimate effects of ozone loss on plants

    (D) CFCs are not the primary cause of ozone depletion in such areas

    (E) ozone levels are beginning to stabilize at the poles

GO ON TO THE NEXT PAGE

KAPLAN

19. Scientists apparently believe which of the following about the "volcanic gases" mentioned in line 60?

    (A) They contribute more to global warming than to ozone loss.

    (B) They pose a greater long-term threat than CFCs.

    (C) They are hastening ozone loss at present.

    (D) They are of little long-term consequence.

    (E) They contain molecules that are less destructive of ozone than CFCs.

20. The author's reference to the long life of chlorine molecules (lines 66–68) is meant to show that

    (A) CFCs are adaptable to a variety of industrial uses

    (B) there is more than adequate time to develop a long-term strategy against ozone loss

    (C) the long-term effects of ozone loss on human health may never be known

    (D) it is doubtful that normal levels of ozone can ever be reestablished

    (E) the positive effects of actions taken against ozone loss will be gradual

21. In the final paragraph, the author tries to emphasize that

    (A) researchers are unlikely to find effective substitutes for CFCs

    (B) human action can alleviate the decline of the ozone layer

    (C) people must to learn to live with the damaging effects of industrial pollutants

    (D) people have more control over ozone depletion than over the greenhouse effect

    (E) atmospheric conditions are largely beyond human control

GO ON TO THE NEXT PAGE

KAPLAN

Questions 22–27 are based on the following passage.

In this excerpt from a short story, the narrator describes an afternoon visit to the farm of Mrs. Hight and her daughter, Esther. The narrator is accompanied on her visit by William, a fisherman.

Mrs. Hight, like myself, was tired and thirsty. I brought a drink of water, and remembered some fruit that was left from my lunch. She revived vigorously, and told me the history of her later years
(5) since she had been been struck in the prime of her life by a paralyzing stroke, and her husband had died and left her with Esther and a mortgage on their farm. There was only one field of good land, but they owned a large area of pasture and some
(10) woodland. Esther had always been laughed at for her belief in sheep-raising when one by one their neighbors were giving up their flocks. When everything had come to the point of despair she had raised some money and bought all the sheep
(15) she could, insisting that Maine lambs were as good as any, and that there was a straight path by sea to the Boston market. By tending her flock herself she had managed to succeed; she had paid off the mortgage five years ago, and now what they did
(20) not spend was in the bank. "It has been stubborn work, day and night, summer and winter, and now she's beginning to get along in years," said the old mother. "She's tended me along with the sheep, and she's been good right along, but she should
(25) have been a teacher."

We heard voices, and William and Esther entered; they did not know that it was so late in the afternoon. William looked almost bold, like a young man rather than an ancient boy. As for
(30) Esther, she might have been Joan of Arc* returned to her sheep*, touched with age and gray. My heart was moved by the sight of her face, weather-worn and gentle, her thin figure in its close dress, and the strong hand that clasped a shepherd's staff,
(35) and I could only hold William in new awe; this silent fisherman who alone knew the heart that beat within her. I am not sure that they acknowledged even to themselves that they had always been lovers. Esther was untouched by the fret and
(40) fury of life; she had lived in sunshine and rain among her sheep and been refined instead of

coarsened, while her patience with an angry old mother, stung by defeat and mourning her lost activities, had given back a self-possession and
(45) habit of sweet temper. I had seen enough of Mrs. Hight to know that nothing a sheep might do could vex a person who was used to the severities of her companionship.

*Joan of Arc (1412–31): a young shepherdess who led the French army against the English during the Hundred Years' War

22. The main purpose of the passage is to

(A) suggest some of the essential attributes of a character

(B) speculate about a romantic link between two people

(C) show that people's lives are determined by events beyond their control

(D) identify the major causes of Mrs. Hight's unhappiness

(E) recount an incident that changed the narrator's life

23. Mrs. Hight's description of Esther's sheep-raising efforts (lines 8–17) reveals her daughter's

(A) desire to succeed no matter what the cost

(B) humility and grace in accepting defeat

(C) considerable regard for her neighbors' opinions

(D) calm determination in meeting difficulties

(E) dogged refusal to admit a mistake

GO ON TO THE NEXT PAGE

KAPLAN

24. In lines 37–39, the narrator speculates that Esther and William may be

    (A) resigned to being permanently separated from one another
    (B) apprehensive about each other's true feelings
    (C) impatient to make a formal commitment to one another
    (D) ambivalent in their regard for one another
    (E) unaware of the extent of their attachment

25. The narrator is most impressed with Esther's

    (A) aloofness and reserve
    (B) serenity and devotion
    (C) lively sense of humor
    (D) stubborn pride
    (E) material success

26. Lines 39–48 are meant to convey Mrs. Hight's

    (A) strength in the face of adversity
    (B) inability to carry on a conversation
    (C) dissatisfaction with her life
    (D) distrust of her neighbors
    (E) ingratitude toward her daughter

27. The *person* referred to in line 47 is

    (A) the narrator
    (B) William
    (C) Esther
    (D) Mrs. Hight
    (E) Mrs. Hight's husband

IF YOU FINISH BEFORE TIME IS CALLED, YOU MAY CHECK YOUR WORK ON THIS SECTION ONLY. DO NOT TURN TO ANY OTHER SECTION IN THE TEST. **STOP**

KAPLAN

SECTION TWO

Time—25 Minutes
26 Questions

For each of the following questions, choose the best answer and darken the corresponding oval on the answer sheet.

1. Liz is ---- person who loves to attend parties and is always full of ----.

   (A) a saturnine . . . melancholy
   (B) a querulous . . . zest
   (C) a convivial . . . bonhomie
   (D) an eloquent . . . vitriol
   (E) an affable . . . choler

2. Negritude, a literary movement emphasizing the importance and value of African culture and history, was founded in Paris in the 1930s by a group of ---- students from Martinique, Senegal, and other French-speaking colonies.

   (A) animated
   (B) didactic
   (C) expatriate
   (D) radical
   (E) sophisticated

3. Maria's performance was so ---- that even Mr. Rhodes, her teacher and harshest critic, was forced to ---- her talent.

   (A) magnificent . . . denigrate
   (B) tentative . . . concede
   (C) superb . . . deny
   (D) indifferent . . . praise
   (E) compelling . . . laud

4. Though the Greek author Thucydides used psychological insight rather than documented information to ---- speeches to historical figures, he is still considered an impartial and ---- historian.

   (A) dictate . . . endless
   (B) transmit . . . illustrious
   (C) disseminate . . . relevant
   (D) attribute . . . accurate
   (E) promote . . . inventive

5. Clint Eastwood made his reputation playing tough, ---- characters, notable for their expressive yet ---- speech.

   (A) laconic . . . pithy
   (B) narcissistic . . . obtuse
   (C) pragmatic . . enthusiastic
   (D) esoteric . . . trite
   (E) monotonous . . . interesting

6. Though George Balanchine's choreography stayed within a classical context, he challenged convention by recombining ballet idioms in ---- ways.

   (A) naive
   (B) effective
   (C) redundant
   (D) unexpected
   (E) awkward

GO ON TO THE NEXT PAGE

KAPLAN

7. While many Americans enjoy ---- lifestyle, the official number of Americans living in poverty has been ---- for several years.

    (A) an opulent . . . increasing
    (B) a leisurely . . . developing
    (C) an acerbic . . . varying
    (D) a provincial . . . ignored
    (E) a peripheral . . . stabilized

8. The participants allowed the debate to degenerate into ---- dispute; the urgency of the topic precluded the cordiality expected at such events.

    (A) an inconsequential
    (B) a depraved
    (C) an acrimonious
    (D) a prudent
    (E) a reticent

9. He claimed to usher in a new era of literature, but his novels were mostly ----, resembling those of many other contemporary authors.

    (A) realistic
    (B) emotional
    (C) pastoral
    (D) theoretical
    (E) derivative

10. Nearly all epiphytic ferns are ---- tropical rain-forests; while they do not require soil, they cannot survive without constant moisture.

    (A) uprooted to
    (B) steeped in
    (C) appointed to
    (D) decorative in
    (E) endemic to

GO ON TO THE NEXT PAGE

Questions 11–12 refer to the following passage.

Surprisingly, recent studies have demonstrated that sufferers from gum disease are actually at increased risk for <u>atherosclerosis</u>, the narrowing of the arteries that may lead to heart attack and
(5) stroke. Though scientists are not yet sure about the reasons, some researchers have hypothesized that bacteria in the gums may enter the blood-stream and establish themselves in the arteries, contributing to the formation of plaque, the mate-
(10) rial that helps create <u>blockages</u>. Three specific types of bacteria, in fact, have been identified in an analysis of plaque. It now seems that regular brushing and flossing may result in health benefits extending far beyond the teeth and gums.

11. Which of the following is introduced by the author to help confirm the hypothesis cited in lines 6–10?

(A) Regular brushing and flossing promote good dental hygiene.

(B) Plaque helps create the blockages associated with atherosclerosis.

(C) Sufferers from gum disease are at an increased risk of heart attack and stroke.

(D) Three types of bacteria have been identified in an analysis of plaque.

(E) Atherosclerosis is characterized by a narrow-ing of the arteries

12. The author's purpose in writing this passage was most likely to

(A) entertain

(B) persuade

(C) inform

(D) amuse

(E) argue

Questions 13–14 refer to the following passage.

Folklorists have found that holidays and holiday customs often bear interesting traces of their ori-gins. For example, the beginning of the European April Fools' Day is linked to the replacement of
(5) the Julian calendar by the Gregorian calendar in the year 1582. The new calendar changed New Year's Day from March 25 to January 1. However, people who refused to accept the change contin-ued to celebrate New Year's as an eight-day festival
(10) that concluded with the exchange of gifts on April 1. According to folklore, these laggards were derid-ed by their more progressive contemporaries, who called them "April Fools."

13. As used in the passage, *bear* (line 2) most nearly means

√(A) carry

(B) endure

(C) tolerate

(D) abide

(E) generate

14. The "laggards" cited in line 11 were

(A) people who mocked those who failed to adopt the new Gregorian Calendar

(B) the holidays that marked the beginning of the year under the Julian calendar

√(C) those who continued to observe the Julian calendar

(D) folklorists who described the origins of April Fools Day

(E) people who advocated the adoption of the Gregorian Calendar

GO ON TO THE NEXT PAGE

KAPLAN

Questions 15–26 are based on the following passage.

The author of the following passage is Juan Carlos Langlois, an Argentine artist whose work has been exhibited in Latin America, North America and Europe.

With the spread of industry, the exodus of people from the countryside, and the resultant transformation of the urban landscape, city-dwellers of the twentieth century have found themselves liv-
(5) ing in an increasingly colorless environment. Veiled in soot, towns and suburbs have lapsed into grimy taciturnity as an all-pervading drabness has overcome our great, sprawling urban complexes.

From the time of the first industrial revolution,
(10) Western societies have favored the use of somber, neutral colors in their towns and cities, judging them to be more functional. This anti-color attitude has been accentuated by the desire to imitate the supposed canons of Greek and Roman classi-
(15) cism. As we now know, however, the city-dwellers of antiquity loved color. Our vision of the temples and market-places of old, built solely in white marble, is wrong. On the contrary, judging by the rich and subtle palette found in the art of ancient
(20) civilizations, the use of color as a symbolic language seems to have been an important development in human culture. In later times, Romanesque and Gothic architecture also featured great use of color—witness the cathedrals of
(25) Siena, Florence, and Venice, with their stained-glass windows, frescoes, mosaics, and precious colored marble.

The facades embellished with traditional paintings still to be seen today in many countries of the
(30) world are an indication of the extent to which other peoples continue to nourish their spiritual and imaginative vision through contact with color. This extraordinary ornamental richness can be seen in the cities of Islam, the villages of Greece,
(35) the cities, villages and temples of India and Southeast Asia, and the fishing villages of the Caribbean, to name but a few examples. Sensitivity of this kind has found little place in the monotonous environments of our great western
(40) cities.

Fortunately, in recent decades the notion of bringing decorative color back into building projects has been gaining some ground. Bold and judicious use of color has an important role to
(45) play in the public art of our urban streets, providing a favorable background for a revived form of "urbanity" in its original, positive sense. The whole city becomes more understandable and more convivial as color, the poetry of the street,
(50) triumphs over drabness.

Public murals and trompe-l'oeil* facades, which are able to strike a chord in the collective memory by alluding to the important political, religious or artistic events of our cultures, are gradually mak-
(55) ing a comeback. The first influential muralists of the twentieth century were three great Mexican artists—Diego Rivera, José Clemente Orozco, and David Alfaro Siqueiros. In the 1920s, in search of an art form that would be monumental yet
(60) human and popular, they began to paint gigantic frescoes that retraced the major episodes in the history of Mexico. Their initiative brought them many commissions in their own country and, later, in the United States, where they inspired a
(65) vast program of publicly financed commissions in the 1930s, designed to provide work for unemployed American artists during the Great Depression. More than 2,500 murals were completed throughout the United States over the next
(70) few years under New Deal programs begun by the administration of Franklin D. Roosevelt.

During the 1960s, the creation of murals in public places became the spearhead of an authentic popular art movement. This movement was a
(75) community response to the need for expression felt by ethnic and other minority groups to whom access to visual creativity and expression had previously been barred. In 1967, a mural conceived as a "collage" of portraits, photographs and poetic
(80) verse was created on a derelict building in the southern suburbs of Chicago by a group of black American artists led by William Walker. Entitled "Wall of Respect," the work paid tribute to public figures who had fought for Civil Rights for black
(85) Americans. This group effort by minority artists

GO ON TO THE NEXT PAGE

KAPLAN

inspired other similar projects in American cities such as Los Angeles, San Francisco, Baltimore, and New York, and marked a new point of departure for public mural painting in this country.

(90) Improving the quality of life in the city is one of the primary objectives of street art. Color can help to save, rehabilitate or otherwise give new life to neighborhoods and other urban sites doomed to demolition, dereliction or anonymity. The aim is *(95)* to provide the city-dweller with the opportunity to participate in the rebirth of a more human environment. By its very nature as communal space, the street lends itself to collective creativity which, in turn, leads to an enhanced sense of *(100)* community pride and well-being.

*Trompe l'oeil (literally, "deception of the eye"): a highly decorative style of mural painting that often depicts architectural or other three-dimensional forms

15. The "transformation of the urban landscape" (lines 2–3) most likely refers to the

   (A) diversity of urban ethnic populations
   (B) spread and greater density of urban areas
   (C) loss of manufacturing jobs in cities
   (D) improved visual appearance of cities
   (E) loss of parks in modern cities

16. In lines 6–7, the phrase "lapsed into grimy taciturnity" refers to the

   (A) growing violence of city life
   (B) decay of urban areas
   (C) unresponsiveness of politicians to city problems
   (D) increasing development of rural areas
   (E) passive acceptance by city-dwellers of their surroundings

17. Which of the following best explains why "somber, neutral colors" (lines 10–11) came into wider use in western cities?

   (A) They were intended to accentuate other, bolder colors.
   (B) They were viewed as more modern than the colors of Greece and Rome.
   (C) They were considered more beautiful than brighter colors.
   (D) They were judged more suitable for an industrial environment.
   (E) They recalled the muted colors of Romanesque and Gothic architecture.

18. The author suggests that the admiration of Western societies for "the supposed canons of Greek and Roman classicism" (lines 14–15) was

   (A) a reaction to the widespread use of functional colors
   (B) based on a mistaken belief about the use of color in antiquity
   (C) consistent with our love of the colors of Siena, Florence, and Venice
   (D) founded on respect for the art of ancient civilizations
   (E) inspired by their use of color as a symbolic language

19. In line 16, *vision* most nearly means

   (A) image
   (B) display
   (C) fixation
   (D) personal wish
   (E) clear-sightedness

GO ON TO THE NEXT PAGE

KAPLAN

20. The cities and villages mentioned in lines 34–37 are noted for their

    (A) breathtaking natural scenery
    (B) complex histories
    (C) uniform architecture
    (D) decorative lushness
    (E) religious convictions

21. In line 38, the word *sensitivity* most nearly means

    (A) sense of community spirit
    (B) imaginative use of color
    (C) understanding of different cultures
    (D) consideration for other people
    (E) knowledge of art history

22. *Judicious* in line 44 is best understood as meaning

    (A) controversial
    (B) objective
    (C) determined
    (D) informed
    (E) judgmental

23. The phrase "strike a chord in the collective memory" (line 52) is used to signify the

    (A) adaptability of people living in unfamiliar surroundings
    (B) willingness of people to make sacrifices for the good of a community
    (C) loyalty shown by people living in small communities
    (D) tendency of city-dwellers to lose touch with their cultural roots
    (E) ability of art to portray the variety and history of a culture

24. The reference in paragraph 5 to the painters Diego Rivera, José Clemente Orozco, and David Alfaro Siquieros serves to

    (A) highlight the poor quality of mural painting in the United States
    (B) indicate the wide range of colors and styles to be found in mural painting
    (C) shed light on the revival of mural painting in two countries
    (D) show the important role that artists have played in Mexican history
    (E) emphasize the lack of government funding for public mural painting

25. William Walker's "Wall of Respect" project is described as a "new point of departure" (line 89) because

    (A) artists who began painting murals went on to success in other art forms
    (B) public mural painting had never before been attempted in the United States
    (C) other minority groups were inspired to undertake similar community projects
    (D) the project popularized a new use for derelict buildings
    (E) the artists involved led a revival of the civil rights movement

26. The author most likely considers the street an appropriate location for art because the street

    (A) encourages a natural reserve in city-dwellers
    (B) carries few traces of past events
    (C) is naturally a place of shared activities
    (D) forces people to be more alert about their surroundings
    (E) features subjects that are interesting to paint

IF YOU FINISH BEFORE TIME IS CALLED, YOU MAY CHECK YOUR WORK ON THIS SECTION ONLY. DO NOT TURN TO ANY OTHER SECTION IN THE TEST.   STOP

SECTION THREE

Time—20 Minutes
16 Questions

For each of the following questions, choose the best answer and darken the corresponding oval on the answer sheet.

Questions 1–12 are based on the following passages.

The following two passages discuss closely linked periods in European history. In Passage 1, the author describes the organization of the guild, an important feature of town life in medieval Europe. The author of Passage 2 identifies a fundamental social change that began taking place in Italian towns in the late 1200s.

Passage 1

The membership of guilds in medieval European towns was made up of masters, journeymen, and apprentices. Each guild differed from town to town in its social and political influence,
(5) but its primary economic function was the same everywhere—to protect the merchant and artisan, not just from the competition of foreign merchants, but also from the competition of fellow guild members. Town markets were closed to for-
(10) eign products, and individual members were prevented from growing rich at the expense of others.

Each guild adopted strict rules, including fixed hours of work, fixed prices and wages, limits on the numbers of workers in workshops, and regular
(15) workshop inspections. These tightly enforced rules had the effect of dampening personal ambition and initiative. No one was allowed to employ methods of production that were cheaper or more efficient than those used by fellow guild members.
(20) In fact, technical progress and those who favored it were looked on with suspicion.

Each local guild was organized hierarchically. The dominant members were the masters—small merchant proprietors of workshops who owned
(25) their tools, raw materials, products, and all the profits from the sale of those products. Journeymen were wage-earning workers who had completed an apprenticeship. Apprentices were brought into a trade under a master's direction.
(30) The number of masters in each local guild was limited, determined by the needs of the local market and by certain requirements, including citizenship, that were hard to fulfill.

The master functioned as a small, independent
(35) entrepreneur whose primary capital included a house, a workshop, tools, and equipment. The number of workshop employees was restricted, usually to one or two apprentices and journeymen. If a master happened to inherit or marry
(40) into a fortune, it could not be used against other masters, because the guild system left no room for competition. But material inequality among guild merchants was rare. For most of them, the economic structure of the guild meant the same kind
(45) of existence and the same measured resources. While it gave them a secure position, it also prevented them from rising above it. In this sense, the guild system might be described as non-capitalist.

Passage 2

Throughout most of Europe in the late Middle
(50) Ages, human consciousness as we know it today was really only half awake. People thought of themselves as members of a family, organization, or community, but not as individuals. In most countries, the different classes of society lived
(55) apart, each with its own sense of values. Throughout their lives, people tended to remain in the class into which they were born. But in Italy social fluidity appeared early. By the late 1200s, Italy was brimming with the notion of individual-
(60) ity. The Italians of the next two centuries—the period that we now call the Renaissance—were unafraid of being and appearing different from their neighbors.

Italian towns, primarily because of their control
(65) of the Mediterranean trade, were the busiest in Europe. Town crafts included such sophisticated trades as goldsmithing and stonecarving. Competition between artisans grew so acute that masterpieces began to proliferate, and love of art
(70) spread throughout society. A few merchants made great fortunes, lent their money to foreign princes, and thus became international bankers.

GO ON TO THE NEXT PAGE

Italy was a place in which the potential for individual achievement—for a privileged few, any-
(75) way—seemed unlimited. Since there was no central Italian government, wealthy merchants were unchecked in their political and social ambitions. They competed for civic power and fame, sponsored public works and cultural institutions, hired
(80) armies, and forged alliances. The typical Italian merchant was fluent in Latin and Greek and read the classic works of Rome and Greece. It was in these circles that private, secular education got its start.
(85) The story of the Medici family of Florence illustrates these changes. Giovanni, an obscure merchant born in 1360, created the family banking fortune. His son Cosimo became ruler of Florence by scheming against rivals in other Florentine
(90) families. Cosimo's grandson and heir, Lorenzo the Magnificent, was an able politician, a famous patron of the arts and learning, and a reputable scholar and poet. The Medici family's rise to prominence coincided with the decline of the
(95) guild and the growth of capitalist individualism in Italy.

1. The most important function of the "rules" discussed in lines 12–15 was probably to

   (A) guarantee that masters retained strict control over their employees

   (B) broaden the political influence of guilds within a town

   (C) minimize competition among local artisans and merchants

   (D) stimulate the development of more efficient production methods

   (E) improve the quality of merchandise in local markets

2. The "requirements" mentioned in line 32 had the effect of

   (A) opening local markets to foreign products

   (B) controlling the number of those who advanced beyond journeyman status

   (C) enlarging the number of those qualified to become town citizens

   (D) prohibiting trade with foreign merchants

   (E) encouraging economic rivalry among small entrepreneurs

3. In line 45, the word *measured* most nearly means

   (A) deliberate

   (B) inadequate

   (C) rhythmical

   (D) cautious

   (E) limited

4. The author of Passage 1 describes the guild system as an economic system that was

   (A) open and permissive

   (B) innovative and energetic

   (C) fluid and unpredictable

   (D) restrictive and stable

   (E) unfair and exploitative

5. In describing human consciousness in most of Europe as being "only half awake" (line 51), the author of Passage 2 seeks to

   (A) contrast prevailing social conditions in Europe to those in Italy

   (B) criticize a lack of interest in education in medieval European society

   (C) imply that some people have always opposed social progress

   (D) stress the role of individuality in contemporary society

   (E) suggest that a common belief about medieval Europe is wrong

GO ON TO THE NEXT PAGE ▷

6. The author of Passage 2 uses the term "social fluidity" in line 58 mainly to describe the

(A) dangerous conditions of urban life in Italy

(B) intense competition between families in Italian towns

(C) great disparities of wealth among social classes in Italy

(D) rapid spread of democratic institutions in Italy

(E) unfixed character of social life in Italy

7. The meaning of the word *acute* in line 68 is

(A) chaotic

(B) dangerous

(C) wise

(D) keen

(E) sudden

8. The author discusses the Medici primarily to illustrate which of the following?

(A) The guild system in Italy rewarded individual effort and competitiveness.

(B) There were few restraints on the aspirations of people in Italy.

(C) Political power in Italy was held by a small number of wealthy families.

(D) Family rivalry in Florence was a major social phenomenon.

(E) It was easy for individuals to capture wealth and power in Italy.

9. The author's discussion of the Medici family (lines 85–96) is

(A) nostalgic

(B) disapproving

(C) dispassionate

(D) ironic

(E) defensive

10. Both passages seek to explain the

(A) expanding role of commerce in Italian towns during the Middle Ages

(B) economic structure of the guild system during the Middle Ages

(C) growing importance of individuality in the Middle Ages

(D) circumstances of merchants during the Middle Ages

(E) fast growth of capitalism during the Middle Ages

11. What position would the author of Passage 1 most likely take regarding the description of European society in lines 49–53 of Passage 2?

(A) The structure of the medieval guild and its effects support the description.

(B) The description underestimates the extent to which the medieval guild system favored individual initiative.

(C) Trying to describe the complexities of human consciousness is not an appropriate task for historians.

(D) The accuracy of the description cannot be determined without further investigation.

(E) It is unwise to describe European society in such sweeping terms.

12. The merchants discussed in Passage 1 are most different from those discussed in Passage 2 in their

(A) concern for the economic welfare of their towns

(B) interest in exercising their rights as citizens

(C) views regarding the right to own private property

(D) patriotic loyalty to their towns

(E) attitudes regarding personal ambition

GO ON TO THE NEXT PAGE

KAPLAN

Questions 13–14 refer to the following passage.

I am a shameless word maniac. You can imagine, then, my excitement when a friend told me about the "Word a Day" website in the Internet. This wonderful site presents an unusual word
(5) every day, along with a definition and a word history. The researchers who write the material often feature a weekly theme. Last week, for example, the site featured such choice items as *octothorpe* (the eight-pointed pound sign on your telephone
(10) keyboard), *ennead* (a group of nine), and *doyenne* (the senior woman of a group, derived from the Latin word for "ten").

13. The word *shameless* (line 1) serves to

(A) emphasize the writer's interest in a humorous way

(B) show that the author defies those who disapprove of such interests

(C) illustrate the author's delight at discovering the "Word a Day" website

(D) provide an example of a word featured on the website

(E) reveal a regrettable characteristic of the author's personality

14. The author cites the words *octothorpe*, *ennead*, and *doyenne* (lines 8–10) to serve as examples primarily because they

(A) have similar origins

(B) are highly unusual words

(C) are favorite entries of the author

(D) were featured on the "Word a Day" website

(E) are related to a single theme

Questions 15–16 refer to the following passage.

We have recently witnessed a dramatic shift in the image and mission of museums. For over a century, these institutions presented themselves as elitist temples of art. Even the architecture of
(5) museum buildings recalled, more often than not, the sacred shrines of Greco-Roman antiquity. Now, however, museums have developed blockbuster shows for the masses, and they have put vigorous efforts into merchandising, as the size of
(10) the typical museum gift shop shows. Perhaps most important, many museums have now adopted an educational mission, reaching out to young audiences whom the museums, quite sensibly, view as the patrons of the future.

15. The word *blockbuster* (line 7) serves to emphasize

(A) the similarity between the appeal of art and films

(B) the tendency of modern museums to avoid exhibits of Greco-Roman art

(C) the tremendous financial rewards of a successful museum exhibition

(D) the efforts of modern museums to appeal to a large audience

(E) the increasing sense of an educational mission in modern museums

16. Which of the following would the author most likely cite as a significant change in the mission of museums?

(A) The growing role of the museum gift shop

(B) The move towards exhibits that appeal to many people

(C) The increasing focus on commerce

(D) The move away from classically inspired architecture

(E) The recent focus on education

IF YOU FINISH BEFORE TIME IS CALLED, YOU MAY CHECK YOUR WORK ON THIS SECTION ONLY. DO NOT TURN TO ANY OTHER SECTION IN THE TEST.

Practice Test A: **Answer Key**

SECTION ONE

1. B	10. A	19. C
2. A	11. B	20. E
3. D	12. B	21. B
4. D	13. E	22. A
5. E	14. D	23. D
6. D	15. C	24. E
7. B	16. B	25. B
8. C	17. D	26. C
9. B	18. A	27. C

SECTION TWO

1. C	10. E	19. A
2. C	11. D	20. D
3. E	12. C	21. B
4. D	13. A	22. D
5. A	14. C	23. E
6. D	15. B	24. C
7. A	16. B	25. C
8. C	17. D	26. C
9. E	18. B	

SECTION THREE

1. C	7. D	13. A
2. B	8. B	14. E
3. E	9. C	15. D
4. D	10. D	16. E
5. A	11. A	
6. E	12. E	

Answers and Explanations

SECTION ONE

1. B

The clue words here are *reelect* and *change*. If those polled are planning to reelect their legislators, then they are not eager for a change in leadership. The public could not have been (A) *partial to a change in leadership,* since they're intending to bring back the same people. And if they were (D) *confident of* or (E) *receptive to* replacing their legislators, they would vote for someone other than the current office holders. (B) and (C) are the only remaining options. If anything, the public is getting used to keeping the same people around, so (C) doesn't. But if *the public was wary of a change* (that is, cautious or nervous about it), voters might well decide *to reelect their legislators.*

inured to: accustomed to something

receptive: open, welcoming

partial to: having a preference or liking for

2. A

The missing word has to describe an animal that can run at high speed and climb any tree. We could predict that a word like *nimble* would work. (A) *agile* matches our prediction. None of the other choices makes sense—the mountain lion certainly isn't a *passive* creature if it can run at high speed and climb any tree. It makes no sense to call the lion a *capricious* animal. And while the lion may very well be an *attentive* or *dominant* creature, these choices don't make sense in the context of the sentence.

capricious: inconsistent, impulsive

3. D

The sentence says that *organic farming* is *labor intensive,* that is, it requires a lot of work by human beings (as opposed to machines). It is *thus initially quite—.* If the sentence ended right after the blank, (E) might be the best answer, but *although* signals a contrast: Since the second clause is concerned with how expensive organic farming is compared to conventional farming, the blank must have something to do with expense, not labor. *Costly* means "expensive," so (D) is correct.

arduous: laborious, involving very hard work

4. D

We know that Rivera used *bold, dramatic forms,* so one possible prediction for the first blank would be something like "vivid" or "creative." But none of the answer choices has a first word that matches this prediction. And it's hard to tell what Rivera did to the *generation of young artists.* We won't be able to pick a choice based on one blank.

We'll just have to see which answer choice contains two words that go together *and* make sense when we plug them into the sentence. The other important hint is that the overall tone of the sentence is positive, so whichever pair we choose will probably be positive as well. Choice (D) is the only answer that contains two positive words. When we plug them into the sentence, the two words do reinforce each other: An *influential* artist would be *inspiring* to other painters.

In (A), a famous artist could make it hard for younger artists. But nothing in the sentence indicates that Rivera's fame or his *bold, dramatic forms displaced* other artists. In (B), *convoluted* doesn't really fit with *bold* and *dramatic.* And (C) and (E) both contain highly negative words: *antagonistic* and *thwarting.*

convoluted: complex, intricate

antagonistic: hostile, opposing

thwarting: blocking, hindering

5. E

The backbone of this sentence is a contrast: *Although the Druids . . . were—, they preferred to use— teaching methods to educate the young.* The two words in the correct answer should contrast with each other somehow. The only answer choice that contains two contrasting words is (E). *The Druids . . . were literate*—they knew how to read—but they imparted *information orally,* that is, by speaking, rather than by writing. The word pairs in (A) and (B) may have a relation in some contexts, but they never contrast each other.

literate: able to read and write

oral: using speech

enduring: lasting

haphazard: random

KAPLAN

6. D

The clue words here are *either* and *or*. This offers a choice of two options which do not mean the same thing. If one of the options is a *localized . . . form,* the other has to be a *[nonlocalized]* form. So the correct answer will mean "nonlocalized."

Let's say you didn't know the word *localized.* You probably do know the word *local.* It means near you, in your area, and not all over the place. So *localized* will have something to do with a limited space. The answer has to be "nonlocalized," so (A) and (C) won't work. (D) *diffuse* means "spread out," the opposite of *localized,* so it's correct.

localized: restricted to a given area

diffuse: spread out

7. B

The clue words here are *even though.* There must be a strong contrast between the way Veronica's friends describe her and the way the author of the sentence sees her. So the words that go in the blanks should be the opposite of *amiable and frank.* We might predict that the correct answer would be something like "disagreeable and secretive." No matter what, both words should certainly be negative. That lets us eliminate (A), (C), and (D) right away, since each of them contains a positive word. And in (E), *frugal* and *mysterious* aren't really negative or positive. Therefore, (B) must be the right answer. A *rude* person is certainly not *amiable;* a *calculating* person isn't *frank,* either.

gregarious: sociable, friendly

frugal: thrifty

calculating: scheming

amiable: pleasing, agreeable

frank: open, honest

8. C

It seems pretty clear that the second blank is going to be filled by something like "definite." On the basis of that prediction alone, choice (D) is wrong.

That still leaves us with four choices in the second words that more or less match the prediction. We need to look at the first blank. The word *despite* is a major clue word. There will be an opposition or contrast between the two parts of the sentence. To contrast with the fact that there is still no definite *relationship between sunspot cycles and the Earth's weather,* the first blank should probably set up

a phrase like *educated guessing.* Though *clear* makes sense in (B), it's out, because *educated confusion* doesn't make sense. And (E) won't work, because it wouldn't set up a contrast either. The only remaining choices are (A) and (C). (C) makes the internal logic of the sentence work better. *Conjecture* is pretty close to *guessing* and contrasts very well with *proven.* Also, *proven* is closer to the meaning of *definite* that we had in mind.

tenuous: flimsy, slender

conjecture: speculation, guessing

Captive Breeding Passages

9. B

In Passage 1, the author writes that the programs were once used simply to provide animals for the zoos, but are now often considered "an insurance policy for endangered species." This matches (B) nicely. Notice that (A) and (D) are related to the old purpose of the breeding programs—keeping zoos stocked, but the question relates to how the programs are regarded now. (C) is the opinion of Author 2, not author 1, while (E) is out of the scope of the passage. The author never discusses the drawbacks (or lack of such drawbacks) of the breeding programs.

10. A

The author of Passage 1 is quite objective, and never actually says whether she considers captive breeding programs a good idea. So the phrase, "so the thinking goes" shows that the thoughts are not her own. She doesn't necessarily believe that a captive breeding program can introduce endangered species back into the wild, (A). (B) is a distortion of the word *thinking.* Here the word is used to refer to the thought that such an effort would be successful, not the thought and research involved in implementing such an effort. (C) and (E) are too negative, since the author never indicates whether she believes the reintroduction could work. (D) is out of scope, since we don't learn whether such an effort has been attempted.

11. B

Author 2 is very down on captive breeding programs and feels that they are ineffective and distract people from the more important goal of preserving environments. In other words, he is highly critical, (B). (A) and (C) are the opposite of what we're looking for. (D) doesn't fit, since the author does take a stand, and so can't be described as *impartial*. There's no support that the outlook is *unique*, (E), since we don't know if other people believe the same thing.

12. B

Passage 1 states that zoos consider captive breeding an insurance policy, since animals can be reintroduced into places where they have become extinct. Passage 2, however, states that captive breeding is too expensive and produces "mixed results at best." Author 2 feels that preserving habitats is the only way to "guarantee lasting safety for endangered species." So he would likely say that the "insurance policy" of captive breeding will be unsuccessful because it ignores the deeper problem of disappearing habitats. This matches (B) well.

Author 2 might agree that the policy would have harmful effects, but there is no way to know that these effects couldn't be known in advance, (A). The phrase *important component* makes (C) wrong, since the author doesn't feel that captive breeding is a good idea at all, even as a component of a larger program. (D) is out of scope, since Author 2 never refers to natural evolution. He does say that the programs are expensive, but he doesn't say that that's why the programs would be unsuccessful, (E).

Ozone Passage

Here's a straightforward but somewhat sobering science passage on the topical subject of damage to the ozone layer. Paragraph 1 summarizes the problem; the layer of ozone, which protects the earth from the sun's ultraviolet rays, is being depleted. Paragraph 2 explains the chemical reaction that causes the problem. Paragraph 3 traces the problem from the first time scientists noticed that something was wrong to the point that the public became aware of it. Paragraph 4 identifies industry-produced CFCs as the chief culprits in ozone depletion, and paragraph 5 lists some of the threats the problem poses to life on Earth. Paragraphs 6 and 7 give us the latest news—even though CFCs are being phased out, the long lifespan of CFC molecules means that the effects on the ozone layer can be expected to worsen for the time being. There's a note of optimism at the end of the passage, though—the author advocates continued effort to improve the situation.

13. E

The author describes the *function* of the ozone layer (in lines 6–9). We're told that the ozone layer "protects the Earth from UV radiation," which is "harmful to all living organisms." Choice (E) is the closest analogy here. It captures the idea of something which constantly provides protection against a life-threatening force. The *evacuation plan* mentioned in (A) only helps in *emergencies.* None of the other choices—(B) *information desks,* (C) *traffic lights,* or (D) *suspension bridge supports*—are facilities designed to provide protection against specific threats.

14. D

The author uses *tenuous* to describe the quality of the atmosphere at the ozone layer. Even though the ozone layer is several miles thick, leading us to expect that the atmosphere would be thick too, we're told that the atmosphere is *tenuous.* And so *tenuous* here means (D) *thin,* the opposite of "thick."

(A) *doubtful* is the closest wrong answer because of its negative connotation, but it is not specific enough. (B) *tense* doesn't fit in a discussion of atmosphere. (C) *clear* would contradict the passage by implying that there was no atmosphere at all at this level. Finally, (E) *hazy* is a term that would apply more to the weather than to atmospheric density.

15. C

The "seasonal variations" noticed in 1958 were initially regarded as the "natural effects of wind and temperature" (line 25). According to the passage, it was only much later that the connection between CFCs and ozone depletion became known (lines 31–33). Therefore, we can infer that in 1958, these seasonal variations *were not regarded as a threat,* making (C) correct and (B), (D), and (E) wrong. No *other ozone depletants* are mentioned (A).

16. B

The key word in line 26 is *while,* because it indicates a contrast. We're told that *while* the low October levels stayed *constant,* ozone levels as a whole *diminished,* or fell. *Unlike* the overall figures, in other words, the October levels did not fluctuate—they remained (B) *steady.* (A) *gentle* and (C) *pestering* are unlikely words to use to describe atmospheric measurements. (D) *unerring* suggests that the accuracy of scientists' measurements is the issue. (E) presents a contradiction—the October levels couldn't be both low *and considerable* in size.

17. D

The author's point is implied in the first two lines of the paragraph. We're told that CFCs represent a sizeable market. Then we're told that in spite of this, people began to question the risks to human health when CFCs were implicated in ozone depletion. So the author's point in mentioning the CFC market is that the dangers of using CFCs *overshadowed* the *economic* considerations (D).

(A) can't be inferred from the context. The author doesn't explicitly blame industry for the problem. (B) is out because the author makes no mention of *benefits.* (C) gets the issue wrong; it was the health risks, not *industry profits,* that *turned public opinion.* And (E) distorts the author's point of view, since ozone depletion, not *job losses,* is the author's main concern.

18. A

Here the author's giving us a progress report on ozone depletion in the 1990s. We're told that the layer was "depleting faster than expected" in addition to natural events "making the problem worse" (lines 57–58). (A) summarizes this idea that the situation is worsening.

Paragraph 6 describes the problem as a whole, without relating it to any particular species, even though threats to *marine species* (B) and *plant life* (C) are mentioned elsewhere. (D) goes against the gist of the passage, which basically identifies *CFCs* as the main culprits. Finally, we're told that the ozone layer is depleting over the Arctic, (E).

19. C

Lines 57–58 say that scientists believe that natural events are "making the problem worse," and the volcanic gases emitted by the Pinatubo volcano are mentioned as one example. (C) is the correct answer.

(A) *global warming* isn't mentioned until paragraph eight. (B) distorts the author's point; *CFCs* are still the biggest *threat.* Since the gases are adding to a *long-term* problem, (D) must be wrong. Finally, (E) can't be inferred here, since the author tells us nothing about how *destructive* the *molecules* in volcanic gases are.

20. E

Even stopping all CFC production today wouldn't solve the problem, we're told, because CFCs can live for up to 400 years. (E) captures the underlying point here; measures against ozone depletion may take years to have an effect.

Choice (A) doesn't fit with the passage at all. (B) is too positive; the author's saying that the problem's going to take years to fix, not that there's plenty of time to deal with it. There's no mention of the implications for *human health* (C) in paragraph 7. (D), finally, is too extreme. The author never states that the problem is insoluble.

21. B

The last paragraph focuses on what scientists are doing about the problem. Even if things are bad, the author says, "nobody can say that the situation will not improve" (lines 76–77) if people lend a hand. (B) captures this positive note.

(A) exaggerates the obstacles to research discussed at the beginning of the paragraph. Choices (C) and (E) just accept ozone depletion as a fact of life, which is not the author's position at all. And finally, ozone depletion and *the greenhouse effect* are never compared in terms of our *control over* them (D).

Mrs. Hight Passage

This fiction passage is about Mrs. Hight and her daughter Esther, who live together on a farm. Through a conversation with Mrs. Hight, paragraph 1 gives us some background detail on how Esther saved the family farm by raising sheep singlehandedly. Paragraph 2 centers on the narrator's admiration for Esther, for her achievement on the farm, and her steadfast loyalty to her mother.

22. A

From line 10 onward, the story of the passage is really about Esther—her success with sheep farming, and her patience in looking after her mother. The purpose of the passage is to (A) *suggest some of the essential attributes* of her character—determination, good nature, and so on.

Both (B), the *romance* between William and Esther, and (D), *the causes of Mrs. Hight's unhappiness*, are topics only briefly touched on. (C) is not supported by the story at all—Esther's success in sheep raising seems to show that people's lives are very much under *their own control.* And (E) is too extreme—there's no indication that the visit to the farm has *changed the narrator's life* in any major way.

23. D

In *Mrs. Hight's* words, we're told that even though raising the sheep had been "stubborn work," Esther had been "good right along" (lines 24). Choice (D) captures Esther's approach here—not only did she overcome *difficulties* with *determination*—she kept *calm* throughout.

(A) is too extreme; Esther didn't put *success* before all other considerations. She wasn't *defeated* (B), and she did-n't bow to her *neighbors' opinions* (C). And her success suggests that her efforts were not a *mistake* (E).

24. E

The author speculates that William and Esther had "always been lovers" but had not acknowledged it "even to them-selves." In other words, she thinks that William and Esther have a strong attachment that they're not fully aware of. (E) captures this situation.

(B) is wrong because it's their *own* feelings that William and Esther haven't acknowledged, which also makes (C) *a formal commitment* unlikely as yet. (D) *ambivalence* is wrong because there's no suggestion of uncertainty or contradictory feelings. Finally, there's no evidence of a *permanent separation* (A).

25. B

This question touches again on the qualities Esther showed in managing to raise sheep *and* look after her mother at the same time. We're told that she had been "refined instead of coarsened" by her work, and had shown "patience," "self-possession," and "sweet temper" in caring for her mother. (B) *serenity and devotion* fits the bill here.

(B) *aloofness and reserve* sounds like the opposite of "sweet temper." Esther's (C) *sense of humor* is never mentioned, and the author doesn't seem particularly im-pressed by her (E) *material success*. Finally, (D) *stubborn pride* exaggerates Esther's determination in overcoming adversity, without acknowledging her good points.

26. C

Mrs. Hight, we're told in lines 42–43, was an "angry old mother, stung by defeat and mourning her lost activities." (C) captures the point here—Mrs. Hight is difficult to live with because she's *dissatisfied* with the way her life has run.

(A) *strength in adversity* applies to Esther, but not to her mother. (B) *carrying on a conversation* doesn't seem to be a problem for Mrs. Hight. Mrs. Hight is angry because of her own defeats—not because she (D) *distrusts her neighbors* or (E) *lacks gratitude towards her daughter*.

27. C

The author's focus at the end of the passage is on Esther's relationship with her mother. It's (C) *Esther* who will prob-ably find sheep easier to deal with than the "severity" of Mrs. Hight's company. None of the other characters deals with sheep, or interacts closely with Mrs. Hight.

SECTION TWO

1. C

How would you describe someone who likes to *"attend parties"*? Probably as (C) *convivial*, (E) *affable*, or (a little less likely) (D) *eloquent*. You certainly would not describe her as (A) *saturnine* or (B) *querulous*. Now you've elimi-nated (A) and (B). Looking at (C), (D), and (E), this per-son would have to be full of (C) *bonhomie*. She definitely wouldn't be full of (D) *vitriol* or (E) *choler*.

convivial: sociable

affable: friendly, approachable

eloquent: well-spoken

saturnine: gloomy

querulous: complaining, irritable

bonhomie: good nature, geniality

vitriol: bitterness

choler: anger

2. C

The clue here is that Negritude *was founded in Paris* and the students who created it were from *French-speaking colonies*. Thus they must have been (C) *expatriates*. Nothing in the sentence suggests they were (A) *animated*, (D) *radical*, or (E) *sophisticated*.

expatriates: people who've left their native land

didactic: factual to the point of dullness; instructive

3. E

There are two things to look for in this sentence. The first is the construction *so—that*. It tells us that whatever word fills the first blank *forced* [Mr. Rhodes] to—her talent. The second is the clue word *even*. If Maria's teacher was her harshest critic, and even he was forced to say something about her talent, chances are that the performance was too good to criticize. Therefore, we can predict that both words will be positive.

Although *praise* appears in choice (D), *indifferent* is not the kind of strongly positive word that would be suitable for the first blank. Similarly, the first word in (B), *tentative*, wouldn't fit the first blank. The first words in (A), (C), and (E) are all strongly positive words, but the second words in (A) and (C) are negative. (E) is the only choice with positive words for both blanks.

tentative: hesitant

denigrate: to put down or insult

indifferent: mediocre

compelling: riveting

laud: to honor or praise highly

concede: to admit

4. D

The clue words *though* and *still* point to a contrast between what Thucydides did and how he is viewed today. We know that he is still considered an impartial and—historian. Since *impartial* is a good thing for historians to be, the second blank will probably be filled by another positive word. That doesn't help us much, though, since none of the second words in the answer choices is negative. But in (A), it doesn't make much sense to attach *endless* to *historian*. (E) can go, too. How can you *promote* a speech to a historical figure?

With (A) and (E) out of the running, let's go to the first blank. Thucydides used speculation or invention rather than documented fact, to—speeches to historical figures. So Thucydides must have ascribed to historical figures words that they never actually spoke. The only choice that gives us that meaning when plugged into the first blank is (D): Thucydides *attributed* speeches to historical figures that they may never have made. Historians are supposed to be impartial and *accurate*, so (D) fills the sentence well all the way around. (B) doesn't work; Thucydides may be considered *illustrious*, but there is no evidence in the sen-

tence that he *transmitted* speeches to historical figures. Nor does (C) work; the sentence never hints that Thucydides *disseminated* speeches.

impartial: fair, not taking sides

illustrious: notable

transmit: to send

disseminate: to distribute

5. A

The key to completing a sentence is to tie up loose ends without adding any new or unrelated information. The clue word *yet* should help you limit the choices up front. The second word will be something not usually associated with *expressive*. The first word will be one that goes well with *tough*. That lets you eliminate (C) and (E) based on their second blanks.

That leaves (A), (B), and (D) for the first blank. Someone *tough* isn't necessarily be (B) *narcissistic* or (E) *monotonous*. But he could very well be (A) *laconic*. The two words in (A), *laconic* and *pithy*, best fit our predictions.

laconic: using as few words as possible, curt

pithy: concise and to the point

narcissistic: self-centered and vain

obtuse: blunt, dull, or stupid

pragmatic: practical

esoteric: relating to knowledge that few people have

6. D

The problem with the wrong choices here is that they add new information and don't fit the logic of the existing sentence. We're told that Balanchine stayed within the format of a particular style of dance, but that he challenged convention by doing something new or creative within the established form. (D) *unexpected* ties the whole sentence together—Balanchine's choreography was unexpected and unconventional, but still stayed within the context of classical ballet.

naive: innocent, inexperienced

redundant: repetitive

7. A

The first clause says that *Americans enjoy—lifestyle*. Since *enjoy* is a very positive verb, the first blank should be filled by a positive adjective. This eliminates (C), (D), and (E).

Now, if the sentence simply read *the official number of Americans has been—for several years,* you might generally predict that the blank would be filled by any verb or adjective having to do with quantity, e.g., *increasing,* decreasing, or stable. But the clue word *while* expresses a contrast or opposition between how Americans are depicted in the two main clauses. So if the first clause describes the lifestyle in positive terms, the second clause must describe it in negative terms. Therefore, we can predict that the official number of Americans living in poverty has been rising or increasing. In (B), *leisurely,* which means "without haste," doesn't work as well in the first blank; nor does it seem quite right to say that *the official number . . . has been developing.* That leaves us with (A) as the right choice.

acerbic: sharp or bitter

provincial: unsophisticated or closed-minded

peripheral: on the periphery or outer boundary, not essential

opulent: wealthy or luxurious

leisurely: without haste

8.   C

A *debate* is normally orderly and rational, but this one apparently *degenerate[d] into—dispute.* What we have of the sentence before filling in the blank implies that this *debate* became a bitter argument. Therefore, something like *bitter* should go in the blank. (A) won't work; since the sentence talks about the urgency, or pressing importance, of the topic, the dispute would hardly be inconsequential. (B) *depraved* seems a bit far-fetched. (D) *prudent* means "careful," which would go better with rational debate than with an uncordial dispute. And in (E), a *reticent* dispute means just the opposite of the tumultuous argument we predicted. But (C) *acrimonious* fulfills the prediction exactly.

degenerate: to deteriorate or sink to a lower level

preclude: to prevent

cordiality: affection and kindness

inconsequential: insignificant

depraved: sinful or corrupt

prudent: careful

reticent: silent, reserved

acrimonious: bitter

9.   E

This unnamed novelist had delusions of grandeur. *He claimed to usher in a new era of literature,* that is, to be the first to write in a new style or format. But *his novels … [resembled] those of many other contemporary authors.* To complete this sentence correctly, you need a choice that reinforces the existing content of the sentence. Whatever fills the blank must support the idea that the author wasn't as innovative as he thought. (E) *derivative* fits the sentence well.

derivative: taken or received from another source

pastoral: relating to the countryside, especially to shepherds or to an idyllic scene

10.   E

You don't have to know anything about *epiphytic ferns* to complete this sentence. The heart of a sentence completion is its internal logic, not its scientific topic or specialized technical vocabulary. Look at the parts of the sentence you do understand, and try to figure out how they might fit together with the rest of the sentence. Whatever *epiphytic ferns* are, we know that *they do not require soil* and that *they cannot survive without constant moisture.* What could either of those statements have to do with *tropical rainforests? Tropical rainforests* are extremely humid, so they're probably good places to find plants that need *constant moisture.* Look for an answer that means "found in" or "native to." You should be able to rule out most of the choices, because they don't fit that predicted meaning. But (E) *endemic to* fits; it means "native to" or "found only in."

endemic: native, found only in

steep: to soak or saturate

Gum and Heart Disease Passage

11.   D

The hypothesis in question is that gum bacteria enters the bloodstream and helps to form plaque which block arteries. After explaining the hypothesis, the author states that three types of bacteria have been identified in this plaque. This acts as evidence in support of the hypothesis, since it makes it quite feasible that bacteria contributes to plaque formation.

(A) relates to good dental hygiene, but it does nothing to confirm the hypothesis about plaque. (B) is tempting, but it actually describes the hypothesis itself, not the *evidence* of the hypothesis, which is what you're being asked. Similarly, (C) is an effect of the hypothesis, not evidence for the hypothesis. (E) is a definition of the term athero-sclerosis, not evidence for the hypothesis in question.

12. C

The passage is quite scientific and factual, and describes recent findings in medicine. So, the author's purpose was probably to *inform* (C) the reader. (A) and (D) are closely related, and don't fit with the fairly dry presentation of factual information in the passage. The author doesn't recommend any particular course of action or argue against another point of view, so it doesn't make sense that the author attempted to *persuade* (B) or *argue* (E). (C) is correct: The passage is quite scientific and factual, and describes recent findings in medicine. So, the author's purpose was probably to *inform* the reader.

Origin of April Fool's Passage

13. A

Start by paraphrasing the sentence: "The author is stating that holidays often keep or retain traces of their origins." (A) is a close match—the holidays carry traces of their origins. (B) might be tempting, but notice it is the *traces* that endure, while the sentence is about what the holidays themselves do. (C) and (D) are common meanings of *bear*, as in "I just can't bear it," but they don't make sense here. Likewise, (E) refers to another common meaning, as in "to bear fruit," that doesn't fit either.

14. C

Laggards are people who move slowly, or lag behind. You don't need to know that to answer this question however. The passage states that the "progressive" adopters of the new calendar made fun of the laggards by calling them April Fools. So, the laggards are the people who *didn't* adopt the new calendar, (C).

(A) and (E) describe the people who invented the term April Fool's, while the question is asking about the laggards to whom the term referred. (B) misses the point that laggards are people, not holidays, and (D) refers to modern folklorists, while the laggards lived in the sixteenth century.

Murals Passage

This passage is about the lack of decorative color in our cities. Paragraph 1 tells us that modern cities have become "increasingly colorless environments." Paragraph 2 explains why—not only were somber colors believed to be more *functional*, but architects adopted them in order to imitate the traditions of ancient Greece and Rome. Midway through paragraph 2, however, we're told that the architects were wrong—that the ancients *had* used a lot of color in their cities. In fact, according to paragraph 3, vibrant colors are used almost everywhere outside the monotonous cities of the west. Paragraphs 4–6 state, however, that color in various forms is coming back; we're told that the work of Mexican mural painters sparked a revival of mural painting in the United States, and the work of William Walker is listed as the first of several mural projects by minority groups undertaken during the 1960s. Paragraph 7 concludes the passage by affirming the benefits of street art.

15. B

Resultant is the key word here. We're told that the transformation of the landscape was a result of "the spread of industry" and "the exodus of the people from the countryside." (B)'s the correct answer here. If industry was growing, and people were moving from the country into the towns, we can infer that *urban areas were spreading* and *growing in density*.

Ethnic diversity (A) is discussed later in the passage. *Loss of manufacturing jobs* (C) goes against the idea of industry spreading. *Improved visual appearance* (D) goes against the author's critique of "an increasingly colorless environment." *Loss of parks* (E) isn't mentioned at all.

16. B

The author explains the phrase in question in lines 6–8. "Veiled in soot," we're told, towns have "lapsed into grimy taciturnity," as "all-pervading drabness" overcomes our "urban complexes." (B) captures the idea here.

City violence (A) isn't an issue in the passage at all. *Politicians* (C) aren't explicitly blamed for the situation and neither are *city-dwellers* (E). It's the state of our cities, not who's responsible, that the author is interested in. Finally, (D)'s out because the author's talking about urban areas, not *rural* ones.

17. D

Two things we're told about "somber, neutral colors" are relevant here. One, they've been widely used since the Industrial Revolution. Two, they were judged to be "more functional." Choice (D) captures these points.

(B) is wrong because we're also told that somber, neutral colors were favored because people wanted to imitate *Greek and Roman* traditions. There's no basis for (C) in the passage. (A) takes the word *accentuated* (line 13) out of context; the author's point is that somber colors have been used almost exclusively. Finally, we're told that *Romanesque and Gothic architecture* featured "great use of color" (line 24), so (E) is out.

18. B

Western societies' admiration for Greek and Roman classicism was based on *mistaken beliefs.* We're told that somber, neutral colors were used for a long time out of a desire to imitate the Greeks and Romans, but historians now know that they loved color. Therefore (B) is correct.

(A) is wrong because we're told that these beliefs *accentuated* the *widespread* preference for *functional colors.* The cathedrals of *Siena, Florence, and Venice* (C) are described as featuring "great use of color"—so admiring the ancients for *neutral* colors wouldn't be a consistent attitude. Nor was a *respect for ancient art* (D) the basis of somber color schemes, since we're told that ancient art used a "rich and subtle palette." (E) is wrong for the same reason—using color as a *symbolic language* is using a lot of color, and the admiration for the Greek and Roman canons was based on the idea that they used somber, neutral colors.

19. A

The word *vision* relates to the reverence for Greek and Roman classicism. We're told that our "vision" of marble market places in ancient Rome was all wrong. So *vision* in this context means (A) *image*—our mental picture of what ancient Rome was like.

(B) *display* doesn't make sense. Neither does (D) *personal wish.* (C)'s too extreme; we're not obsessed with the classical colors—we just have a certain idea about them that happens to be wrong. Finally, (E) *clear-sightedness* doesn't fit with the author's acknowledgement that the vision is wrong.

20. D

In line 33, we're told that "extraordinary ornamental richness" can be seen in the cities and villages mentioned. The phrase "to name but a few examples" is the giveaway. The cities and villages are listed as *examples of* the (D) *decorative lushness* the author's discussing in the paragraph as a whole.

The author is interested in colorful architecture, not (C) *architecture* that is all the same. (A) *natural scenery* is never discussed in the passage. (B) *complex history* only figures later in paragraph 5 in the discussion of mural painting. Finally, (E) *religious convictions* is a bit of a distortion—we're told that people from these societies derive spiritual nourishment from all the different colors they use.

21. B

The way he introduces the word—"*sensitivity* of this kind"—tells us that the author's referring to a sensitivity that he has just discussed. The topic of the paragraph is the decorative use of color in different cultures—something that has little place in "our great western cities." So the author is talking about *sensitivity* in the (B) *use of color* in our cities. (A), (C), and (D) all suggest possible meanings for sensitivity in other contexts. But the author is talking specifically about the extent to which different societies use decorative color here. Finally, (E) is incorrect. We're told that all these people from different cultures are nourished by "contact with color," not that they're all versed in *art history*.

22. D

In lines 43–47, we're told that "bold and *judicious*" use of color makes cities better places to live. *Judicious,* then, is a positive quality. (D) *informed,* meaning "knowledgeable," is the best choice here, since *judicious* means "resulting in good decisions." (A) *controversial* and (E) *judgmental* are both poor choices because both have negative connotations. (B) *objective* conflicts with the word *bold*—could a city planner be both bold and objective about a project? Finally, (C) *determined* simply restates the idea of being bold.

23. E

The author uses the metaphor "striking a chord" here to illustrate how murals work. By "alluding to the important political, religious or artistic events of our cultures," murals make us remember historical events that are significant in our cultures. (E) captures this idea.

It's the function of the mural, not the benefits they present for the community—choices (A), (B), (C)—nor the monotony of cities without murals (D), that the author's referring to here.

24. C

In the lines *surrounding* the quote in question, the author's talking about public murals "making a comeback" (lines 55–56). We're told that the three great Mexican artists were the "first influential muralists of the century" and that "their initiative" subsequently inspired American artists. (C)'s the answer here; the author mentions the Mexican artists to explain why there was a *revival in mural painting* in Mexico and the United States.

(A) is wrong because the author never implies any criticism of American mural painting. (B) is wrong because the history of this revival is the issue in paragraph five. (D)'s a distortion. We're never told that the Mexican artists themselves influenced historical events. Finally, paragraph five does mention the Mexican artists inspiring government funding for murals in the United States (E).

25. C

Turning lines 83–90 around, we're told that Walker's project inspired similar projects in various cities. In other words, it was a "point of departure" since it led to other group projects involving *minorities* (C).

There's no evidence for (A) at all. We're told nothing about specific *artists*. (B) contradicts paragraph 5; murals had been commissioned 30 years earlier during the New Deal. (D)'s a bit off the point—the author's more concerned with the revival in murals than with public housing issues. (E) finally, is a distortion; Walker portrayed the *civil rights* pioneers, he didn't *lead* the *movement* himself.

26. C

The question ties quite clearly to the last paragraph's discussion of street art. The author tells us that "by its very nature as communal space" the street "lends itself to collective creativity." So it's the fact that streets are places *shared* by everyone that makes them ideal for this kind of mural painting (C).

(A) *encouraging reserve* goes against the gist of the passage. (B) *carrying few traces of past events* goes against the gist too, since part of the function of murals, according to paragraph five, is to make people aware of their own

cultural history. (D) is wrong because the author describes many urban areas as "doomed to demolition, dereliction, or anonymity." If streets already made people aware of *their surroundings,* then presumably murals wouldn't be necessary. (E) is tempting, but the author doesn't mention using the street scenes themselves as *subjects* for painting.

SECTION THREE

Medieval-Guilds Passages

Unlike many others, these paired passages on medieval European society don't present two different perspectives on a single topic. Rather, the second passage here seems to grow out of the first, by depicting the beginning of the transition away from the historical situation described in Passage 1. Author 1 talks about the closed, stable world of the medieval guild, while Author 2 talks about what was going on in Italy in the 13th century, when that world was giving way to the more open, more fluid world of the Renaissance. So Passage 2 is almost like an outgrowth of Passage 1.

1. C

You're asked about the main function of the rules discussed in lines 12–15. In the passage, we read that these rules had the effect of "dampening personal ambition and initiative," which would protect the merchant and artisan from *competition* with other *merchants and artisans.* So (C) answers the question best.

Choice (A) is perhaps the closest wrong choice, but the impression given in the passage is that the rules imposed as much *control* on masters as on the people under those masters. (B) is out, since the *political influence of the guilds* is never discussed at length. Choices (D) and (E), meanwhile, work against the thrust of Passage 1, which is that the guild system discouraged the *development* and innovation.

2. B

We move to the third paragraph of Passage 1. In the last sentence, we read that "the number of masters in each local guild was limited . . . by certain requirements . . . that were hard to fulfill." So the requirements had the effect of limiting the number of masters, or, as correct choice (B) has it, of *controlling the number of those who advanced beyond journeyman status.*

Choices (A) and (E) both contradict the passage, which claims that the guilds kept *foreign products* out of *local markets* (A) and actually discouraged *economic rivalry* (E). (C) is a distortion, since the guild requirements insisted only that one be a *citizen* to become a master. And in (D), the requirements mentioned in line 32 have to do with becoming a master, not with *trade* restrictions.

3.   E

This question asks about the adjective *measured* in line 45. It is used to describe the resources of guild merchants. The author has just written about restrictions on the number of workshop employees a merchant could employ, and limits on the amount of their personal wealth they could use against other masters. So their resources were (E) *limited*. (A) *deliberate* and (C) *rhythmical* are other dictionary definitions of *measured,* but neither can be used to describe the word *resources* as it is used in this context. (B) *inadequate* is a close wrong choice, but the passage implies that these resources, while subject to strict limits, were still adequate to get the job done. (D)'s suggestion of *cautious,* meanwhile, is off the mark, since it's not the resources that were cautious.

4.   D

This question is asking us to characterize the author's general description of the guild system in economic terms. The author writes at great length of the restrictions the system placed on the guilds. And although these restrictions prevented guild members from "rising above" their position, they did ensure that those positions would be "secure." So choice (D), which incorporates both the *restrictiveness* and the security, or *stability,* looks good as our answer.

(A), (B), and (C) are the opposite of what we want; they seem to describe the post-guild situation that appeared in Italy described in Passage 2—a situation variously described as (A) *open* and (C) *fluid,* and one whose emphasis on competition led to the kind of (B) *innovation* that the guild system tended to stifle. Choice (E), on the other hand, goes too far in the other direction.

5.   A

We switch to an examination of Passage 2. The author wants to contrast what was going on in most of Europe with the new developments in Italy. Individuality was replacing group mentality, openness was replacing restrictiveness, and fluidity was replacing social rigidity. So (A) is the best answer.

(B) brings up the red herring of *education,* which isn't discussed until the end of paragraph three. (C) is a distortion, since the author's purpose is to describe the new attitudes in Italy rather than condemn the attitudes in the rest of medieval Europe. (D) is on the right track with its mention of *individuality,* but the author is not interested in *contemporary society.* Finally, (E) fails because the author isn't debunking a *common belief about medieval Europe.*

6.   E

The author sets up Italy's new *social fluidity* (line 58) as a contrast to what was going on in the rest of Europe, where social life was rigidly fixed. So it's the *unfixed* quality of *social life in Italy* that the author is describing with the term *social fluidity,* making (E) the best choice.

(A) misses the mark, since the author nowhere indicates that she regards life in Italy at this time as *dangerous.* As for (B), the discussion of rivalries *between Italian families* doesn't come until much later. (C) is a distortion, since the phenomenon described by the author isn't the disparity in *wealth between classes,* but how individuals could jump from one class to another. (D) is closer in spirit, but it tries to fool you by playing to your outside knowledge, since nothing about *democratic institutions* is discussed by Author 2.

7.   D

What is described as *acute* in line 68? The competition between artisans, competition that was so sharp, or *keen,* as correct choice (D) says, that it spurred the artisans on to the creation of masterpieces.

As for (A) and (B): Although the competition described definitely could be characterized as energetic, it's not depicted as either out of control or perilous. (C) *wise* could perhaps be seen as a definition of the word *acute* in some contexts, but how can competition itself be described as *wise*? (E) *sudden* has sort of the opposite problem; it could be said to fit the context but there's no way that *sudden* is a synonym for *acute,* which means sharp, penetrating, or extreme.

8.   B

Author 2 tells us explicitly in lines 85–86 that the story of the Medici family is meant to illustrate "these changes." She means the changes mentioned in the previous paragraph, that showed how in Italy "the potential for individual achievement . . . seemed unlimited." Therefore (B) is the right choice.

Choice (A) is a distortion, since the Medici family's success is linked to the decline of the *guild system,* which actually hampered the kind of *individual effort* they represent. Although (C) and (D) are true statements, neither is something that the example of the Medicis is meant primarily to illustrate in the passage. (E), meanwhile, is another distortion; no one said that it was *easy* to become successful in Italy at this time, just that it was possible.

9.   C

This question asks us to characterize the author's discussion of the Medici family. If you go back and examine that discussion, you'll see that the facts are reported without any kind of emotional slant, so (C) *dispassionate* is the best characterization.

(A) *nostalgic* implies a fondness for old times, but clearly there's nothing affectionate in this description. (B) *disapproving* suggests that the author is passing judgment on the Medicis, but there's no evidence of any such negative evaluation. Finally, choices (D) *ironic* and (E) *defensive* indicate emotions toward the Medici family that are just not supported by the sober delivery of facts.

10.   D

You're asked for a common denominator of the two passages. Passage 1 talks about the guild system and the limits it placed on medieval European merchants. Passage 2 deals with the throwing off of limits for artisans and merchants in Italy in the late Middle Ages. So both passages explain the circumstances of *merchants during the Middle Ages,* choice (D).

All of the wrong choices fail because they don't accurately describe something that's discussed in both passages. Choice (A) can't be the answer, since *Italy* isn't even mentioned in Passage 1. On the other hand, (B) talks about the *structure of the guild system,* which the author of Passage 2 never discusses. (C)'s mention of the *growing importance of individuality* misses the mark, since Passage 1 is about how the guild system discouraged individuality.

Similarly, (E)'s mention of capitalism's *fast growth* runs afoul of the thrust of Passage 1.

11.   A

We're looking for a likely position taken by Author 1, so we must keep in mind what we know of Author 1. He regards the guild system as closed, restrictive, and stifling of individuality and innovation. So what would he think of the description of most of European society in the first two lines of Passage 2? That's where we hear that human consciousness (in most of Europe) was "half awake," and that people regarded themselves in terms of groups rather than as individuals. Well, this description jibes pretty well with the situation described by Author 1. So (A) looks right.

(B) is way off, since Author 1 tells us how the guild system discouraged *individual initiative.* Meanwhile, there's no evidence that Author 1 has such a restrictive view of the *historian's* job as choice (C) would imply. The wishy-washiness of (D) is also unfounded; we do have evidence that Author 1 would agree with Author 2's *description.* And the general statement in (E) seems unlike our Author 1, who was perfectly willing to make *sweeping* statements about the entire system of medieval guilds.

12.   E

The merchants discussed in Passage 1 are very different from the Italian merchants discussed in Passage 2, and this question wants to know in what way they are most different. Well, the merchants in Passage 1 were working within the closed system of the guild, which had numerous restrictions that actually discouraged individual initiative. On the other hand, the merchants in Passage 2 "were unchecked in their political and social ambitions" (lines 76–77). So individual *ambitions* were radically different, making choice (E) the best answer.

Since we don't hear anything about either kind of merchant's attitude towards the *towns* they lived in, we really can't choose either (A) or (D), both of which deal with such attitudes. As for (B), we know nothing about attitudes toward *citizenship* rights. And as for (C), both types of merchant seem to have had *private property,* so it's unclear how their views on the subject would have been vastly different.

Word a Day Passage

13. A

The word *shameless* usually means someone who *should* be ashamed but isn't. That's not the case here. In this passage, the author certainly doesn't believe that loving words is something to be ashamed of. Instead, the word *shameless* serves to show that the person is really into this hobby. It's also supposed to be mildly humorous, since it's silly to consider an interest in words a shameful hobby. All of this is nicely summed up by (A).

(B) and (E) are too literal, since it seems unlikely anyone would actually disapprove of an interest in words, or consider it regrettable. Although the author seems delighted about the website (C), the term *shameless* doesn't emphasize this. There's no reason to think that the word *shameless* was featured on the website (D).

14. E

Before mentioning the words in question, the passage states that the website often features a weekly theme. He then lists three words, all of which relate to numbers in some way. So, these three words are examples of choices that center on a weekly theme—a great match for (E).

The words in question are all unusual words (B) featured on the website (D), and all have origins related to numbers (A). However, these answer choices miss the point of this example—that the website often features words that relate to a theme. (After all, the author could have picked could have picked many different words as examples, all of them with a similar origin, or very difficult, or from the website. But he chose these because they have a similar theme.) (C) is out of scope, since the author never implies that these three words are his favorites from the website.

Museums Passage

15. D

The word *blockbuster* usually refers to movies that sell a lot of tickets. Here, the author is drawing a comparison to museum exhibits that are aimed at "the masses," as opposed to the "elitist" outlook of the past. This fits (D) well.

(A) is out of the scope of the passage, since the word "blockbuster" is the only hint of a comparison of movies and museum exhibits. The author mentions Greco-Roman architecture, but never discusses "exhibits of Greco-Roman art," choice (B). The author concentrates on the attempts of the museums to attract large crowds, rather than the financial outcomes of such an effort, so (C) is out. As for (E), thought it's an important point in the passage, it doesn't relate to the word *blockbuster*.

16. E

The author lists many facets of recent changes in the image and mission museums. At the end of the passage, however, he uses the phrase "perhaps most important" to describe educational outreach efforts. So, although (A), (B), (C), and (D) are all mentioned in the text, only (E) is described as the most important.

SAT Practice Test B
Answer Sheet

Remove (or photcopy) this answer sheet and use it to complete the practice test. See the answer key following the test when finished. The "Compute Your Score" section at the back of the book will show you how to find your score.

Start with number 1 for each section. If a section has fewer questions than answer spaces, leave the extra spaces blank.

SECTION 1

1. Ⓐ Ⓑ Ⓒ Ⓓ Ⓔ	11. Ⓐ Ⓑ Ⓒ Ⓓ Ⓔ	21. Ⓐ Ⓑ Ⓒ Ⓓ Ⓔ	31. Ⓐ Ⓑ Ⓒ Ⓓ Ⓔ
2. Ⓐ Ⓑ Ⓒ Ⓓ Ⓔ	12. Ⓐ Ⓑ Ⓒ Ⓓ Ⓔ	22. Ⓐ Ⓑ Ⓒ Ⓓ Ⓔ	32. Ⓐ Ⓑ Ⓒ Ⓓ Ⓔ
3. Ⓐ Ⓑ Ⓒ Ⓓ Ⓔ	13. Ⓐ Ⓑ Ⓒ Ⓓ Ⓔ	23. Ⓐ Ⓑ Ⓒ Ⓓ Ⓔ	33. Ⓐ Ⓑ Ⓒ Ⓓ Ⓔ
4. Ⓐ Ⓑ Ⓒ Ⓓ Ⓔ	14. Ⓐ Ⓑ Ⓒ Ⓓ Ⓔ	24. Ⓐ Ⓑ Ⓒ Ⓓ Ⓔ	34. Ⓐ Ⓑ Ⓒ Ⓓ Ⓔ
5. Ⓐ Ⓑ Ⓒ Ⓓ Ⓔ	15. Ⓐ Ⓑ Ⓒ Ⓓ Ⓔ	25. Ⓐ Ⓑ Ⓒ Ⓓ Ⓔ	35. Ⓐ Ⓑ Ⓒ Ⓓ Ⓔ
6. Ⓐ Ⓑ Ⓒ Ⓓ Ⓔ	16. Ⓐ Ⓑ Ⓒ Ⓓ Ⓔ	26. Ⓐ Ⓑ Ⓒ Ⓓ Ⓔ	36. Ⓐ Ⓑ Ⓒ Ⓓ Ⓔ
7. Ⓐ Ⓑ Ⓒ Ⓓ Ⓔ	17. Ⓐ Ⓑ Ⓒ Ⓓ Ⓔ	27. Ⓐ Ⓑ Ⓒ Ⓓ Ⓔ	37. Ⓐ Ⓑ Ⓒ Ⓓ Ⓔ
8. Ⓐ Ⓑ Ⓒ Ⓓ Ⓔ	18. Ⓐ Ⓑ Ⓒ Ⓓ Ⓔ	28. Ⓐ Ⓑ Ⓒ Ⓓ Ⓔ	38. Ⓐ Ⓑ Ⓒ Ⓓ Ⓔ
9. Ⓐ Ⓑ Ⓒ Ⓓ Ⓔ	19. Ⓐ Ⓑ Ⓒ Ⓓ Ⓔ	29. Ⓐ Ⓑ Ⓒ Ⓓ Ⓔ	39. Ⓐ Ⓑ Ⓒ Ⓓ Ⓔ
10. Ⓐ Ⓑ Ⓒ Ⓓ Ⓔ	20. Ⓐ Ⓑ Ⓒ Ⓓ Ⓔ	30. Ⓐ Ⓑ Ⓒ Ⓓ Ⓔ	40. Ⓐ Ⓑ Ⓒ Ⓓ Ⓔ

right

wrong

SECTION 2

1. Ⓐ Ⓑ Ⓒ Ⓓ Ⓔ	11. Ⓐ Ⓑ Ⓒ Ⓓ Ⓔ	21. Ⓐ Ⓑ Ⓒ Ⓓ Ⓔ	31. Ⓐ Ⓑ Ⓒ Ⓓ Ⓔ
2. Ⓐ Ⓑ Ⓒ Ⓓ Ⓔ	12. Ⓐ Ⓑ Ⓒ Ⓓ Ⓔ	22. Ⓐ Ⓑ Ⓒ Ⓓ Ⓔ	32. Ⓐ Ⓑ Ⓒ Ⓓ Ⓔ
3. Ⓐ Ⓑ Ⓒ Ⓓ Ⓔ	13. Ⓐ Ⓑ Ⓒ Ⓓ Ⓔ	23. Ⓐ Ⓑ Ⓒ Ⓓ Ⓔ	33. Ⓐ Ⓑ Ⓒ Ⓓ Ⓔ
4. Ⓐ Ⓑ Ⓒ Ⓓ Ⓔ	14. Ⓐ Ⓑ Ⓒ Ⓓ Ⓔ	24. Ⓐ Ⓑ Ⓒ Ⓓ Ⓔ	34. Ⓐ Ⓑ Ⓒ Ⓓ Ⓔ
5. Ⓐ Ⓑ Ⓒ Ⓓ Ⓔ	15. Ⓐ Ⓑ Ⓒ Ⓓ Ⓔ	25. Ⓐ Ⓑ Ⓒ Ⓓ Ⓔ	35. Ⓐ Ⓑ Ⓒ Ⓓ Ⓔ
6. Ⓐ Ⓑ Ⓒ Ⓓ Ⓔ	16. Ⓐ Ⓑ Ⓒ Ⓓ Ⓔ	26. Ⓐ Ⓑ Ⓒ Ⓓ Ⓔ	36. Ⓐ Ⓑ Ⓒ Ⓓ Ⓔ
7. Ⓐ Ⓑ Ⓒ Ⓓ Ⓔ	17. Ⓐ Ⓑ Ⓒ Ⓓ Ⓔ	27. Ⓐ Ⓑ Ⓒ Ⓓ Ⓔ	37. Ⓐ Ⓑ Ⓒ Ⓓ Ⓔ
8. Ⓐ Ⓑ Ⓒ Ⓓ Ⓔ	18. Ⓐ Ⓑ Ⓒ Ⓓ Ⓔ	28. Ⓐ Ⓑ Ⓒ Ⓓ Ⓔ	38. Ⓐ Ⓑ Ⓒ Ⓓ Ⓔ
9. Ⓐ Ⓑ Ⓒ Ⓓ Ⓔ	19. Ⓐ Ⓑ Ⓒ Ⓓ Ⓔ	29. Ⓐ Ⓑ Ⓒ Ⓓ Ⓔ	39. Ⓐ Ⓑ Ⓒ Ⓓ Ⓔ
10. Ⓐ Ⓑ Ⓒ Ⓓ Ⓔ	20. Ⓐ Ⓑ Ⓒ Ⓓ Ⓔ	30. Ⓐ Ⓑ Ⓒ Ⓓ Ⓔ	40. Ⓐ Ⓑ Ⓒ Ⓓ Ⓔ

right

wrong

SECTION 3

1. Ⓐ Ⓑ Ⓒ Ⓓ Ⓔ	11. Ⓐ Ⓑ Ⓒ Ⓓ Ⓔ	21. Ⓐ Ⓑ Ⓒ Ⓓ Ⓔ	31. Ⓐ Ⓑ Ⓒ Ⓓ Ⓔ
2. Ⓐ Ⓑ Ⓒ Ⓓ Ⓔ	12. Ⓐ Ⓑ Ⓒ Ⓓ Ⓔ	22. Ⓐ Ⓑ Ⓒ Ⓓ Ⓔ	32. Ⓐ Ⓑ Ⓒ Ⓓ Ⓔ
3. Ⓐ Ⓑ Ⓒ Ⓓ Ⓔ	13. Ⓐ Ⓑ Ⓒ Ⓓ Ⓔ	23. Ⓐ Ⓑ Ⓒ Ⓓ Ⓔ	33. Ⓐ Ⓑ Ⓒ Ⓓ Ⓔ
4. Ⓐ Ⓑ Ⓒ Ⓓ Ⓔ	14. Ⓐ Ⓑ Ⓒ Ⓓ Ⓔ	24. Ⓐ Ⓑ Ⓒ Ⓓ Ⓔ	34. Ⓐ Ⓑ Ⓒ Ⓓ Ⓔ
5. Ⓐ Ⓑ Ⓒ Ⓓ Ⓔ	15. Ⓐ Ⓑ Ⓒ Ⓓ Ⓔ	25. Ⓐ Ⓑ Ⓒ Ⓓ Ⓔ	35. Ⓐ Ⓑ Ⓒ Ⓓ Ⓔ
6. Ⓐ Ⓑ Ⓒ Ⓓ Ⓔ	16. Ⓐ Ⓑ Ⓒ Ⓓ Ⓔ	26. Ⓐ Ⓑ Ⓒ Ⓓ Ⓔ	36. Ⓐ Ⓑ Ⓒ Ⓓ Ⓔ
7. Ⓐ Ⓑ Ⓒ Ⓓ Ⓔ	17. Ⓐ Ⓑ Ⓒ Ⓓ Ⓔ	27. Ⓐ Ⓑ Ⓒ Ⓓ Ⓔ	37. Ⓐ Ⓑ Ⓒ Ⓓ Ⓔ
8. Ⓐ Ⓑ Ⓒ Ⓓ Ⓔ	18. Ⓐ Ⓑ Ⓒ Ⓓ Ⓔ	28. Ⓐ Ⓑ Ⓒ Ⓓ Ⓔ	38. Ⓐ Ⓑ Ⓒ Ⓓ Ⓔ
9. Ⓐ Ⓑ Ⓒ Ⓓ Ⓔ	19. Ⓐ Ⓑ Ⓒ Ⓓ Ⓔ	29. Ⓐ Ⓑ Ⓒ Ⓓ Ⓔ	39. Ⓐ Ⓑ Ⓒ Ⓓ Ⓔ
10. Ⓐ Ⓑ Ⓒ Ⓓ Ⓔ	20. Ⓐ Ⓑ Ⓒ Ⓓ Ⓔ	30. Ⓐ Ⓑ Ⓒ Ⓓ Ⓔ	40. Ⓐ Ⓑ Ⓒ Ⓓ Ⓔ

right

wrong

Practice Test B

SECTION ONE

Time—25 Minutes
28 Questions

For each of the following questions, choose the best answer and darken the corresponding oval on the answer sheet.

1. More insurers are limiting the sale of property insurance in coastal areas and other regions ---- natural disasters.

   (A) safe from
   (B) according to
   (C) despite
   (D) which include
   (E) prone to

2. Roman legions ---- the mountain ---- of Masada for three years before they were able to seize it.

   (A) dissembled . . . bastion
   (B) assailed . . . symbol
   (C) besieged . . . citadel
   (D) surmounted . . . dwelling
   (E) honed . . . stronghold

3. Unlike his calmer, more easygoing colleagues, the senator was ----, ready to quarrel at the slightest provocation.

   (A) whimsical
   (B) irascible
   (C) gregarious
   (D) ineffectual
   (E) benign

4. Although historians have long thought of Genghis Khan as a ---- potentate, new research has shown he was ---- by many of his subjects.

   (A) tyrannical . . . abhorred
   (B) despotic . . . revered
   (C) redundant . . . venerated
   (D) jocular . . . esteemed
   (E) peremptory . . . invoked

5. Jill was ---- by her employees because she often ---- them for not working hard enough.

   (A) deified . . . goaded
   (B) loathed . . . berated
   (C) disregarded . . . eulogized
   (D) cherished . . . derided
   (E) execrated . . . lauded

6. Reconstructing the skeletons of extinct species like dinosaurs is ---- process that requires much patience and effort by paleontologists.

   (A) a nascent
   (B) an aberrant
   (C) a disheveled
   (D) a worthless
   (E) an exacting

GO ON TO THE NEXT PAGE

KAPLAN

7. Nearly ---- by disease and the destruction of their habitat, koalas are now found only in isolated parts of eucalyptus forests.

(A) dispersed

(B) compiled

(C) decimated

(D) infuriated

(E) averted

8. Deep ideological ---- and internal power struggles ---- the government.

(A) disputes . . . facilitated

(B) similarities . . . protracted

(C) distortions . . . accelerated

(D) agreements . . . stymied

(E) divisions . . . paralyzed

GO ON TO THE NEXT PAGE

Questions 9–10 refer to the following passage.

The Latin Quarter became a distinct geographi-
cal area of Paris in the 13th Century with the
founding of the Sorbonne.* Because of an association with students—and later with artists—the
(5) Latin Quarter became known as a bohemian area
where the conventions of society were generally
disregarded. Until the 19th Century, the Latin
Quarter and the lives of its inhabitants were all
but ignored by the larger society. This changed in
(10) 1845 when Henri Murger, sometimes called the
first bohemian, wrote a series of stories about the
Latin Quarter that was printed in the Parisian
journal, Corsaire-Satan. Thanks to Murger's
romantic depiction, the Latin Quarter gained a
(15) foothold in the popular imagination, and the
loose lifestyles previously regarded as scandalous,
suspect, and dangerously unconventional now
seemed enviable.

* The University of Paris

9. According to the passage, those who live a
bohemian lifestyle would most likely

(A) ignore the mores of society
(B) attend a university
(C) make a living in the arts
(D) write stories for a Parisian newspaper
(E) be dangerous to society

10. In line 16, the word *loose* most nearly means

(A) disorganized
(B) unfastened
(C) needing structure
(D) replete
(E) unrestrained

Question 11 refers to the following passage.

The start of every presidential season sends the
candidates flocking to Iowa—the home of one of
the most important caucuses in the campaign season. Since surfacing in 1976 as the first chance for
(5) voters to express a preference for the candidates of
each party, the Iowa caucus has brought the presidential candidates to the Midwest for a chance at
gaining nationwide recognition. In the past, several candidates have launched national campaigns
(10) after winning the caucus. Two recent examples are
Jimmy Carter and Bill Clinton, whose superior
showing drove them from obscurity all the way to
the White House.

11. The author makes reference to Jimmy Carter and
Bill Clinton to make the point that

(A) a surprising result in the Iowa caucus can
jumpstart a lackluster campaign
(B) obscure candidates can become well-known
after winning the Iowa caucus
(C) well-established candidates will be hurt if
they do not win the Iowa caucus
(D) presidential candidates who win the Iowa
caucus will win the presidency
(E) the Iowa caucuses assures all candidates
national exposure

GO ON TO THE NEXT PAGE

KAPLAN

Questions 12–18 are based on the following passage.

In this excerpt, a Nobel Prize–winning scientist discusses ways of thinking about extremely long periods of time.

There is one fact about the origin of life that is reasonably certain. Whenever and wherever it happened, it started a very long time ago, so long ago that it is extremely difficult to form any realis-
(5) tic idea of such vast stretches of time. The short-ness of human life necessarily limits the span of direct personal recollection.

Human culture has given us the illusion that our memories go further back than that. Before
(10) writing was invented, the experience of earlier generations, embodied in stories, myths and moral precepts to guide behavior, was passed down verbally or, to a lesser extent, in pictures, carvings, and statues. Writing has made more pre-
(15) cise and more extensive the transmission of such information and, in recent times, photography has sharpened our images of the immediate past. Even so, we have difficulty in contemplating steadily the march of history, from the beginnings of civiliza-
(20) tion to the present day, in such a way that we can truly experience the slow passage of time. Our minds are not built to deal comfortably with peri-ods as long as hundreds or thousands of years.

Yet when we come to consider the origin of life,
(25) the time scales we must deal with make the whole span of human history seem but the blink of an eyelid. There is no simple way to adjust one's thinking to such vast stretches of time. The immensity of time passed is beyond our ready
(30) comprehension. One can only construct an impression of it from indirect and incomplete descriptions, just as a blind man laboriously builds up, by touch and sound, a picture of his immediate surroundings.

(35) The customary way to provide a convenient framework for one's thoughts is to compare the age of the universe with the length of a single earthly day. Perhaps a better comparison, along the same lines, would be to equate the age of our
(40) earth with a single week. On such a scale the age of the universe, since the Big Bang, would be about two or three weeks. The oldest macroscopic fossils (those from the start of the Cambrian

Period*) would have been alive just one day ago.
(45) Modern man would have appeared in the last ten seconds and agriculture in the last one or two. Odysseus** would have lived only half a second before the present time.

Even this comparison hardly makes the longer
(50) time scale comprehensible to us. An alternative is to draw a linear map of time, with the different events marked on it. The problem here is to make the line long enough to show our own experience on a reasonable scale, and yet short enough for
(55) convenient reproduction and examination. But perhaps the most vivid method is to compare time to the lines of print themselves. Let us make a 200-page book equal in length to the time from the start of the Cambrian to the present; that is,
(60) about 600 million years. Then each full page will represent roughly 3 million years, each line about ninety thousand years and each letter or small space about fifteen hundred years. The origin of the earth would be about seven books ago and the
(65) origin of the universe (which has been dated only approximately) ten or so books before that. Almost the whole of recorded human history would be covered by the last two or three letters of the book.

(70)   If you now turn back the pages of the book, slowly reading one letter at a time—remember, each letter is fifteen hundred years—then this may convey to you something of the immense stretches of time we shall have to consider. On this scale the
(75) span of your own life would be less than the width of a comma.

*Cambrian: the earliest period in the Paleozoic era, beginning about 600 million years ago
**Odysseus: the most famous Greek hero of antiquity; he is the hero of Homer's *The Odyssey*, which describes the aftermath of the Trojan War (ca. 1200 B.C.)

GO ON TO THE NEXT PAGE

12. The phrase to a *lesser extent* in line 13 indicates that, before the invention of writing, the wisdom of earlier generations was

(A) rejected by recent generations when portrayed in pictures, carvings, or statues

(B) passed down orally, or not at all

√(C) transmitted more effectively by spoken word than by other means

(D) based on illusory memories that turned fact into fiction

(E) more strongly grounded in science than in the arts

13. The author most likely describes the impact of writing (lines 14–17) in order to

(A) illustrate the limitations of the human memory

√(B) provide an example of how cultures transmit information

(C) indicate how primitive preliterate cultures were

(D) refute an opinion about the origin of human civilization

(E) explain the difference between historical facts and myth

14. The word *ready* in line 29 most nearly means

(A) set

(B) agreeable

(C) immediate

(D) apt

(E) willing

15. The analogy of the "blind man" (line 32) is presented primarily to show that

(A) humans are unable to comprehend long periods of time

(B) myths and legends fail to give an accurate picture of the past

(C) human history is only a fraction of the time since life began

(D) humans refuse to learn the lessons of the past

(E) long periods of time can only be understood indirectly

16. In lines 40–44, the author mentions the Big Bang and the Cambrian Period in order to demonstrate which point?

√(A) The age of the earth is best understood using the time scale of a week.

(B) Agriculture was a relatively late development in human history.

(C) No fossil record exists before the Cambrian Period.

(D) Convenient time scales do not adequately represent the age of the earth.

(E) The customary framework for thinking about the age of the universe should be discarded permanently.

17. According to lines 52–56, one difficulty of using a linear representation of time is that

(A) linear representations of time do not meet accepted scientific standards of accuracy

(B) prehistoric eras overlap each other, making linear representation deceptive

(C) the more accurate the scale, the more difficult the map is to copy and study

√(D) there are too many events to represent on a single line

(E) our knowledge of pre-Cambrian time is insufficient to construct an accurate linear map

GO ON TO THE NEXT PAGE

KAPLAN

18. The author of this passage discusses several kinds
of time scales primarily in order to illustrate the

  (A) difficulty of assigning precise dates to past
  events

  (B) variety of choices faced by scientists
  investigating the origin of life

  (C) evolution of efforts to comprehend the
  passage of history

  (D) immensity of time since life began on earth

  (E) development of the technology of
  communication

GO ON TO THE NEXT PAGE

Questions 19–21 refer to the following passages.

Passage 1

Musicologists and linguists argue about the relationship between music and language. Prominent ethnomusicologist Bruno Nettl has concluded that like language, music is a "series of
(5) symbols." However, music has traditionally been used purely to express emotions, while language has also been used for more functional, prosaic tasks. This distinction was especially evident in the Romantic era of Western music, when many com-
(10) posers and critics felt that music could stand by itself to connote emotions without any extra-musical references.

Passage 2

The fundamental building blocks of both language and music are quite similar, as are the
(15) manners in which these components are combined to form a cohesive whole. In the same way that an entire piece of music can be divided into phrases, and further subdivided into specific notes, language can be subdivided into para-
(20) graphs, sentences, and words. A single note can have different meanings depending on the piece; a lone word can have different meanings depending on the context in the sentence. Words and notes are also similar in that they have little intrinsic
(25) meaning, but instead act as symbols to convey larger ideas.

19. Author 1 most likely cites the Romantic era of western Music (line 9) in order to establish that

(A) our modern perception of Romantic music is different from the one held during the Romantic era

(B) unlike language, Romantic music is not used functionally

(C) composers of Romantic music always used music to express emotion

(D) during the Romantic era it was a commonly held opinion that music was itself sufficient to carry emotion

(E) the music of the Romantic era is compromised because it does not contain extra-musical references

20. In both passages, the authors state that music and language are

(A) symbols

(B) subdivided sections

(C) functional parts

(D) clues

(E) conveyers of emotion

21. Which of the following statements would Authors 1 and 2 most likely disagree about?

(A) Music and language can both be subdivided into several parts.

(B) Although significantly similar, music and language have several fundamentally distinct aspects.

(C) A group of notes used in a musical composition has the same meaning in a piece by a different composer.

(D) Language is not an effective means to express emotions.

(E) The meaning of a particular word is solely dependent on context.

GO ON TO THE NEXT PAGE ⟩

KAPLAN

Questions 22–28 are based on the following passage.

The following excerpt is from a speech delivered in 1873 by Susan B. Anthony, a leader in the women's rights movement of the 19th century.

Friends and fellow-citizens: I stand before you tonight under indictment for the alleged crime of having voted at the last Presidential election, with-out having a lawful right to vote. It shall be my
(5) work this evening to prove to you that in thus vot-ing, I not only committed no crime, but, instead, simply exercised my citizen's rights, guaranteed to me and all United States citizens by the National Constitution, beyond the power of any State to
(10) deny.

The Preamble of the Federal Constitution says: "We, the people of the United States, in order to form a more perfect union, establish justice, insure domestic tranquillity, provide for the com-
(15) mon defense, promote the general welfare, and secure the blessings of liberty to ourselves and our posterity, do ordain and establish this Constitution for the United States of America."

It was we, the people; not we, the white male
(20) citizens; nor yet we, the male citizens; but we, the whole people, who formed the Union. And we formed it, not to give the blessings of liberty, but to secure them; not to the half of ourselves and the half of our posterity, but to the whole people—
(25) women as well as men. And it is a downright mockery to talk to women of their enjoyment of the blessings of liberty while they are denied the use of the only means of securing them provided by this democratic-republican government—the
(30) ballot.

For any State to make sex a qualification that must ever result in the disfranchisement* of one entire half of the people is a violation of the supreme law of the land. By it the blessings of lib-
(35) erty are forever withheld from women and their female posterity. To them this government had no just powers derived from the consent of the gov-erned. To them this government is not a democra-cy. It is not a republic. It is an odious aristocracy;
(40) a hateful oligarchy of sex; this oligarchy of sex, which makes father, brothers, husband, sons, the oligarchs over the mother and sisters, the wife and

daughters of every household—which ordains all men sovereigns, all women subjects, carries dis-
(45) sension, discord and rebellion into every home of the nation.

Webster, Worcester and Bouvier all define a citi-zen to be a person in the United States, entitled to vote and hold office.
(50) The one question left to be settled now is: Are women persons? And I hardly believe any of our opponents will have the hardihood to say they are not. Being persons, then, women are citizens; and no State has a right to make any law, or to enforce
(55) any old law, that shall abridge their privileges or immunities. Hence, every discrimination against women in the constitutions and laws of the several States is today null and void, precisely as is every one against Negroes.

*disfranchisement: to deprive of the right to vote

22. In the first paragraph, Anthony states that her action in voting was

(A) illegal, but morally justified
(B) the result of her keen interest in national pol-itics
(C) legal, if the Constitution is interpreted cor-rectly
(D) an illustration of the need for a women's rights movement
(E) illegal, but worthy of leniency

23. Which best captures the meaning of the word *promote* in line 15?

(A) further
(B) organize
(C) publicize
(D) commend
(E) motivate

GO ON TO THE NEXT PAGE

24. By saying "we, the people . . . the whole people, who formed the Union" (lines 20–21), Anthony means that

    (A) the founders of the nation conspired to deprive women of their rights

    (B) some male citizens are still being denied basic rights

    (C) the role of women in the founding of the nation is generally ignored

    (D) society is endangered when women are deprived of basic rights

    √(E) all people deserve to enjoy the rights guaranteed by the Constitution

25. By "the half of our posterity" (line 20), Anthony means

    (A) the political legacy passed down from her era

    (B) future generations of male United States citizens

    (C) those who wish to enjoy the blessings of liberty

    √(D) current and future opponents of the women's rights movement

    (E) future members of the democratic-republican government

26. In lines 31–46, Anthony's argument rests mainly on the strategy of convincing her audience that

    (A) any state that denies women the vote undermines its status as a democracy

    (B) women deprived of the vote will eventually raise a rebellion

    √(C) the nation will remain an aristocracy if the status of women does not change

    (D) women's rights issues should be debated in every home

    (E) even an aristocracy cannot survive without the consent of the governed

27. The word *hardihood* in line 52 could best be replaced by

    (A) endurance

    (B) vitality

    √(C) nerve

    (D) opportunity

    (E) stupidity

28. When Anthony warns that "no State . . . shall abridge their privileges" (line 54–55), she means that

    (A) women should be allowed to live a life of privilege

    (B) women on trial cannot be forced to give up their immunity

    (C) every state should repeal its outdated laws

    √(D) governments may not deprive citizens of their rights

    (E) the rights granted to women must be decided by the people, not the state

IF YOU FINISH BEFORE TIME IS CALLED, YOU MAY CHECK YOUR WORK ON THIS SECTION ONLY. DO NOT TURN TO ANY OTHER SECTION IN THE TEST.

STOP

SECTION TWO

Time—25 Minutes   For each of the following questions, choose the best answer and darken the
27 Questions   corresponding oval on the answer sheet.

1. The rain is so rare and the land is so ---- that few of the men who work there see much ---- in farming.

    (A) plentiful . . hope
    (B) barren . . difficulty
    (C) productive . . profit
    (D) infertile . . future
    (E) dry . . danger

2. The principal declared that the students were not simply ignoring the rules, but openly ---- them.

    (A) accepting
    (B) redressing
    (C) reviewing
    (D) flouting
    (E) discussing

3. Some critics believe that the ---- of modern art came with dadaism, while others insist that the movement was a ----.

    (A) zenith . . . sham
    (B) pinnacle . . . triumph
    (C) decline . . . disaster
    (D) acceptance . . . success
    (E) originality . . . fiasco

4. She would never have believed that her article was so ---- were it not for the ---- of correspondence which followed its publication.

    (A) interesting . . . dearth
    (B) inflammatory . . . lack
    (C) controversial . . . spate
    (D) commonplace . . . influx
    (E) insignificant . . . volume

5. The writings of the philosopher Descartes are ----; many readers have difficulty following his complex, intricately woven arguments.

    (A) generic
    (B) trenchant
    (C) reflective
    (D) elongated
    (E) abstruse

6. The prisoner was ---- even though he presented evidence clearly proving that he was nowhere near the scene of the crime.

    (A) abandoned
    (B) indicted
    (C) exculpated
    (D) exhumed
    (E) rescinded

7. Many biologists are critical of the film's ---- premise that dinosaurs might one day return.

    (A) scientific
    (B) tacit
    (C) speculative
    (D) unwitting
    (E) ambiguous

8. It is ---- that a people so capable of treachery and brutality should also exhibit such a tremendous capacity for heroism.

    (A) unfortunate
    (B) explicable
    (C) paradoxical
    (D) distressing
    (E) appalling

GO ON TO THE NEXT PAGE

Questions 9–10 refer to the following passage.

One of the hazards of swimming in the ocean is an unexpected encounter with a jellyfish. Contact with the poison in a jellyfish's tentacles can result in sharp, lingering pain, or even death if the per-
(5) son stung is highly allergic. While everyone, including the jellyfish, would like to avoid these encounters, they are not uncommon. This is hardly surprising considering that jellyfish live in every ocean in the world and have done so for more
(10) than 650 million years. The animals are likely so widespread because of their extreme adaptability—they are quite hardy and can withstand a wide range of temperatures and conditions in their environment.

9. The author uses the phrase *including the jellyfish* (line 6) in order to

   (A) introduce a small note of humor to an otherwise serious discussion

   (B) encourage the reader's sympathy for the jellyfish

   (C) ridicule humans' fear of jellyfish

   (D) emphasize the danger that jellyfish pose for swimmers

   (E) contrast the jellyfish's reaction to the encounter to that of humans

10. According to the passage, encounters between humans and jellyfish in the ocean are relatively common because jellyfish

   (A) are more than 650 million years old

   ✓(B) live in all the world's oceans

   (C) are extremely robust

   (D) have poisonous tentacles

   (E) can endure a range of temperatures

Questions 11–13 refer to the following passages.

Passage 1

Walter O'Malley and architect Emil Praeger created baseball's most popular and beautiful stadium when they built the Dodgers' new home after the team moved from Brooklyn to Los
(5) Angeles in 1958. In contrast to the solely functional appeal of other stadiums, Dodger Stadium was built on a 300-acre site covered by 3,400 trees, creating a fantastic space in which fans can watch a baseball game. Over the past 40 years,
(10) more than 110 million people have watched the Dodger baseball team at Dodger Stadium. In fact, the Dodgers set the all time Major League Baseball attendance mark, drawing three million fans to the ballpark.

Passage 2

(15) Originally designed to host baseball games, Dodger Stadium has since been utilized for a dizzying array of events. Many non-baseball sporting events have taken place in the stadium, such as boxing, basketball, even a ski-jump com-
(20) petition! A host of entertainers have also performed there, ranging from Elton John and the Beatles to the internationally renowned opera stars Jose Carreras, Placido Domingo, and Luciano Pavarotti. Even Pope John Paul II performed a
(25) Mass in 1987 in the stadium. More than just a place to watch a baseball game, Dodger Stadium has become a meeting place for the citizens of Los Angeles.

GO ON TO THE NEXT PAGE

KAPLAN

11. The author of Passage 2 most likely mentions the mass performed by Pope John Paul (lines 10–11) in order to emphasize the

    (A) worldwide popularity of baseball

    (B) predominance of religious activities in Dodger Stadium

    (C) inappropriate nature of holding a religious events in a sporting arena

    (D) importance of religious events to the Los Angeles community

    (E) diversity of activities that occur at Dodger Stadium

12. Author 2 would most likely react to Passage 1's characterization of Dodger Stadium as a "fantastic space in which fans can watch a baseball game" (lines 7–9) by stating that

    (A) baseball fans would enjoy non-baseball events more

    (B) the natural surroundings explain why Dodger Stadium broke the attendance record

    (C) its pleasant atmosphere is also the reason why non-baseball events are popular

    (D) the enjoyable atmosphere is the only reason that fans watch baseball games there

    (E) concert goers would also enjoy baseball games

13. When discussing Dodger Stadium, both passages emphasize the

    (A) contrast between Dodger Stadium and other baseball stadiums

    (B) reasons that people go to Dodger Stadium

    (C) pastoral landscape of Dodger Stadium

    (D) diverse events that occur at Dodger Stadium

    (E) importance of Dodger Stadium as a meeting place for Los Angeles

Questions 14–15 refer to the following passage.

Connecting the northern frontier of Pakistan with Afghanistan, the Khyber Pass is one of the most noteworthy mountain passes in the world. At its narrowest point in the north, the pass is walled
(5) on either side by precipitous cliffs up to 300 meters in height, though the pass itself is only 3 meters wide. Because it is only 53 kilometers long, the Pass offers the best land route between India and Pakistan. This has led to a long and often vio-
(10) lent history—conquering armies have used the Khyber as an entry point for their invasions of India, Pakistan, and Afghanistan. Today there are two highways that snake their way through the Khyber Pass, one for motor traffic and another for
(15) traditional caravans.

14. Which of the following topics is NOT addressed by the passage?

    (A) the origin of the pass

    (B) the countries that border the pass

    (C) the length of the pass

    (D) the role of the pass in history

    (E) the uses of the pass today

15. In line 13, the word *snake* most directly emphasizes the

    (A) function of the Khyber Pass as a means to connect two points

    (B) danger of crossing the Khyber Pass

    (C) Khyber Pass as a direct route through the Hindu Kush mountains

    (D) relatively short length of the Khyber Pass

    (E) winding quality of the Khyber Pass

GO ON TO THE NEXT PAGE

KAPLAN

Questions 16–27 are based on the following passage.

In the following passage, a nineteenth-century American writer recalls his boyhood in a small town along the Mississippi River.

My father was a justice of the peace, and I supposed he possessed the power of life and death over all men and could hang anybody that offended him. This was distinction enough for me as a
(5) general thing; but the desire to be a steamboatman kept intruding, nevertheless. I first wanted to be a cabin boy, so that I could come out with a white apron on and shake a tablecloth over the side, where all my old comrades could see me. Later I
(10) thought I would rather be the deck hand who stood on the end of the stage plank with a coil of rope in his hand, because he was particularly conspicuous.

But these were only daydreams—too heavenly
(15) to be contemplated as real possibilities. By and by one of the boys went away. He was not heard of for a long time. At last he turned up as an apprentice engineer or "striker" on a steamboat. This thing shook the bottom out of all my Sunday-
(20) school teachings. That boy had been notoriously worldly and I had been just the reverse—yet he was exalted to this eminence, and I was left in obscurity and misery. There was nothing generous about this fellow in his greatness. He would always
(25) manage to have a rusty bolt to scrub while his boat was docked at our town, and he would sit on the inside guard and scrub it, where we could all see him and envy him and loathe him.

He used all sorts of steamboat technicalities in
(30) his talk, as if he were so used to them that he forgot common people could not understand them. He would speak of the "labboard" side of a horse in an easy, natural way that would make you wish he was dead. And he was always talking about "St.
(35) Looy" like an old citizen. Two or three of the boys had long been persons of consideration among us because they had been to St. Louis once and had a vague general knowledge of its wonders, but the day of their glory was over now. They lapsed into
(40) a humble silence, and learned to disappear when the ruthless "cub" engineer approached. This fellow had money, too, and hair oil, and he wore a showy brass watch chain, a leather belt, and used no suspenders. No girl could withstand his
(45) charms. He "cut out" every boy in the village. When his boat blew up at last, it diffused a tranquil contentment among us such as we had not known for months. But when he came home the next week, alive, renowned, and appeared in
(50) church all battered up and bandaged, a shining hero, stared at and wondered over by everybody, it seemed to us that the partiality of Providence for an undeserving reptile had reached a point where it was open to criticism.
(55) This creature's career could produce but one result, and it speedily followed. Boy after boy managed to get on the river. Four sons of the chief merchant, and two sons of the county judge became pilots, the grandest position of all. But
(60) some of us could not get on the river—at least our parents would not let us.

So by and by I ran away. I said I would never come home again till I was a pilot and could return in glory. But somehow I could not manage
(65) it. I went meekly aboard a few of the boats that lay packed together like sardines at the long St. Louis wharf, and very humbly inquired for the pilots, but got only a cold shoulder and short words from mates and clerks. I had to make the best of this
(70) sort of treatment for the time being, but I had comforting daydreams of a future when I should be a great and honored pilot, with plenty of money, and could kill some of these mates and clerks and pay for them.

GO ON TO THE NEXT PAGE

KAPLAN

16. The author makes the statement that "I supposed he . . . offended him" (lines 1–4) primarily to suggest the

    (A) power held by a justice of the peace in a frontier town

    (B) naive view that he held of his father's importance

    (C) respect in which the townspeople held his father

    (D) possibility of miscarriages of justice on the American frontier

    (E) harsh environment in which he was brought up

17. As used in line 4, the word *distinction* most nearly means

    (A) difference

    (B) variation

    (C) prestige

    (D) desperation

    (E) clarity

18. The author decides that he would rather become a deck hand than a cabin boy (lines 6–13) because

    (A) the job offers higher wages

    (B) he believes that the work is easier

    (C) he wants to avoid seeing his older friends

    (D) deck hands often go on to become pilots

    (E) the job is more visible to passersby

19. The author most likely mentions his "Sunday-school teachings" in lines 18–20 to emphasize

    (A) the influence of his early education in later life

    (B) his sense of injustice at the engineer's success

    (C) his disillusionment with longstanding religious beliefs

    (D) his determination to become an engineer at all costs

    (E) the unscrupulous nature of the engineer's character

20. The author most likely concludes that the engineer is not "generous" (line 23) because he

    (A) has no respect for religious beliefs

    (B) refuses to share his wages with friends

    (C) flaunts his new position in public

    (D) takes a pride in material possessions

    (E) ignores the disappointment of other people's ambitions

21. The author most probably mentions the use of "steamboat technicalities" (line 29) in order to emphasize the engineer's

    (A) expertise after a few months on the job

    (B) fascination for trivial information

    (C) ignorance on most other subjects

    (D) desire to appear sophisticated

    (E) inability to communicate effectively

22. The word *consideration* in line 36 most nearly means

    (A) generosity

    (B) deliberation

    (C) contemplation

    (D) unselfishness

    (E) reputation

23. According to the passage, the "glory" of having visited St. Louis (lines 35–39) was over because

    (A) the boys' knowledge of St. Louis was much less detailed than the engineer's

    (B) St. Louis had changed so much that the boys' stories were no longer accurate

    (C) the boys realized that traveling to St. Louis was not a mark of sophistication

    (D) the engineer's account revealed that the boys' stories were lies

    (E) travel to St. Louis had become too commonplace to be envied

GO ON TO THE NEXT PAGE →

24. The author describes the engineer's appearance (lines 41–44) primarily in order to

    (A) suggest one reason why many people found the engineer impressive

    (B) convey the way steamboatmen typically dressed

    (C) emphasize the inadequacy of his own wardrobe

    (D) contrast the engineer's behavior with his appearance

    (E) indicate his admiration for fashionable clothes

25. In lines 51–54, the author's response to the engineer's survival is one of

    (A) thankfulness for what he believes is God's providence

    (B) astonishment at the engineer's miraculous escape

    (C) reflection on the occupational hazards of a steamboating career

    (D) outrage at his rival's undeserved good fortune

    (E) sympathy for the extent of the engineer's wounds

26. The major purpose of the passage is to

    (A) sketch the peaceful life of a frontier town

    (B) relate the events that led to a boy's first success in life

    (C) portray the unsophisticated ambitions of a boy

    (D) describe the characteristics of a small-town boaster

    (E) give a humorous portrayal of a boy's conflicts with his parents

27. At the end of the passage, the author reflects on

    (A) his new ambition to become either a mate or a clerk

    (B) the wisdom of seeking a job in which advancement is easier

    (C) the prospect of abandoning a hopeless search for fame

    (D) the impossibility of returning home and asking his parents' pardon

    (E) his determination to keep striving for success in a glorious career

IF YOU FINISH BEFORE TIME IS CALLED, YOU MAY CHECK YOUR WORK ON THIS SECTION ONLY. DO NOT TURN TO ANY OTHER SECTION IN THE TEST.

STOP

SECTION THREE

Time—20 Minutes
17 Questions

For each of the following questions, choose the best answer and darken the corresponding oval on the answer sheet.

Questions 1–13 are based on the following passages.

The controversy over the authorship of Shakespeare's plays began in the 18th century and continues to this day. Here, the author of Passage 1 embraces the proposal that Francis Bacon actually wrote the plays, while the author of Passage 2 defends the traditional attribution to Shakespeare himself.

Passage 1

Anyone with more than a superficial knowledge of Shakespeare's plays must necessarily entertain some doubt concerning their true authorship. Can scholars honestly accept the idea that such master-
(5) works were written by a shadowy actor with limited formal education and a social position that can most charitably be called "humble"? Obviously, the author of the plays must have traveled widely, yet there is no record that Shakespeare ever left his
(10) native England. Even more obviously, the real author had to have intimate knowledge of life within royal courts and palaces, yet Shakespeare was a commoner, with little firsthand experience of the aristocracy. No, common sense tells us that
(15) the plays must have been written by someone with substantial expertise in the law, the sciences, classics, foreign languages, and the fine arts—someone, in other words, like Shakespeare's eminent contemporary, Sir Francis Bacon.
(20) The first person to suggest that Bacon was the actual author of the plays was Reverend James Wilmot. Writing in 1785, Wilmot argued that someone of Shakespeare's educational background could hardly have produced works of such erudi-
(25) tion and insight. But a figure like Bacon, a scientist and polymath* of legendary stature, would certainly have known about, for instance, the circulation of the blood as alluded to in *Coriolanus*. And as an aristocrat, Bacon would have possessed
(30) the familiarity with court life required to produce a *Love's Labour's Lost*.

Delia Bacon (no relation to Sir Francis) was next to make the case for Francis Bacon's authorship. In 1856, in collaboration with Nathaniel

(35) Hawthorne, she insisted that it was ridiculous to look for the creator of Hamlet among "that dirty, doggish group of players, who come into the scene [of the play Hamlet] summoned like a pack of hounds to his service." Ultimately, she concluded
(40) that the plays were actually composed by a committee consisting of Bacon, Edmund Spenser, Walter Raleigh, and several others.

Still, some might wonder why Bacon, if indeed the plays were wholly or partly his work, would
(45) not put his own name on them. But consider the political climate of England in Elizabethan times. Given that it would have been politically and personally damaging for a man of Bacon's position to associate himself with such controversial plays, it
(50) is quite understandable that Bacon would hire a lowly actor to take the credit—and the consequences.

But perhaps the most convincing evidence of all comes from the postscript of a 1624 letter sent to
(55) Bacon by Sir Tobie Matthew. "The most prodigious wit that I ever knew . . . is your lordship's name," Matthew wrote, "though he be known by another." That name, of course, was William Shakespeare.

*polymath: a person of wide and varied learning

Passage 2

(60) Over the years, there have been an astonishing number of persons put forth as the "true author" of Shakespeare's plays. Some critics have even gone so far as to claim that only a "committee" could have possessed the abundance of talent and
(65) energy necessary to produce Shakespeare's thirty-seven plays. Among the individual figures most seriously promoted as "the real Shakespeare" is Sir Francis Bacon. Apparently, the fact that Bacon wrote most of his own work in academic Latin
(70) does nothing to deter those who would crown him the premier stylist in the English language.

GO ON TO THE NEXT PAGE

Although the entire controversy reeks of scholarly gamesplaying, the issue underlying it is worth considering: How could an uneducated actor cre-
(75) ate such exquisite works? But the answer to that is easy. Shakespeare's dramatic gifts had little to do with encyclopedic knowledge, complex ideas, or a fluency with great systems of thought. Rather, Shakespeare's genius was one of common sense
(80) and perceptive intuition—a genius that grows not out of book-learning, but out of a deep understanding of human nature and a keen grasp of basic emotions, passions, and jealousies.

One of the most common arguments advanced
(85) by skeptics is that the degree of familiarity with the law exhibited in a *Hamlet* or a *Merchant of Venice* can only have been achieved by a lawyer or other man of affairs. The grasp of law evidenced in these plays, however, is not a detailed knowl-
(90) edge of formal law, but a more general understanding of so-called "country law." Shakespeare was a landowner—an extraordinary achievement in itself for an ill-paid Elizabethan actor—and so would have been knowledgeable about legal mat-
(95) ters related to the buying, selling, and renting of real estate. Evidence of such a common understanding of land regulations can be found, for instance, in the gravedigging scene of *Hamlet*.

So no elaborate theories of intrigue and secret
(100) identity are necessary to explain the accomplishment of William Shakespeare. Scholars who have made a career of ferreting out "alternative bards" may be reluctant to admit it, but literary genius can flower in any socioeconomic bracket.
(105) Shakespeare, in short, was Shakespeare—an observation that one would have thought was obvious to everyone.

1. In line 2, *entertain* most nearly means

    (A) amuse
    (B) harbor
    (C) occupy
    (D) cherish
    (E) engage

2. In Passage 1, the author draws attention to Shakespeare's social standing as a "commoner" (line 13) in order to cast doubt on the Elizabethan actor's

    (A) aptitude for writing poetically
    (B) knowledge of foreign places and habits
    (C) ability to support himself by playwriting
    ✓(D) familiarity with life among persons of high rank
    (E) understanding of the problems of government

3. *Coriolanus* and *Love's Labour's Lost* are mentioned in lines 28–31 as examples of works that

    (A) only Francis Bacon could have written
    (B) exhibit a deep understanding of human nature
    (C) resemble works written by Francis Bacon under his own name
    (D) portray a broad spectrum of Elizabethan society
    ✓(E) reveal expertise more likely held by Bacon than Shakespeare

4. In Passage 1, the quotation from Delia Bacon (lines 36–39) conveys a sense of

    ✓(A) disdain for the disreputable vulgarity of Elizabethan actors
    (B) resentment at the way Shakespeare's characters were portrayed
    (C) regret that conditions for Elizabethan actors were not better
    (D) doubt that Shakespeare could actually have created such unsavory characters
    (E) disappointment at the incompetence of Elizabethan actors

GO ON TO THE NEXT PAGE ▷

KAPLAN

5. The author of Passage 1 maintains that Bacon did not put his own name on the plays attributed to Shakespeare because he

(A) regarded writing as an unsuitable occupation for an aristocrat

(B) wished to protect himself from the effects of controversy

(C) preferred being known as a scientist and politician rather than as a writer

(D) did not want to associate himself with lowly actors

(E) sought to avoid the attention that fame brings

6. In the first paragraph of Passage 2, the author calls into question Bacon's likely ability to

(A) write in a language with which he was unfamiliar

(B) make the transition between scientific writing and playwriting

(C) produce the poetic language evident in the plays

(D) cooperate with other members of a committee

(E) singlehandedly create thirty-seven plays

7. The word *premier* in line 71 most nearly means

(A) earliest

(B) influential

(C) inaugural

(D) greatest

(E) original

8. In line 77, the word *encyclopedic* most nearly means

(A) technical

(B) comprehensive

(C) abridged

(D) disciplined

(E) specialized

9. The author of Passage 2 cites Shakespeare's status as a landowner in order to

(A) prove that Shakespeare was a success as a playwright

(B) refute the claim that Shakespeare had little knowledge of aristocratic life

(C) prove that Shakespeare didn't depend solely on acting for his living

(D) dispute the notion that Shakespeare was a commoner

(E) account for Shakespeare's apparent knowledge of the law

10. In lines 101–104, the author maintains that literary genius

(A) is not dependent on a writer's external circumstances

(B) must be based on an inborn comprehension of human nature

(C) is enhanced by the suffering that poverty brings

(D) frequently goes unrecognized among those of modest means and position

(E) can be stifled by too much book-learning and academic training

GO ON TO THE NEXT PAGE ⟩

KAPLAN

11. Author 2 would probably respond to the speculation in the fourth paragraph of Passage 1 (lines 43–52) by pointing out that

   (A) Shakespeare's plays would not have seemed particularly controversial to Elizabethan audiences

   (B) The extent and range of Bacon's learning has been generally exaggerated

   √(C) such scenarios are farfetched and unnecessary if one correctly understands Shakespeare's genius

   (D) Bacon would not have had the knowledge of the lower classes required to produce the plays

   (E) the claim implies that Shakespeare was disreputable when in fact he was a respectable landowner

12. Author 1 would probably respond to the skepticism expressed by Author 2 in lines 68–71 by making which of the following statements?

   (A) The similarities between English and Latin make it plausible that one person could write well in both languages.

   (B) Plays written in Latin would not have been likely to attract a wide audience in Elizabethan England.

   (C) The premier stylist in the English language is more likely to have been an eminent scholar than an uneducated actor.

   (D) Writing the plays in Latin would have shielded Bacon from much of the political damage he wanted to avoid.

   (E) The style of the plays is notable mostly for the clarity of thought behind the lines rather than their musicality or beauty.

13. In lines 105–106, *observation* most nearly means

   (A) inspection

   (B) measurement

   (C) research

   (D) comment

   (E) memorandum

GO ON TO THE NEXT PAGE

KAPLAN

Questions 14–15 refer to the following passage.

I am compelled by the stories of women in history. In my dreams, I stand on the coastline and these women come to me in rowboats—gentle waves rolling inexorably to the shore. They ask
(5) how I will remember them and how I will remember them to others in my artwork. Sometimes I am surprised by the things that are important to them. Into the sands of my sleep, they trace images of struggles won and lost, children reared,
(10) loves pursued; when I wake, I struggle to hold my head still, hoping to keep the sands from shifting so that I can remember well the ideas gifted to me.

14. The image of the "waves" (line 4) most clearly expresses

 (A) the narrator's impression of the women in the rowboats
 (B) the need of the women in the rowboat to be heard
 (C) the narrator's inner discomfort at being interrupted in her dream
 (D) the importance of the women in the rowboat
 (E) the narrator's sense of being confounded by the stories of the women

15. The "images" ("struggles won … loves pursued") (lines 9–10) are examples of

 (A) the narrator's own artwork
 (B) reflections of the women in the water
 (C) the inspiration captured in the dream
 (D) the narrator's memorial to the women
 (E) factual accounts of history

Questions 16–17 refer to the following passage.

The struggle to balance a family life and a career is significant in many women's lives. This tension is a theme in *The Yellow Wallpaper*, written by Charlotte Perkins Gilman in 1892. In this short
(5) story, the narrator struggles to fulfill her role as mother and wife at the expense of her work, a sublimation that ultimately makes her depressed. Though women today certainly have more options and freedom than those of Gillman's time, they
(10) still often face the conflict between being caretakers and having careers—a conflict that Charlotte Perkins Gilman chronicled over 100 years ago.

16. In line 6, the word *expense* most nearly means

 (A) burden
 (B) taxation
 (C) expenditure
 (D) sacrifice
 (E) income

17. In the last sentence, the author suggests that

 (A) modern women rarely use their new freedom to its fullest potential
 (B) there has been little progress in the women's rights movement in more than 100 years
 (C) if women do not balance their family lives and careers they will become depressed
 (D) women will never be able to hold meaningful careers
 (E) the issues in Gilman's short story have relevance today

IF YOU FINISH BEFORE TIME IS CALLED, YOU MAY CHECK YOUR WORK ON THIS SECTION ONLY. DO NOT TURN TO ANY OTHER SECTION IN THE TEST.

Practice Test B: **Answer Key**

SECTION ONE

1. E	11. B	21. B
2. C	12. C	22. C
3. B	13. B	23. A
4. B	14. C	24. E
5. B	15. E	25. B
6. E	16. A	26. A
7. C	17. C	27. C
8. E	18. D	28. D
9. A	19. D	
10. E	20. A	

SECTION TWO

1. D	10. B	19. B
2. D	11. E	20. C
3. A	12. C	21. D
4. C	13. B	22. E
5. E	14. A	23. A
6. B	15. E	24. A
7. C	16. B	25. D
8. C	17. C	26. C
9. A	18. E	27. E

SECTION THREE

1. B	10. A
2. D	11. C
3. E	12. C
4. A	13. D
5. B	14. A
6. C	15. C
7. D	16. D
8. B	17. E
9. E	

Answers and Explanations

SECTION 1

1. E

It's easy enough to understand that *insurers* don't like to insure property in places where *natural disasters* are likely to happen. The term *prone to* (E) means "having a tendency to," so it is correct.

2. C

If it took *Roman legions* three years to seize Masada, we can predict that they spent a long time "surrounding or isolating" *the mountain* "fortress or stronghold" *of Masada* before they were finally able to take it. (C) is the best choice. (B) *assailed*, meaning "attacked," would make sense in the first blank, and (E) *stronghold* and (A) *bastion* would fit, too. But (A), (B), and (E)'s other blank's words don't make sense when plugged in.

besieged: surrounded with armed forces

citadel: fortress

assailed: attacked

bastion: fortified area

dissembled: concealed

honed: sharpened

3. B

If the senator was *unlike* "his calmer, more easygoing colleagues" and "ready to quarrel at the slightest provocation," it's fair to infer that he was short-tempered or extremely irritable. The best choice is (B)—*irascible*.

irascible: easily angered

whimsical: fanciful, erratic, or unpredictable

gregarious: sociable, friendly

ineffectual: futile, unproductive

benign: harmless or gentle

4. B

You don't have to know that *Genghis Khan* was a violent dictator to get this question right. What's important to know is that the first word of the sentence, *although*, implies that the two blanks have to contain words that contrast with each other. (B) is the best choice—although historians had thought that Genghis Khan was a *despotic* potentate, new research shows that many of his subjects nevertheless *revered* him. Although (A) *tyrannical* is synonymous with *despotic*, (A)'s second-blank choice, *abhorred*, doesn't provide the predicted contrast. Choice (C) *venerated* doesn't really contrast with *redundant*. And in (E), it doesn't make sense to say that Khan's subjects *invoked* him despite his *peremptory* reputation.

despotic: oppressive, dictatorial

potentate: dictator

revered: worshipped, adored

abhorred: hated

venerated: highly respected

peremptory: putting an end to debate

invoke: call upon for help

5. B

The word *because* in the middle of the sentence lets us know that the words in the blanks will be consistent in meaning, which means that they will share the same type of charge. We can predict two positive words, like Jill was "appreciated" by her employees because she often "forgave" the fact that they were lazy, or two negative words like Jill was "disliked" by her employees because she often "scolded" them for being lazy. (B) matches the latter prediction—Jill was *loathed* by her employees because she often *berated* them for not working hard enough. No other choice besides (B) contains two like, or similar, charges.

loathed: hated

berated: scolded

deified: made godlike

lauded: praised or celebrated

derided: made fun of

execrated: condemned, cursed

6. E

If reconstructing the skeletons of extinct species like dinosaurs . . . requires much patience and effort by paleontologists, we can predict that such an activity is a "painstaking or tough, demanding process." (E) *exacting* is our best choice.

exacting: requiring extreme accuracy

nascent: introductory or starting

aberrant: abnormal

7. C

Because of disease and the destruction of their habitat, koalas are now found only in isolated parts of eucalyptus forests. The word in the blank must mean something like *killed off* or *destroyed*, since things like disease and habitat destruction are destructive processes. (C) is our best choice—nearly *decimated*, or wiped out, by disease and habitat destruction, koalas are now found only in isolated parts of eucalyptus forests. (A) *dispersed*, meaning "scattered," may have been a little tempting, but there's no reason to assume that the koalas were scattered around the forests due to disease and habitat destruction.

compiled: categorized, collected, arranged

averted: avoided

8. E

Looking at the first blank first, if there were internal power struggles [in] the government, then it's likely that the government had something like deep ideological "differences" or "conflicts." For the second blank, we can predict that these conflicts and power struggles harmed or crippled the government. Although (C)'s first-blank choice, *distortions*, sounds negative, like "differences" or "conflicts," (A) and (E) make more sense. We can easily imagine deep ideological *disputes* or divisions going hand in hand with internal power struggles, but it's hard to imagine ideological *distortions*.

Now we can turn to (A) and (E)'s second-blank choices. (A) doesn't make sense—why would deep ideological disputes and internal power struggles *facilitate* the government? (E) is the best choice—deep ideological divisions and internal power struggles *paralyzed* the government.

facilitate: assist

stymied: frustrated, impeded

Latin Quarter Passage

9. A

The word *bohemian* is first mentioned in sentence 5, "a bohemian area where the conventions of society were generally disregarded." You can infer from this that bohemians were not concerned with the accepted and traditional customs of the society in which they lived (A). If you weren't sure what *mores* were, you should have held on to this and gone to the other choices to eliminate them.

The Latin Quarter is inhabited not only by students, but also by artists, so (B) and (C) must either both be correct (impossible) or both be wrong. Even though Murger, referred to as the first bohemian, did write stories, there's no indication that this is true of all bohemians (D). Choice (E) is out because, although the last sentence says that the bohemian lifestyle was regarded by the larger society as "dangerously unconventional," the author doesn't seem to endorse this view.

mores: accepted and traditional customs of a social group

10. E

The context for the word *loose* is the last sentence: "The loose lifestyles that the world had previously regarded as scandalous, suspect, and dangerously unconventional now seemed enviable." So these are lifestyles that don't conform to the customs of the larger society. The bohemians, in other words, do not limit their behavior (E).

(A) and (B) are common meanings of the word *loose*, but they don't fit here. (C) might be tempting, but it's a little too negative, the author has generally positive feelings towards the bohemians. (D) *replete*, means full, which doesn't work.

Iowa Caucus Passage

11. B

Jimmy Carter and Bill Clinton appear in the final sentence. They are cited as examples of two candidates who were "obscure" before the Iowa caucus, but whose victory helped launch their run for the presidency. (B) reflects this.

The author doesn't say that the campaigns of Jimmy Carter or Bill Clinton were lackluster, or that their wins were *surprising* (A). Watch out for (C); the passage mentions only the positive impact of unknown candidates winning the Iowa caucus, not the negative effects of famous candidates not winning it. (D) and (E) are far too extreme; the author states neither that the Caucus winner will win the presidential election, nor that the Caucus *assures* candidates national exposure.

Time Passage

Next up is a fairly abstract science passage. This particular passage is perhaps a little bit harder than the ones you're going to encounter on Test Day—but don't be intimidated by the subject matter. Even if your passage is written by a Nobel Prize winner, it's going to contain ideas that you can relate to, and probably some ideas that you've seen before.

The topic of the passage is how difficult it is to comprehend long stretches of time. Paragraph 2 tells us that our minds aren't built to handle the idea of thousands of years passing. We have *some* conception of the past through the art, writing, and photography of previous generations, but the scale of longer time periods eludes us. Paragraphs 4 and 5 attempt to bridge this gap by providing a few everyday yardsticks; the time the human race has been around is compared to a few seconds in a week, or a few letters in a book.

12. C

Before writing, we're told, the wisdom of generations was passed down in two ways: verbally, and "to a lesser extent," in pictures, carvings, and statues. This means that the wisdom of the past was transmitted less effectively by nonverbal means, and thus (C) *more effectively by the spoken word than by other means*.

Choices (A) and (B) distort this idea. Nowhere are we told that wisdom was *rejected*. And since spoken words *and* pictures were both used, it was obviously not an all or nothing proposition. (E) doesn't make much sense. How could there be an emphasis on *science* before writing existed? (D), finally, makes no sense at all—the author never says that all ancient wisdom was *fiction*.

13. B

This asks about the purpose of a detail. The question asks why the author discusses the impact of writing. Looking at the lines around the line reference given, we're told that writing has made the transmission of information about the past a lot more precise and extensive. Pictures and photography are also mentioned as ways in which the ex-

perience of the past has been passed down. So choice (B) is correct here—writing is mentioned as an *example* of how cultures record knowledge about the past.

(A) is a distortion; The author is showing us something about the past, not why we remember hardly anything. He never implies any criticism of *preliterate cultures*, so choice (C) is out too. Choices (D) and (E) are never mentioned.

14. C

The word *ready* can mean several things—choices (A), (C), (D), and (E) are all possible meanings. In this context, however, it most nearly means *immediate*, choice (C). In the sentence before the cited line, the author says, "there is no simple way" to understand vast stretches of time. And in the sentence following the cited line, the author compares the way we understand time to the way a blind man "laboriously" constructs a picture of his surroundings. This implies that our understanding of time is a difficult and time-consuming task, not something we can do readily or immediately.

15. E

Give the context a quick scan. Once again, the author's talking about how difficult it is to understand vast stretches of time. We're told that it's like a blind man building up a sensory picture of his surroundings. This is an indirect process, so (E) is right.

Choice (C) is dealt with later in paragraph 4, so you can eliminate it right away. Choice (A) is too sweeping. The author never says that human beings are completely unable to comprehend time.

16. A

Inference skills are required here. What is the author's underlying point in mentioning *the Big Bang and the Cambrian Period*? The author introduces this discussion by saying that a week provides a better yardstick for the age of the earth than a day. The Big Bang and the Cambrian Period are used as examples to support this point. So (A) is right—it's the point about the time scale that the author's trying to demonstrate.

Choices (D) and (E) both distort the point in different ways. The author is not suggesting that the time scale of a day should be totally abandoned—just that the week is a better scale. The development of (B) agriculture is another supporting example like the Big Bang and the Cambrian

Period, but it's not the author's central point here. Finally, fossils have nothing to do with the question at hand, so (C) is easily eliminated.

17. C

A more straightforward comprehension question this time. When we go back to the lines referred to, we're told about the problem with linear maps: When you produce one that's big enough to show us on it, the map becomes too big to study and reproduce conveniently. (C) gets the right paraphrase here. Notice especially the match in synonyms for "convenient reproduction" and "examination."

(A), (B), and (E) aren't supported—there's nothing about scientific standards, overlapping periods, or ignorance about pre-Cambrian times in the passage. (D) doesn't address the problem. The question is about getting our human experience on the map.

18. D

The overall point here is that life started on earth so long ago that it is difficult for us to comprehend. Everything that follows is meant to illustrate this point, including the time scales. Don't let the material confuse you. The point is (D)—the immensity of time since the origin of life.

(C) is tricky because it's an aspect of the larger argument, but it's not the whole point. The other wrong choices mention issues that the author hardly touches on. In paragraphs 4 to 6, the author is not concerned with *getting dates right* (A), the *question of how life actually began* (B), or the (E) *development of communication*.

Music and Language Passages

19. D

The author includes lines 5–12 as evidence that in the Romantic era, folks believed that music by itself could signify *emotion* (D).

There is no evidence in the passage to support (A). While you know what the perception was during the Romantic era, there's no mention of the current perception. As for (B), though the author states that language is used functionally as opposed to music, this claim is not made specifically for Romantic Music. (C) is too extreme—the author isn't saying that Romantic music composers *always* used music to connote emotions. And (E) expresses a negativity absent from the passage.

20. A

Both authors mention the *symbolic* nature of music and language (A). Passage 1 says "Nettl has concluded that like language, music is a 'series of symbols.'" Passage 2 says something similar in the last line.

Only the author of Passage 2 compares both to *subdivided sections* (B). Only the author of Passage 1 compares both to *functional parts* (C). As for (D), clues are never mentioned. (E) fits Passage 2 pretty well, but Passage 1 never links emotions and language. (A) is the answer.

21. B

The wrong answer here will be something that the authors agree on, or something that is not mentioned at all in one of the passages. Author 1 would agree with (B), while author 2 would disagree.

Author 2 would agree with (A) and (E), but you don't know how Author 1 would feel; she might agree, or she might disagree. Author 2 would probably disagree with (C), since context is so important, but there's no telling what Author 1 would think about the statement. (D) is too extreme—you don't know that Author 1 would agree with this.

Susan B. Anthony Passage

This humanities passage is from a speech by Susan B. Anthony, a 19th-century women's rights leader. Anthony admits at the outset that she was recently charged with the "crime" of voting. Her intention is to prove that her vote was no crime, but rather the exercise of her Constitutional rights, which no state should be allowed to impinge upon. This generates the passage's big idea: that Anthony—and by extension all women—should be allowed to vote. You may have found Anthony's style a little dated or confusing. Don't worry; the questions will help you focus on specific details.

22. C

The important thing here is to see what exactly Anthony is saying. The question stem is keyed to the first paragraph. In the second sentence she states that she "not only committed no crime, but . . . simply exercised my citizen's rights, guaranteed me . . . by the National Constitution." The words *no crime* are the first important clue. You can immediately rule out (A) and (E) because they say she believes the act was illegal. The second part of the line discusses the Constitution, so (C) is clearly a restatement of her argument.

(B) and (D) both make sense, but she does not state these points in the first paragraph. Therefore, they are wrong.

23. A

The most common meaning of *promote* is "to move up"—to a higher position, rank, or job. This doesn't make sense, though, in the phrase "promote the general welfare." "General welfare" means the good of all people, so to (A) *further* it, makes the most sense.

(B) *organize* and (C) *publicize* both could apply to the general welfare, but not as well as (A). They refer more to promotion as you would do with a concert or sports event. (D) *commend* means "praise," which seems silly in the context given, as does (E) *motivate*.

24. E

Anthony points out that no subgroup was excluded by the wording of the preamble of the Constitution. "we formed it . . . to secure [the blessings of liberty,] not to the half of ourselves . . . but to . . . women as well as men." Therefore (E) is correct. All people are entitled to the rights of the Constitution.

Anthony never claims that the Founding Fathers plotted to deny women their rights (A). (B) is incorrect because the author's concern is women's rights and not rights of any other group. Though some male citizens may still be denied basic rights, (B) goes against the gist of what is being said. (C) is like (A) in that it's a claim Anthony never makes. Finally, though (D) is a point that Anthony does make, she doesn't make it until the next paragraph.

25. B

We're still looking at the same part of the passage.

Look at the structure of the quoted sentence: "We didn't do it only for X, but for X *and* Y." "Posterity" means *future generations*, which would include men and women. So the X, the "half of our posterity," refers to the posterity of those who already enjoy the blessings of liberty. In other words, *males*. (B) is the right choice.

(A) has nothing to do with what Anthony is discussing. Since the construction of the sentence makes it clear that the "half of our posterity" is not the whole of those who

want to vote, (C) is out. There's no way of saying that one-half of the people are and will be *opponents of women's rights*, so (D) is wrong. And (E) wrongly suggests that in the *future*, one half of the country's population will be members of government.

26. A

Reread the keyed paragraph. Anthony is saying that a state that prohibits women from voting violates federal law—the Constitution. Therefore it becomes "an odious aristocracy, a hateful oligarchy." Neither of these things is a democracy. (A) is the correct answer.

Anthony mentions *rebellion*, but she doesn't mean the kind of violent rebellion (B) talks about. (C) is wrong because of the word *remain*. The nation is not and never has been an *aristocracy*. (D) plays off the same sentence as (B) does, but instead of going too far, it doesn't go far enough. Anthony wants the laws against women voting repealed; she doesn't want them merely discussed. (E) is totally wrong because at no point is Anthony arguing that an aristocracy should be preserved.

27. C

You might readily associate *hardihood* with (A) *endurance* and (B) *vitality*, but a quick check back in context shows you these aren't correct. Anthony says she doesn't believe her opponents would have the —— to say women aren't "persons." Saying such an offensive thing would take a lot of *nerve*, choice (C). It might also take a lot of *stupidity* (E), but that's too strong a word, considering Anthony's diplomatic tone.

28. D

The stem keys you to the second to last sentence of the passage. *Abridge* means "deprive," so Anthony is saying that no state can deprive citizens of their rights. (D) states exactly this.

In (A), *privilege* means "luxury," but voting is a basic right, not a luxury. (B) comes out of nowhere; there's no discussion of *courts* in this passage. (C) plays off Anthony's reference to "any old law." She's not talking about any *outdated laws* in this passage; she means any law that prohibits women from voting. Anthony never addresses how the laws will be changed, only that they must be changed, so (E) is out.

antagonism: hostility

SECTION TWO

1. D

This is not a difficult question. The use of the word *and* tells us that we're looking for a word to fill the first blank that is consistent with scarcity of rain—a word like *dry*. We can, therefore, eliminate (A) and (C) at once. Since farming conditions are bad, our second blank should express the idea that there's no point in trying to work there. By that criterion, choices (B) and (E) can be eliminated. This leaves us with (D) *future*. (D)'s first word, *infertile*, also fits perfectly, so (D) is the correct answer.

barren: not productive

2. D

The structural clue in this sentence is *not only . . . but*, which suggests that the students were doing something even worse than ignoring the rules. The only word that fits here is *flouting*, choice (D).

flouting: mocking, treating with contempt

3. A

The word *while* following the comma in the second part of the sentence tells us that there will be a contrast between what some critics believe about dadaism and what others insist the movement was. The best choice is (A): some critics believe that the *zenith* of modern art came with dadaism, while others insist the movement was a *sham*. Other choices have single words that would make sense in one of the blanks, but none of the pairs except (A) expresses the contrast that is implied by the sentence.

zenith: highest point

sham: hoax

4. C

It is clear that the content of the journalist's article either had no impact, in which case there was little or no response from the public, or it attracted a great deal of attention and was followed by a lot of correspondence. (C) is the correct answer. The author would never have thought her article was so *controversial* were it not for the *spate* of correspondence. The other answer choices are wrong because they sound contradictory when plugged into the sentence. For example, in choice (A), if the article were *interesting*, one would expect it to be followed by a lot of correspondence—not by a *dearth*, or lack of it. In choice (D), if the article were *commonplace* (ordinary), why would an *influx* of letters follow its publication?

spate: a sudden flood or rush

dearth: lack

inflammatory: likely to arouse strong feeling or anger

influx: flow coming in

5. E

If many readers have difficulty following Descartes's complex, intricately woven arguments, then it's likely that his writings are something like "complicated," "esoteric," or "obscure." The best choice is (E) *abstruse*.

abstruse: difficult to understand

generic: common, general

trenchant: extremely perceptive, insightful

6. B

The phrase *even though* indicates contrast. So, even though the prisoner presented evidence clearly proving that he was nowhere near the scene of the crime, he was (B) *indicted*, or formally charged with committing the crime.

exculpated: absolved, proved to be innocent

exhumed: removed from a grave

rescinded: cancelled, taken back

7. C

A premise is a proposition which is used as the basis for an argument—or a story. If scientists are critical of the premise for a movie, we can infer that they are so because they consider it to be unscientific, without basis in fact, or *speculative*. (C) is the answer. (A) is wrong, because if the premise were scientific then it would hardly be open to criticism by scientists. (B) is wrong because there's no reason to think that the theme of the return of the dinosaurs is *tacit*, or unexpressed, in the movie.

tacit: silent; understood but unexpressed

8. C

In this sentence we find a description of two contradictory characteristics which exist in the same group of people. On the one hand, they are brutal; on the other, they are heroic. Such an occurrence is termed a paradox and therefore (C) *paradoxical* is the answer. Choices (A), (D), and (E) are wrong; it is *unfortunate, distressing*, and *appalling* that they are brutal—but not that they are heroic.

paradoxical: opposed to common sense but nonetheless true

explicable: able to be explained

Jellyfish Passage

9.   A

Since it's clear that a jellyfish couldn't have any feelings about its encounter with humans, the author is apparently using this image to make the reader smile (A). (Even if you don't think it's funny, you should note that this is the author's intent.)

The author doesn't ask us to feel *sympathy* for either the jellyfish or humans (B), and doesn't discuss whether or not humans are *afraid* of jellyfish (C). Though the author does discuss the danger of jellyfish (D), the quote in question doesn't accomplish that purpose. The passage never discusses how humans or jellyfish *react* to these encounters (E).

10. B

The third and fourth sentences contain the key here. You learn there that the relatively common encounters are not surprising because jellyfish "live in every ocean in the world" (B).

(A), (C), (D), and (E) are all details from the passage, but none of them helps to explain why encounters are so common.

Dodger Stadium Passage

11. E

The author of Passage 2 is making the point that all kinds of different events take place at Dodger stadium, and the Papal Mass at Dodger Stadium is one example of a non-baseball event that occurred there (E).

The *world-wide popularity* of baseball (A), and the *disapproval of this event* by Major League Baseball (C) are never mentioned. (B) is too extreme—you don't know that *religious events* occur more often than sporting and entertainment. (In fact, that seems pretty unlikely.) The author

also does not give an opinion about the *importance of religious events* to the Los Angeles area (D).

12. C

Author 1 talks a lot about why Dodger Stadium is a great place to see baseball, while Author 2 goes into the different kinds of events that take place there. So, Author 2 would probably make the point that Dodger Stadium is a great place to see non-baseball activities for the same reasons that it's great for baseball (C).

Author 2 doesn't indicate a *preference* among baseball fans for non-baseball events (A). Only Passage 1 mentions baseball's *attendance records*, so (B) doesn't fit. (D) goes too far, and (E) *concert goers* are never mentioned.

13. B

Both passages mention the events that people to the baseball field (B). Passage 1 mentions why people go to baseball games while Passage 2 all the non-baseball events in the stadium.

Neither author *contrasts* Dodger Stadium to other stadiums (A). (C) is mentioned by Author 1 but not by Author 2. (D) and (E) are mentioned by Author 2 but not by Author 1.

Khyber Pass Passage

14. A

For this question, eliminate everything that *does* appear, and you'll be left with the answer. The passage answers (B) (Pakistan and Afghanistan), (C) (53 kilometers), (D) (was used in several wars), and (E) (two roads pass through today). The *origin* of the pass (A), is never mentioned.

15. E

Function questions ask you to consider what a statement adds to the author's reasoning. What claim or argument does it relate to and what does it add to the author's argument? Here, the word *snakes* implies a *twisting, turning* path, like a snake (E).

Although the Khyber Pass *connects* two points, the use of the word *snake* is not referring to that, so (A) is out. And while crossing the Khyber Pass may be *dangerous* (B), that doesn't follow from the word snake, either. (C) is the opposite of what you're looking for; the word implies that the pass is anything but direct. (D) comes from the wrong part of the passage. The short length of the Khyber Pass is mentioned earlier in the passage but this is not why the author stated that the path *snakes*.

Twain Passage

This excerpt from Mark Twain's *Life on the Mississippi* should be amusing and easy to read. All the humor comes from the same technique—using deadpan, matter-of-fact language to describe the exaggerated daydreams and jealousies of a boy's life.

The central point here is the author's envy of the engineer, and many of the questions focus on this. The author starts with his own glamorous ideas about steamboating, then spends most of the passage on the show-off engineer. The passage finishes with the author's own failure to find work as a pilot. The slightly old-fashioned style isn't hard to follow, but several questions focus on the author's figurative use of words.

16. B

The key word in the sentence is *supposed*. Of course, a justice of the peace doesn't possess unlimited power, but because of inexperience the author *supposed* he did. (B) accurately uses *naive* (inexperienced, gullible) to characterize the author's misconception. Three of the wrong choices assume that the father really did have unlimited powers and explain this in different ways—frontier justice (A) and (D); public support (C). (E) mistakenly views the boy's description of his father as an indication that the boy's childhood environment was *harsh*.

17. C

Distinction has several meanings, including those in (A), (B), (C), and (E). The key to its use here is context: In the previous sentence the author is talking about his naive ideas of his father's great power. (C) *prestige*, suggesting high status and honor, fits this context; the other three don't. (D) *desparation*, is not a meaning of *distinction* at all.

18. E

This question asks about the literal meaning of the sentence, but inference and context help, too. The sentence explains that the author wanted the job because a deck

hand was "conspicuous," or easily seen. The previous sentence stresses standing "where all my old comrades could see me," so you can deduce that the author wants to be seen and admired in what he imagines is a glamorous profession (E).

(A) and (B) invent advantages that are not mentioned, and miss the humor by suggesting common-sense economic motivations. (C) assumes that if the author could be seen by his "old comrades" in the first job, he must want *not* to be seen by them in a different job; but this is false, since he'd be "conspicuous" in the second job, too. (D) brings in an ambition—becoming a pilot—that the author doesn't develop until the end of the passage.

19. B

Again, context helps. The *Sunday-school* reference is explained in the next sentence. The engineer had been "worldly"—which is what Sunday school probably taught students not to be—and the author had been "just the reverse." In other words, the author followed his *Sunday-school teachings*, the engineer didn't, yet the engineer gets the glory. The underlying idea is that this was *unjust* (B).

(A) is never mentioned. (C) takes the Sunday-school reference literally and misses the humorous tone. (D) invents an ambition that the author never mentions; his reaction is pure envy, not frustrated ambition. (E) misconstrues the reference to the engineer as "worldly"; it means he didn't take Sunday-school seriously, not that he was unscrupulous (dishonest or crooked).

20. C

To get this question, you need to read the sentence that follows. The engineer was not generous because he sat about where "we all could see him and envy him." The implication is that great people should be generous by not showing off or (C) *flaunting* their success.

(A) refers to the Sunday-school comment, but that was about undeserved greatness, not lack of generosity. (B) and (D) interpret *generous* in the literal sense of not caring for money, but the author is using the word figuratively. (E) relates to the author's unfulfilled desire to work on a steamboat, but the engineer is not thinking about the author, he is just showing off.

21. D

The engineer does everything for the purpose of showing off. He talks the jargon of the trade to make himself look knowledgeable, or (D) sophisticated.

Reading between the lines, we realize he's not *an expert* (A), and doesn't care about knowledge for its own sake (B). His (C) *ignorance on other subjects* is not mentioned; in fact, he has a working knowledge of St. Louis. (E) takes literally the phrase about how the engineer "forgot common people could not understand"—he couldn't communicate effectively. But the author says the engineer talked "as if" he forgot common people. In other words he didn't fail to communicate, he chose not to, to impress others.

22. E

The first four choices are all common meanings of *consideration,* but the context makes it clear that the figurative use in (E) is meant. The boys had *consideration* because they knew something about St. Louis, but their glory is over because the engineer knows much more. Prestige, respect, or (E) reputation supplies the meaning that fits. Boys are not likely to have the qualities of generosity, deliberation, contemplation, or unselfishness as a result of knowing a little about St. Louis.

23. A

The context makes it clear that the engineer had, or at least seemed to have, much more familiarity with St. Louis than the other boys with their "vague knowledge"; their "glory" is ended because he can talk rings around them about St. Louis (A).

There's no indication that (B) St. Louis has changed, or that the boys had been lying—their knowledge was "vague," not false (D). Reading between the lines, it's clear that travel to St. Louis was still rare enough to seem enviable (E). As for choice (C), the passage implies just the opposite.

24. A

With his "hair oil . . . showy brass watch chain, [and] leather belt," the engineer was obviously out to impress (A). The next sentence confirms that, telling us "no girl could withstand his charms."

The author never says the young man's dress is *typical* (B). (C) and (E) are both wrong; the emphasis here is on the engineer's charms, not the author's wardrobe or fash-

ion ideas. (D) won't work because the engineer's behavior is as showy and superficial as his clothes.

25. D

As often in these questions, wrong choices give flatfooted, literal interpretations where the author is being humorous. (A) misunderstands the reference to Providence—the author is criticizing *providence,* not thanking it, because it has spared an "undeserving reptile," the engineer. So the author feels resentment, or (D) *outrage,* because the engineer's good luck seems undeserved.

Choice (B) sounds believable at first, but the passage doesn't emphasize the lucky escape—it focuses on people's sense that the engineer got better than he deserved. (C) and (E) are never mentioned.

26. C

The passage focuses on the author's ambition to work on a steamboat and his envy of the engineer. This makes (C) and (D) the strongest choices, so you need to decide between them. Looking at (D), the passage certainly emphasizes the engineer's *boastfulness,* but only within the framework of the author's dreams and ambitions (paragraphs 1 and 5) and the author's reactions to the engineer. So (C) describes the whole passage whereas (D) describes only the long central paragraphs. In a major purpose/major focus question, the answer that sums up the whole passage will be correct.

The (A) *life* of the town is barely suggested. (B) is wrong because the passage's events don't end in *success*—although in reality, Mark Twain did go on to become a pilot. The author's (E) *conflict with his parents* is mentioned only briefly, toward the end of paragraph four.

27. E

The last paragraph discusses the author's failed attempts to become a pilot, and his daydreams that he will still become one, so (E) works best. Mates and clerks are mentioned as ignoring the author, but he never considers becoming either a (A) *mate or a clerk, looking for some other job* (B), *giving up his aim of being a pilot* (C), or *asking his parents' forgiveness* (D).

SECTION THREE

Shakespeare Passages

This paired passages present two opposing arguments on a single subject, the subject here being "Who Really Wrote Shakespeare's Plays?" The author of the first passage maintains that Francis Bacon actually wrote the plays, basing that conclusion on the assertion that Shakespeare didn't have the education and social experience necessary to create such sophisticated plays. The author of the second passage takes issue with that, claiming that Shakespeare's genius grew out of a deep understanding of human nature rather than any wide learning or arcane knowledge.

1. B

A Vocabulary-in-Context question. Here we're asked the definition of the word *entertain* in line 2, where it is used in the phrase "entertain some doubt." Well, when you entertain doubt, or entertain an idea, you are holding it in your head. You are harboring it, in the sense of to harbor as "to be host to." So Choice (B) is correct.

The other choices are all acceptable dictionary definitions of the verb *entertain,* but none fits the context as well as choice (B) does. (A) amuse is a common synonym for *entertain,* but how does one amuse doubt? (C) occupy and (E) engage are closer, but they don't fit the sentence either. One's *mind* is occupied or engaged, but the doubt itself is not occupied or engaged. Meanwhile, (D) cherish adds a sense of valuing the entertained thing, as if it were something desirable.

2. D

The author claims that the person who actually wrote the plays must have had "intimate knowledge of life within royal courts and palaces," but that Shakespeare was just a commoner, without that kind of "firsthand experience" of the aristocracy. He wants to cast doubt on Shakespeare's familiarity with the life of [aristocrats], or Choice (D).

Shakespeare's ability to (A) write poetically and his (C) ability to support himself as a playwright never come up in Passage 1. The knowledge of foreign places mentioned in (B) does come up, but being a commoner is not necessarily related to Shakespeare's apparent lack of travel. Choice (E) is the closest wrong choice, since the aristocracy was the government in Elizabethan England, but the issue is his knowledge of all aspects of aristocratic life.

3. E

Two Shakespearean plays—*Coriolanus* and *Love's Labour's Lost*—are mentioned in lines 28–31 in connection with the allegedly specialized knowledge they contain. They support the point that the educated aristocrat Bacon was a more likely author than was the undereducated commoner Shakespeare. So (E) answers the question best.

Choice (A) is a clever wrong choice, but it's too extreme. The author's not trying to prove that *only* Bacon could have written these plays, just that Bacon was far more likely than Shakespeare to have written them. The deep understanding of human nature mentioned in (B) is something brought up in Passage 2, not Passage 1. The author is not comparing the two plays to works written by Bacon, as (C) claims. And (D) is wrong since nothing about society is mentioned with regard to *Coriolanus.* Also, it's not the broad spectrum of society the author alludes to with regard to *Love's Labour's Lost,* but rather the knowledge of just the upper range of society.

4. A

It's clear that Ms. Bacon is looking down on actors, of which Shakespeare was one, regarding them with the disdain expressed in correct choice (A).

She's not resentful of how the characters are portrayed, choice (B), since she's talking about the characters themselves and what they tell us about real-life actors. Given her opinion of actors, she certainly doesn't regret that [their] conditions weren't better, choice (C). (D) is closer, but it's a distortion. She never doubts that anyone could create such characters; she doubts that the author of the plays could be like such a character. And finally, in (E), there's no evidence in the quote that Ms. Bacon thinks the actors are inept at their art, just that they are vulgar and lowly persons.

5. B

This question sends you back to paragraph 4 of Passage 1, where Bacon's preference for anonymity is explained. The author claims that, because the plays were "controversial," Bacon felt that associating himself with them would have been "politically and personally damaging." So he wished to protect himself from the effects of controversy, (B).

(A) is wrong, since Bacon did publish a lot of writing under his own name. (C) is plausible, but it's not the reason given in paragraph 4 or anywhere else in the first passage.

(D) tries to confuse us by introducing the subject of lowly actors from the preceding paragraph. And (E) is a fabrication since we know that Bacon was already famous from his other writings.

6. C

This question takes us to the first paragraph of Passage 2, where the emphasis is on language ability. The author doubts that Bacon, a writer primarily of academic Latin, would have had the ability to produce the exalted English in which the plays were written. That makes (C) the best answer.

(A) is a distortion. Just because Bacon wrote most of his own work in another language doesn't mean that he was unfamiliar with English. (B)'s emphasis on the difficult switch from scientific writing to playwriting is close, but language rather than the type of writing is the focus. There's no reason to surmise that the author doubts Bacon's ability to cooperate on a committee, choice (D). Finally, (E) is wrong because there is no evidence in the first paragraph that the author has doubts about Bacon's ability to produce that amount of work.

7. D

Back to Vocabulary-in-Context. This question asks about *premier* as it is used in the phrase "premier stylist in the English language." The author definitely wants to indicate the sublime language of the plays here, so *premier* is being used in the sense of "of the first rank," or, as choice (D) has it, greatest. (A), (C), and (E) all play on the sense of *premier* as "first in sequence," (*inaugural*, by the way, means "marking the commencement or beginning") but the author is not referring here to when Shakespeare wrote. He's writing about how well Shakespeare wrote. On the other hand, (B) *influential* misses on two counts—first, it's not a definition of *premier* in any context, and second, the issue of influence on other writers is not brought up here.

8. B

The next Vocabulary-in-Context question concerns the adjective *encyclopedic* in line 77, where it's used to modify the noun "knowledge." The author says that Shakespeare's genius was one of common sense and perceptive intuition, not encyclopedic knowledge, which is related to great book-learning. So the knowledge described as *encyclopedic* is wide-ranging and in-depth—*comprehensive*, (B).

(A) technical is close to the sense of the context, but it's not a synonym of *encyclopedic,* so it really won't work here. (C) won't work either, since abridged (meaning "condensed") cannot describe the kind of exhaustive knowledge the author is describing here. And while it may take discipline to gain encyclopedic knowledge, *encyclopedic* itself cannot be defined as disciplined, so cut (D). Finally, (E) specialized isn't quite right, since it implies a narrowness of focus.

9. E

The reference to *Shakespeare's status as a landowner* comes in the third paragraph of Passage 2, where it is brought up to show that Shakespeare would have been "knowledgeable about legal matters related to . . . real estate." That makes (E) the best answer, "legal matters" being equivalent to the law.

(A) is interesting, since the author does say that owning land was quite an accomplishment for a playwright, but it has nothing to do with his knowledge of the law. (B) is off, since owning land doesn't make one automatically friendly with the highborn set. (C) is wrong, because Shakespeare's financial state is just a side issue; it's not the point of bringing up Shakespeare's landowning status. And (D) doesn't fit, since no one doubts that Shakespeare was a commoner.

10. A

This question directs us to lines 101–104, where the author claims that *literary genius* "can flower in any socioeconomic bracket." That implies that genius has little to do with a person's social and financial position—or, as correct choice (A) has it—genius doesn't depend on a writer's external circumstances.

(B) fails by bringing in the notion of comprehension of human nature from elsewhere in the passage. (C) is a common cliché, but there's no evidence here that the author felt that Shakespeare's genius was enhanced by poverty. In fact, this author implies that Shakespeare wasn't even all that poor. (D) may be a true statement, but recognition of genius isn't really under discussion here; it's the simple existence of genius. And (E) is a distortion; the author claims that at least one kind of genius does not stem from book-learning and academic training, but that doesn't mean that those things would stifle *literary genius.*

11. C

Go back to the fourth paragraph of Passage 1, where our first author claims that Bacon may have "hired a lowly actor" like Shakespeare to put his name to the plays and take the heat of controversy. How would our second author respond to this claim? The second author, remember, writes in the concluding paragraph of Passage 2 that "no elaborate theories of intrigue and secret identity are necessary to explain the accomplishment of William Shakespeare." Surely Author 2 would regard the scenario described in Passage 1 as just this kind of unnecessary theory, so (C) is the best guess for how Author 2 would react.

As for choice (A), Author 2 may or may not agree that the plays were controversial in their time, so (A) won't work. (B) gets the thrust of Author 2's argument wrong. Author 2 denigrates the notion that Bacon wrote the plays not by arguing that Bacon wasn't a great scholar, but by arguing that it didn't require a great scholar to write the plays. (D) tries to turn Author 1's argument on its head. A nice idea, perhaps, but Author 2 shows no hint of doing anything of the kind. And (E) brings up the notion of Shakespeare's social respectability, which really isn't of much concern to Author 2.

12. C

What would be Author 1's reaction to Author 2's *skepticism* that Bacon, the author of Latin treatises, could be the "premier stylist in the English language"? Well, Author 1's repeated assertions of Bacon's scholarly genius and Shakespeare's lack of education are both reflected in choice (C), which makes it a good bet as the correct answer.

(A)'s mention of the similarities between Latin and English is enough to kill this choice, since Author 1 mentions no such similarities in the passage. (B) is a true statement, perhaps, but it doesn't really address the issue. (D) is fairly nonsensical, since it would weaken Author 1's entire theory about why Bacon hired Shakespeare. Finally, (E) makes a good point, but again, there is no hint of this sentiment in Author 1's statements.

13. D

Always check back to the passage to figure out the meaning of a Vocab-in-Context word. Here, the word *observation* refers to the phrase that "Shakespeare, in short, was Shakespeare"—a jokey comment on the author's part. None of the other choices fits the content of an informal remark, so (D) is correct here.

Dream Images Passage

14. A

The dash tells us that the author is continuing a thought. So, the waves must be describing the women rowing to shore. That fits with (A) pretty well.

You might make the point that the women in the boat *need to be heard*—after all, they are talking to the author in her dreams. However, the image of the waves doesn't do much to convey this idea, so (B) is incorrect. *Discomfort* (C) doesn't fit with the word "gentle" in the passage. The women are "women in history," but we do not know that they are generally *important* (D). *Confounded* (E) means confused; this is too negatively charged for this context.

15. C

The list describes things that are "traced" "into the sand of my sleep," which the author then tries to remember when she wakes up. So, these are the ideas that come from the "women of history" (C).

These ideas become the foundations of the author's work, but the ideas themselves do not come from the *author's own artwork* (A). (B) is too literal; the *water* in the dream doesn't relate to the images that the author sees. (D) is similar to (A); these ideas may inspire a memorial by the author, but the images themselves are not the memorial. These accounts come to an artist in her dreams, so they probably cannot be described as strictly *factual* (E).

Yellow Wallpaper Passage

16. D

The word *expense* is used to mean that the narrator has given up something. In particular, she's given up her work in favor of her domestic role. (D) *sacrifice* matches that prediction.

Though the word *burden* (A) might be tempting, it doesn't necessarily indicate that something is given up in order to obtain what something else. So, it doesn't capture the full meaning of what you're looking for here. (B), (C), and (E) have to do with money; a common meaning of *expense*, but not in this context.

17. E

The last phrase *a conflict which Charlotte Perkins Gilman chronicled over 100 years ago*, implies that issues in Gilman's short story are as relevant now as they were in 1892 (E).

The author's tone is generally balanced throughout the passage, so the extremely negative tones of (A), (B), (C), and (D) are all out of place. Also, (C) and (D) make pronouncements about the future, while the text simply describes the present situation.

Compute Your Score

Don't take your scores too literally. They are intended to give you an approximate idea of your performance. There is no way to determine precisely how well you have scored for the following reasons.

- Practice test conditions do not precisely mirror real test conditions.
- Various statistical factors and formulas are taken into account on the real test.
- For each grade, the scaled score range changes from year to year.

Step 1: Figure out your raw score. Refer to your answer sheet for the total number right and the total number wrong for all three Critical Reading sections in the practice test you're scoring. (If you haven't scored your results, do that now, using the answers that follow the test.) Use the chart below to figure out your raw score. As the chart shows, your raw score is equal to the total right in the three sections minus one-fourth of the number wrong in those sections. Round the result to the nearest whole number.

PRACTICE TEST A

	Number Right	Number Wrong	Raw Score
Section One:	☐	− (.25 × ☐)	= ☐
Section Two:	☐	− (.25 × ☐)	= ☐
Section Three:	☐	− (.25 × ☐)	= ☐
Critical Reading Raw Score		=	☐ (rounded up)

PRACTICE TEST B

	Number Right	Number Wrong	Raw Score
Section One:	☐	− (.25 × ☐) =	☐
Section Two:	☐	− (.25 × ☐) =	☐
Section Three:	☐	− (.25 × ☐) =	☐
		Critical Reading Score =	☐
			(rounded up)

Step 2: Find your practice test score. Use the table below to find your practice test score based on your Critical Reading raw score.

FIND YOUR PRACTICE TEST SCORE*

Raw	Scaled	Raw	Scaled	Raw	Scaled
72	800	44	610	16	400
71	800	43	600	15	390
70	800	42	600	14	380
69	800	41	590	13	360
68	800	40	580	12	340
67	790	39	580	11	330
66	790	38	570	10	320
65	780	37	560	9	310
64	780	36	560	8	300
63	770	35	550	7	290
62	760	34	540	6	270
61	750	33	540	5	270
60	750	32	530	4	260
59	730	31	520	3	240
58	720	30	510	2	230
57	710	29	510	1	210
56	700	28	500	0	200
55	700	27	490	neg 1	200
54	690	26	480	neg 2	200
53	680	25	470	neg 3	200
52	670	24	460	neg 4	200
51	660	23	460	neg 5	200
50	650	22	450	neg 6	200
49	640	21	450	neg 7	200
48	630	20	440	neg 8	200
47	630	19	430	neg 9	200
46	620	18	420	neg 10	200
45	620	17	410		

* These numbers are close approximates.

SAT Vocabulary

SAT Root List

Knowing roots can help you in two ways. First, instead of learning one word at a time, you can learn a group of words that contain a certain root. They'll be related in meaning, so if you remember one, it will be easier to remember the others. Second, you can often decode a new vocabulary word by its root. If you can recognize a familiar root, chances are you'll get enough of an idea to answer the question.

A

❑ A, AN—not, without

amoral, atrophy, asymmetrical, anarchy, anesthetic, anonymity, anomaly

❑ AB, A—from, away, apart

abnormal, abdicate, aberration, abhor, abject, abjure, ablution, abnegate, abortive, abrogate, abscond, absolve, abstemious, abstruse, annul, avert, aversion

❑ AC, ACR—sharp, sour

acid, acerbic, exacerbate, acute, acuity, acumen, acrid, acrimony

❑ AD, A—to, toward

adhere, adjacent, adjunct, admonish, adroit, adumbrate, advent, abeyance, abet, accede, accretion, acquiesce, affluent, aggrandize, aggregate, alleviate, alliteration, allude, allure, ascribe, aspersion, aspire, assail, assonance, attest

❑ ALI, ALTR—another

alias, alienate, inalienable, altruism

❑ AM, AMI—love

amorous, amicable, amiable, amity

❑ AMBI, AMPHI—both
ambiguous, ambivalent, ambidextrous, amphibious

❑ AMBL, AMBUL—walk
amble, ambulatory, perambulator, somnambulist

❑ ANIM—mind, spirit, breath
animal, animosity, unanimous, magnanimous

❑ ANN, ENN—year
annual, annuity, superannuated, biennial, perennial

❑ ANTE, ANT—before
antecedent, antediluvian, antebellum, antepenultimate, anterior, antiquity, antiquated, anticipate

❑ ANTHROP—human
anthropology, anthropomorphic, misanthrope, philanthropy

❑ ANTI, ANT—against, opposite
antidote, antipathy, antithesis, antacid, antagonist, antonym

❑ AUD—hear
audio, audience, audition, auditory, audible

❑ AUTO—self
autobiography, autocrat, autonomous

B

❑ BELLI, BELL—war
belligerent, bellicose, antebellum, rebellion

❑ BENE, BEN—good
benevolent, benefactor, beneficent, benign

❑ BI—two
bicycle, bisect, bilateral, bilingual, biped

❑ BIBLIO—book
Bible, bibliography, bibliophile

❑ BIO—life
biography, biology, amphibious, symbiotic, macrobiotics

❑ BURS—money, purse
reimburse, disburse, bursar

C

❑ CAD, CAS, CID—happen, fall
accident, cadence, cascade, deciduous

❑ CAP, CIP—head
captain, decapitate, capitulate, precipitous, precipitate

❑ CARN—flesh
carnal, carnage, carnival, carnivorous, incarnate

❑ CAP, CAPT, CEPT, CIP—take, hold, seize
capable, capacious, recapitulate, captivate, deception, intercept, precept, inception, anticipate, emancipation, incipient, percipient

❑ CED, CESS—yield, go
cease, cessation, incessant, cede, precede, accede, recede, antecedent, intercede, secede, cession

❑ CHROM—color
chrome, chromatic, monochrome

❏ CHRON—time

chronology, chronic, anachronism

❏ CIDE—murder

suicide, homicide, regicide, patricide

❏ CIRCUM—around

circumference, circumlocution, circumnavigate, circumscribe, circumspect, circumvent

❏ CLIN, CLIV—slope

incline, declivity, proclivity

❏ CLUD, CLUS, CLAUS, CLOIS—shut, close

conclude, reclusive, claustrophobia, cloister, preclude, occlude

❏ CO, COM, CON—with, together

coeducation, coagulate, coalesce, coerce, cogent, cognate, collateral, colloquial, colloquy, commensurate, commodious, compassion, compatriot, complacent, compliant, complicity, compunction, concerto, conciliatory, concord, concur, condone

❏ COGN, GNO—know

recognize, cognition, cognizance, incognito, diagnosis, agnostic, prognosis, gnostic, ignorant

❏ CONTRA—against

controversy, incontrovertible, contravene

❏ CORP—body

corpse, corporeal, corpulence

❏ COSMO, COSM—world

cosmopolitan, cosmos, microcosm, macrocosm

❏ CRAC, CRAT—rule, power

democracy, bureaucracy, theocracy, autocrat, aristocrat, technocrat

❏ CRED—trust, believe

incredible, credulous, credence

❏ CRESC, CRET—grow

crescent, crescendo, accretion

❏ CULP—blame, fault

culprit, culpable, inculpate, exculpate

❏ CURR, CURS—run

current, concur, cursory, precursor, incursion

D

❏ DE—down, out, apart

depart, debase, debilitate, declivity, decry, deface, defamatory, defunct, delegate, demarcation, demean, demur, deplete, deplore, depravity, deprecate, deride, derivative, desist, detest, devoid

❏ DEC—ten, tenth

decade, decimal, decathlon, decimate

❏ DEMO, DEM—people

democrat, demographics, demagogue, epidemic, pandemic, endemic

❏ DI, DIURN—day

diary, diurnal, quotidian

❏ DIA—across

diagonal, diatribe, diaphanous

❏ DIC, DICT—speak

diction, interdict, predict, abdicate, indict, verdict

❑ DIS, DIF, DI—not, apart, away

disaffected, disband, disbar, disburse, discern, discordant, discredit, discursive, disheveled, disparage, disparate, dispassionate, dispirit, dissemble, disseminate, dissension, dissipate, dissonant, dissuade, distend, differentiate, diffidence, diffuse, digress, divert

❑ DOC, DOCT—teach

doctrine, docile, doctrinaire

❑ DOL—pain

condolence, doleful, dolorous, indolent

❑ DUC, DUCT—lead

seduce, induce, conduct, viaduct, induct

E

❑ EGO—self

ego, egoist, egocentric

❑ EN, EM—in, into

enter, entice, encumber, endemic, ensconce, enthrall, entreat, embellish, embezzle, embroil, empathy

❑ ERR—wander

erratic, aberration, errant

❑ EU—well, good

eulogy, euphemism, euphony, euphoria, eurythmics, euthanasia

❑ EX, E—out, out of

exit, exacerbate, excerpt, excommunicate, exculpate, execrable, exhume, exonerate, exorbitant, exorcise, expatriate, expedient, expiate, expunge, expurgate, extenuate, extort, extremity, extricate, extrinsic, exult, evoke, evict, evince, elicit, egress, egregious

F

❑ FAC, FIC, FECT, FY, FEA—make, do

factory, facility, benefactor, malefactor, fiction, fictive, beneficent, affect, confection, refectory, magnify, unify, rectify, vilify, feasible

❑ FAL, FALS—deceive

false, infallible, fallacious

❑ FERV—boil

fervent, fervid, effervescent

❑ FID—faith, trust

confident, diffidence, perfidious, fidelity

❑ FLU, FLUX—flow

fluent, flux, affluent, confluence, effluvia, superfluous

❑ FORE—before

forecast, foreboding, forestall

❑ FRAG, FRAC—break

fragment, fracture, diffract, fractious, refract

❑ FUS—pour

profuse, infusion, effusive, diffuse

G

❑ GEN—birth, class, kin

generation, congenital, homogeneous, heterogeneous, ingenious, engender, progenitor, progeny

❑ GRAD, GRESS—step

graduate, gradual, retrograde, centigrade, degrade, gradation, gradient, progress, congress, digress, transgress, ingress, egress

❑ GRAPH, GRAM—writing

biography, bibliography, epigraph, grammar, epigram

❑ GRAT—pleasing

grateful, gratitude, gratis, ingrate, congratulate, gratuitous, gratuity

❑ GRAV, GRIEV—heavy

grave, gravity, aggravate, grieve, aggrieve, grievous

❑ GREG—crowd, flock

segregate, gregarious, egregious, congregate, aggregate

H

❑ HABIT, HIBIT—have, hold

habit, inhibit, cohabit, habitat

❑ HAP—by chance

happen, haphazard, hapless, mishap

❑ HELIO, HELI—sun

heliocentric, helium, heliotrope, aphelion, perihelion

❑ HETERO—other

heterosexual, heterogeneous, heterodox

❑ HOL—whole

holocaust, catholic, holistic

❑ HOMO—same

homosexual, homogenize, homogeneous, homonym

❑ HOMO—man

homo sapiens, homicide, bonhomie

❑ HYDR—water

hydrant, hydrate, dehydration

❑ HYPER—too much, excess

hyperactive, hyperbole, hyperventilate

❑ HYPO—too little, under

hypodermic, hypothermia, hypochondria, hypothesis, hypothetical

I

❑ IN, IG, IL, IM, IR—not

incorrigible, indefatigable, indelible, indubitable, inept, inert, inexorable, insatiable, insentient, insolvent, insomnia, interminable, intractable, incessant, inextricable, infallible, infamy, innumerable, inoperable, insipid, intemperate, intrepid, inviolable, ignorant, ignominious, ignoble, illicit, illimitable, immaculate, immutable, impasse, impeccable, impecunious, impertinent, implacable, impotent, impregnable, improvident, impassioned, impervious, irregular

❑ IN, IL, IM, IR—in, on, into

infusion, ingress, innate, inquest, inscribe, insinuate, inter, illustrate, imbue, immerse, implicate, irrigate, irritate, invade, inaugurate, incandescent, incarcerate, incense, indenture, induct, ingratiate, introvert, incarnate, inception, incisive, infer

❑ INTER—between, among

intercede, intercept, interdiction, interject, interlocutor, interloper, intermediary, intermittent, interpolate, interpose, interregnum, interrogate, intersect, intervene

❑ INTRA, INTR—within
intrastate, intravenous, intramural, intrinsic

❑ IT, ITER—between, among
transit, itinerant, reiterate, transitory

J

❑ JECT, JET—throw
eject, interject, abject, trajectory, jettison

❑ JOUR—day
journal, adjourn, sojourn

❑ JUD—judge
judge, judicious, prejudice, adjudicate

❑ JUNCT, JUG—join
junction, adjunct, injunction, conjugal, subjugate

❑ JUR—swear, law
jury, abjure, adjure, conjure, perjure, jurisprudence

L

❑ LAT—side
lateral, collateral, unilateral, bilateral, quadrilateral

❑ LAV, LAU, LU—wash
lavatory, laundry, ablution, antediluvian

❏ LEG, LEC, LEX—read, speak
legible, lecture, lexicon

❏ LEV—light
elevate, levitate, levity, alleviate

❏ LIBER—free
liberty, liberal, libertarian, libertine

❏ LIG, LECT—choose, gather
eligible, elect, select

❏ LIG, LI, LY—bind
ligament, oblige, religion, liable, liaison, lien, ally

❏ LING, LANG—tongue
lingo, language, linguistics, bilingual

❏ LITER—letter
literate, alliteration, literal

❏ LITH—stone
monolith, lithograph, megalith

❏ LOQU, LOC, LOG—speech, thought
eloquent, loquacious, colloquial, colloquy, soliloquy, circumlocution, interlocutor, monologue, dialogue, eulogy, philology, neologism

❏ LUC, LUM—light
lucid, illuminate, elucidate, pellucid, translucent

❏ LUD, LUS—play
ludicrous, allude, delusion, allusion, illusory

M

☐ MACRO—great
macrocosm, macrobiotics

☐ MAG, MAJ, MAS, MAX—great
magnify, majesty, master, maximum, magnanimous, magnate, magnitude

☐ MAL—bad
malady, maladroit, malevolent, malodorous

☐ MAN—hand
manual, manuscript, emancipate, manifest

☐ MAR—sea
submarine, marine, maritime

☐ MATER, MATR—mother
maternal, matron, matrilineal

☐ MEDI—middle
intermediary, medieval, mediate

☐ MEGA—great
megaphone, megalomania, megaton, megalith

☐ MEM, MEN—remember
memory, memento, memorabilia, reminisce

☐ METER, METR, MENS—measure
meter, thermometer, perimeter, metronome, commensurate

☐ MICRO—small
microscope, microorganism, microcosm, microbe

❑ MIS—wrong, bad, hate

misunderstand, misanthrope, misapprehension, misconstrue, misnomer, mishap

❑ MIT, MISS—send

transmit, emit, missive

❑ MOLL—soft

mollify, emollient, mollusk

❑ MON, MONIT—warn

admonish, monitor, premonition

❑ MONO—one

monologue, monotonous, monogamy, monolith, monochrome

❑ MOR—custom, manner

moral, mores, morose

❑ MOR, MORT—dead

morbid, moribund, mortal, amortize

❑ MORPH—shape

amorphous, anthropomorphic, metamorphosis, morphology

❑ MOV, MOT, MOB, MOM—move

remove, motion, mobile, momentum, momentous

❑ MUT—change

mutate, mutability, immutable, commute

N

❑ NAT, NASC—born

native, nativity, natal, neonate, innate, cognate, nascent, renascent, renaissance

❑ NAU, NAV—ship, sailor
nautical, nauseous, navy, circumnavigate

❑ NEG—not, deny
negative, abnegate, renege

❑ NEO—new
neoclassical, neophyte, neologism, neonate

❑ NIHIL—none, nothing
annihilation, nihilism

❑ NOM, NYM—name
nominate, nomenclature, nominal, cognomen, misnomer, ignominious, antonym, homonym, pseudonym, synonym, anonymity

❑ NOX, NIC, NEC, NOC—harm
obnoxious, noxious, pernicious, internecine, innocuous

❑ NOV—new
novelty, innovation, novitiate

❑ NUMER—number
numeral, numerous, innumerable, enumerate

O

❑ OB—against
obstruct, obdurate, obfuscate, obnoxious, obsequious, obstinate, obstreperous, obtrusive

❑ OMNI—all
omnipresent, omnipotent, omniscient, omnivorous

❑ ONER—burden
onerous, onus, exonerate

❑ OPER—work
operate, cooperate, inoperable

P

❑ PAC—peace
pacify, pacifist, pacific

❑ PALP—feel
palpable, palpitation

❑ PAN—all
panorama, panacea, panegyric, pandemic, panoply

❑ PATER, PATR—father
paternal, paternity, patriot, compatriot, expatriate, patrimony, patricide, patrician

❑ PATH, PASS—feel, suffer
sympathy, antipathy, empathy, apathy, pathos, impassioned

❑ PEC—money
pecuniary, impecunious, peculation

❑ PED, POD—foot
pedestrian, pediment, expedient, biped, quadruped, tripod

❑ PEL, PULS—drive
compel, compelling, expel, propel, compulsion

❑ PEN—almost
peninsula, penultimate, penumbra

❑ PEND, PENS—hang

pendant, pendulous, compendium, suspense, propensity

❑ PER—through, by, for, throughout

perambulator, percipient, perfunctory, permeable, perspicacious, pertinacious, perturbation, perusal, perennial, peregrinate

❑ PER—against, destruction

perfidious, pernicious, perjure

❑ PERI—around

perimeter, periphery, perihelion, peripatetic

❑ PET—seek, go toward

petition, impetus, impetuous, petulant, centripetal

❑ PHIL—love

philosopher, philanderer, philanthropy, bibliophile, philology

❑ PHOB—fear

phobia, claustrophobia, xenophobia

❑ PHON—sound

phonograph, megaphone, euphony, phonetics, phonics

❑ PLAC—calm, please

placate, implacable, placid, complacent

❑ PON, POS—put, place

postpone, proponent, exponent, preposition, posit, interpose, juxtaposition, depose

❑ PORT—carry

portable, deportment, rapport

❑ POT—drink

potion, potable

❑ POT—power

potential, potent, impotent, potentate, omnipotence

❑ PRE—before

precede, precipitate, preclude, precocious, precursor, predilection, predisposition, preponderance, prepossessing, presage, prescient, prejudice, predict, premonition, preposition

❑ PRIM, PRI—first

prime, primary, primal, primeval, primordial, pristine

❑ PRO—ahead, forth

proceed, proclivity, procrastinator, profane, profuse, progenitor, progeny, prognosis, prologue, promontory, propel, proponent, propose, proscribe, protestation, provoke

❑ PROTO—first

prototype, protagonist, protocol

❑ PROX, PROP—near

approximate, propinquity, proximity

❑ PSEUDO—false

pseudoscientific, pseudonym

❑ PYR—fire

pyre, pyrotechnics, pyromania

Q

❑ QUAD, QUAR, QUAT—four

quadrilateral, quadrant, quadruped, quarter, quarantine, quaternary

❑ QUES, QUER, QUIS, QUIR—question

quest, inquest, query, querulous, inquisitive, inquiry

❑ QUIE—quiet

disquiet, acquiesce, quiescent, requiem

❑ QUINT, QUIN—five

quintuplets, quintessence

R

❑ RADI, RAMI—branch

radius, radiate, radiant, eradicate, ramification

❑ RECT, REG—straight, rule

rectangle, rectitude, rectify, regular

❑ REG—king, rule

regal, regent, interregnum

❑ RETRO—backward

retrospective, retroactive, retrograde

❑ RID, RIS—laugh

ridiculous, deride, derision

❑ ROG—ask

interrogate, derogatory, abrogate, arrogate, arrogant

❑ RUD—rough, crude

rude, erudite, rudimentary

❑ RUPT—break

disrupt, interrupt, rupture

S

- ❏ SACR, SANCT—holy

  sacred, sacrilege, consecrate, sanctify, sanction, sacrosanct

- ❏ SCRIB, SCRIPT, SCRIV—write

  scribe, ascribe, circumscribe, inscribe, proscribe, script, manuscript, scrivener

- ❏ SE—apart, away

  separate, segregate, secede, sedition

- ❏ SEC, SECT, SEG—cut

  sector, dissect, bisect, intersect, segment, secant

- ❏ SED, SID—sit

  sedate, sedentary, supersede, reside, residence, assiduous, insidious

- ❏ SEM—seed, sow

  seminar, seminal, disseminate

- ❏ SEN—old

  senior, senile, senescent

- ❏ SENT, SENS—feel, think

  sentiment, nonsense, assent, sentient, consensus, sensual

- ❏ SEQU, SECU—follow

  sequence, sequel, subsequent, obsequious, obsequy, non sequitur, consecutive

- ❏ SIM, SEM—similar, same

  similar, semblance, dissemble, verisimilitude

- ❏ SIGN—mark, sign

  signal, designation, assignation

❑ SIN—curve

sine curve, sinuous, insinuate

❑ SOL—sun

solar, parasol, solarium, solstice

❑ SOL—alone

solo, solitude, soliloquy, solipsism

❑ SOMN—sleep

insomnia, somnolent, somnambulist

❑ SON—sound

sonic, consonance, dissonance, assonance, sonorous, resonate

❑ SOPH—wisdom

philosopher, sophistry, sophisticated, sophomoric

❑ SPEC, SPIC—see, look

spectator, circumspect, retrospective, perspective, perspicacious

❑ SPER—hope

prosper, prosperous, despair, desperate

❑ SPERS, SPAR—scatter

disperse, sparse, aspersion, disparate

❑ SPIR—breathe

respire, inspire, spiritual, aspire, transpire

❑ STRICT, STRING—bind

strict, stricture, constrict, stringent, astringent

❑ STRUCT, STRU—build

structure, construe, obstruct

❑ SUB—under

subconscious, subjugate, subliminal, subpoena, subsequent, subterranean, subvert

❑ SUMM—highest

summit, summary, consummate

❑ SUPER, SUR—above

supervise, supercilious, supersede, superannuated, superfluous, insurmountable, surfeit

❑ SURGE, SURRECT—rise

surge, resurgent, insurgent, insurrection

❑ SYN, SYM—together

synthesis, sympathy, synonym, syncopation, synopsis, symposium, symbiosis

T

❑ TACIT, TIC—silent

tacit, taciturn, reticent

❑ TACT, TAG, TANG—touch

tact, tactile, contagious, tangent, tangential, tangible

❑ TEN, TIN, TAIN—hold, twist

detention, tenable, tenacious, pertinacious, retinue, retain

❑ TEND, TENS, TENT—stretch

intend, distend, tension, tensile, ostensible, contentious

❑ TERM—end

terminal, terminus, terminate, interminable

❑ TERR—earth, land
terrain, terrestrial, extraterrestrial, subterranean

❑ TEST—witness
testify, attest, testimonial, testament, detest, protestation

❑ THE—god
atheist, theology, apotheosis, theocracy

❑ THERM—heat
thermometer, thermal, thermonuclear, hypothermia

❑ TIM—fear, frightened
timid, intimidate, timorous

❑ TOP—place
topic, topography, utopia

❑ TORT—twist
distort, extort, tortuous

❑ TORP—stiff, numb
torpedo, torpid, torpor

❑ TOX—poison
toxic, toxin, intoxication

❑ TRACT—draw
tractor, intractable, protract

❑ TRANS—across, over, through, beyond
transport, transgress, transient, transitory, translucent, transmutation

❑ TREM, TREP—shake
tremble, tremor, tremulous, trepidation, intrepid

❑ TURB—shake

disturb, turbulent, perturbation

U

❑ UMBR—shadow

umbrella, umbrage, adumbrate, penumbra

❑ UNI, UN—one

unify, unilateral, unanimous

❑ URB—city

urban, suburban, urbane

V

❑ VAC—empty

vacant, evacuate, vacuous

❑ VAL, VAIL—value, strength

valid, valor, ambivalent, convalescence, avail, prevail, countervail

❑ VEN, VENT—come

convene, contravene, intervene, venue, convention, circumvent, advent, adventitious

❑ VER—true

verify, verity, verisimilitude, veracious, aver, verdict

❑ VERB—word

verbal, verbose, verbiage, verbatim

❑ VERT, VERS—turn

avert, convert, revert, incontrovertible, divert, subvert, versatile, aversion

❑ VICT, VINC—conquer

victory, conviction, evict, evince, invincible

❑ VID, VIS—see

evident, vision, visage, supervise

❑ VIL—base, mean

vile, vilify, revile

❑ VIV, VIT—life

vivid, vital, convivial, vivacious

❑ VOC, VOK, VOW—call, voice

vocal, equivocate, vociferous, convoke, evoke, invoke, avow

❑ VOL—wish

voluntary, malevolent, benevolent, volition

❑ VOLV, VOLUT—turn, roll

revolve, evolve, convoluted

❑ VOR—eat

devour, carnivore, omnivorous, voracious

SAT Word List

This Word List can boost your knowledge of SAT-level words, and that can help you get more questions right. No one can predict exactly which words will show up on your SAT test. But there are certain words that the test makers favor. The more of these you know, the better.

The best way to improve your vocabulary is to read. Choose challenging, college-level material. If you are concerned mainly about honing your knowledge of SAT words, memorizing the words on the following list can help. Use flashcards. Learn words in groups. And think of hooks that lodge new words in your mind.

ABANDON

noun (uh <u>baan</u> duhn)

total lack of inhibition

With her strict parents out of town, Kelly danced all night with *abandon*.

ABATE

verb (uh <u>bayt</u>)

to decrease, to reduce

My hunger *abated* when I saw how filthy the chef's hands were.

ABET

verb (uh <u>beht</u>)

to aid; to act as an accomplice

While Derwin robbed the bank, Marvin *abetted* his friend by pulling up the getaway car.

ABJURE

verb (aab <u>joor</u>)

to renounce under oath; to abandon forever; to abstain from

After having been devout for most of his life, he suddenly *abjured* his beliefs, much to his family's disappointment.

ABNEGATE

verb (<u>aab</u> nih gayt)

to give up; to deny to oneself

After his retirement, the former police commissioner found it difficult to *abnegate* authority.

ABORTIVE

adj (uh <u>bohr</u> tihv)

ending without results

Her *abortive* attempt to swim the full five miles left her frustrated.

ABROGATE

verb (<u>aab</u> ruh gayt)

to annul; to abolish by authoritative action

The president's job is to *abrogate* any law that fosters inequality among citizens.

ABSCOND

verb (aab <u>skahnd</u>)

to leave quickly in secret

The criminal *absconded* during the night with all of his mother's money.

ABSTEMIOUS

adj (aab <u>stee</u> mee uhs)

done sparingly; consuming in moderation

The spa served no sugar or wheat, but the clients found the retreat so calm that they didn't mind the *abstemious* rules.

ACCEDE

verb (aak <u>seed</u>)

to express approval, to agree to

Once the mayor heard the reasonable request, she happily *acceded* to the proposal.

ACCLIVITY

noun (uh <u>klihv</u> ih tee)

an incline or upward slope, the ascending side of a hill

We were so tired from hiking that by the time we reached the *acclivity*, it looked more like a mountain than a hill.

ACCRETION

noun (uh <u>kree</u> shuhn)

a growth in size, an increase in amount

The committee's strong fund-raising efforts resulted in an *accretion* in scholarship money.

ACME

noun (<u>aak</u> mee)

the highest level or degree attainable

Just when he reached the *acme* of his power, the dictator was overthrown.

ACTUATE

verb (<u>aak</u> choo ayt)

to put into motion, to activate; to motivate or influence to activity

The leaders rousing speech *actuated* the crowd into a peaceful protest.

ACUITY

noun (uh <u>kyoo</u> ih tee)

sharp vision or perception characterized by the ability to resolve fine detail

With unusual *acuity*, she was able to determine that the masterpiece was a fake.

ACUMEN

noun (<u>aak</u> yuh muhn) (uh <u>kyoo</u> muhn)

sharpness of insight, mind, and understanding; shrewd judgment

The investor's financial *acumen* helped him to select high-yield stocks.

ADAMANT

adj (<u>aad</u> uh muhnt) (<u>aad</u> uh mihnt)

stubbornly unyielding

She was *adamant* about leaving the restaurant after the waiter was rude.

ADEPT

adj (uh <u>dehpt</u>)

extremely skilled

She is *adept* at computing math problems in her head.

ADJUDICATE

verb (uh jood ih kayt)

to hear and settle a matter; to act as a judge

The principal *adjudicated* the disagreement between two students.

ADJURE

verb (uh joor)

to appeal to

The criminal *adjured* to the court for mercy.

ADMONISH

verb (aad mahn ihsh)

to caution or warn gently in order to correct something

My mother *admonished* me about my poor grades.

ADROIT

adj (uh droyt)

skillful; accomplished; highly competent

The *adroit* athlete completed even the most difficult obstacle course with ease.

ADULATION

noun (aaj juh lay shuhn)

excessive flattery or admiration

The *adulation* she showed her professor seemed insincere; I suspected she really wanted a better grade.

ADUMBRATE

verb (aad uhm brayt) (uh duhm brayt)

to give a hint or indication of something to come

Her constant complaining about the job *adumbrated* her intent to leave.

AERIE

noun (ayr ee) (eer ee)

a nest built high in the air; an elevated, often secluded, dwelling

Perched high among the trees, the eagle's *aerie* was filled with eggs.

AFFECTED

adj (uh <u>fehk</u> tihd)

phony, artificial

The *affected* hairdresser spouted French phrases, though she had never been to France.

AGGREGATE

noun (<u>aa</u> grih giht)

a collective mass, the sum total

An *aggregate* of panic-stricken customers mobbed the bank, demanding their life savings.

ALGORITHM

noun (<u>aal</u> guh rith uhm)

an established procedure for solving a problem or equation

The accountant uses a series of *algorithms* to determine the appropriate tax bracket.

ALIMENTARY

adj (aal uh <u>mehn</u> tuh ree) (aal uh <u>mehn</u> tree)

pertaining to food, nutrition, or digestion

After a particularly good meal, Sherlock turned to his companion and exclaimed, "I feel quite good, very well fed. It was *alimentary* my dear Watson."

ALLAY

verb (uh <u>lay</u>)

to lessen, ease, reduce in intensity

Trying to *allay* their fears, the nurse sat with them all night.

AMITY

noun (<u>aa</u> mih tee)

friendship, good will

Correspondence over the years contributed to a lasting *amity* between the women.

AMORPHOUS

adj (<u>ay</u> <u>mohr</u> fuhs)

having no definite form

The Blob featured an *amorphous* creature that was constantly changing shape.

ANIMUS

noun (<u>aan</u> uh muhs)

a feeling of animosity or ill will

Though her teacher had failed her, she displayed no *animus* toward him.

ANODYNE

noun (<u>aan</u> uh dyen)

a source of comfort; a medicine that relieves pain

The sound of classical music is usually just the *anodyne* I need after a tough day at work.

ANOMALY

noun (uh <u>nahm</u> uh lee)

a deviation from the common rule, something that is difficult to classify

Among the top-ten albums of the year was one *anomaly*—a compilation of polka classics.

ANTHROPOMORPHIC

adj (aan thruh poh <u>mohr</u> fihk)

suggesting human characteristics for animals and inanimate things

Many children's stories feature *anthropomorphic* animals such as talking wolves and pigs.

ANTIQUATED

adj (<u>aan</u> tih kway tihd)

too old to be fashionable or useful

Next to her coworker's brand-new model, Marisa's computer looked *antiquated*.

APHORISM

noun (<u>aa</u> fuhr ihz uhm)

a short statement of a principle

The country doctor was given to such *aphorisms* as "Still waters run deep."

APLOMB

noun (uh <u>plahm</u>) (uh <u>pluhm</u>)

self-confident assurance; poise

For such a young dancer, she had great *aplomb*, making her perfect to play the young princess.

APOSTATE

noun (uh <u>pahs</u> tayt)

one who renounces a religious faith

So that he could divorce his wife, the king scoffed at the church doctrines and declared himself an *apostate*.

APPOSITE

adj (<u>aap</u> puh ziht)

strikingly appropriate or well adapted

The lawyer presented an *apposite* argument upon cross-examining the star witness.

APPRISE

verb (uh <u>priez</u>)

to give notice to, inform

"Thanks for *apprising* me that the test time has been changed," said Emanuel.

APPROPRIATE

verb (uh <u>proh</u> pree ayt)

to assign to a particular purpose, allocate

The fund's manager *appropriated* funds for the clean-up effort.

ARABLE

adj (<u>aa</u> ruh buhl)

suitable for cultivation

The overpopulated country desperately needed more *arable* land.

ARCANE

adj (ahr <u>kayn</u>)

secret, obscure; known only to a few

The *arcane* rituals of the sect were passed down through many generations.

ARCHIPELAGO

noun (ahr kuh <u>pehl</u> uh goh)

a large group of islands

Between villages in the Stockholm *archipelago*, boat taxis are the only form of transportation.

ARREARS

noun (uh <u>reerz</u>)

unpaid, overdue debts or bills; neglected obligations

After the expensive lawsuit, Dominic's accounts were in *arrears*.

ARROGATE

verb (<u>aa</u> ruh gayt)

to claim without justification; to claim for oneself without right

Lynn watched in astonishment as her boss *arrogated* the credit for her brilliant work on the project.

ASKANCE

adv (uh <u>skaans</u>)

with disapproval; with a skeptical sideways glance

She looked *askance* at her son's failing report card as he mumbled that he had done all the schoolwork.

ASSENT

verb (uh <u>sehnt</u>)

to agree, as to a proposal

After careful deliberation, the CEO *assented* to the proposed merger.

ATAVISTIC

adj (aat uh <u>vihs</u> tik)

characteristic of a former era, ancient

After spending three weeks on a desert island, Roger became a survivalist with *atavistic* skills that helped him endure.

AUTOCRAT

noun (<u>aw</u> toh kraat)

a dictator

Mussolini has been described as an *autocrat* who tolerated no opposition.

AVER

verb (uh <u>vuhr</u>)

to declare to be true, to affirm

"Yes, he was holding a gun," the witness *averred*.

AVUNCULAR

adj (ah <u>vuhng</u> kyuh luhr)

like an uncle in behavior, especially in kindness and warmth

The coach's *avuncular* style made him well-liked.

AWRY

adv (uh <u>rie</u>)

crooked, askew, amiss

Something must have gone *awry* in the computer system because some of my files are missing.

BALK

verb (bawk)

to stop short and refuse to go on

When the horse *balked* at jumping over the high fence, the rider was thrown off.

BALLAST

noun (<u>baal</u> uhst)

a structure that helps to stabilize or steady

Communication and honesty are the true *ballasts* of a good relationship.

BEATIFIC

adj (bee uh <u>tihf</u> ihk)

displaying calmness and joy, relating to a state of celestial happiness

After spending three months in India, she had a *beatific* peace about her.

BECALM

verb (bih <u>kahm</u>)

to stop the progress of, to soothe

The warm air *becalmed* the choppy waves.

BECLOUD

verb (bih <u>klowd</u>)

to make less visible, obscure, or blur

Her ambivalence about the long commute *beclouded* her enthusiasm about the job.

BEDRAGGLE

adj (bih <u>draag</u> uhld)

soiled, wet and limp; dilapidated

The child's *bedraggled* blanket needed a good cleaning.

BEGET

verb (bih <u>geht</u>)

to produce, especially as an effect or outgrowth; to bring about

The mayor believed that finding petty offenders would help reduce serious crime because, he argued, small crimes *beget* big crimes.

BEHEMOTH

noun (buh <u>hee</u> muhth)

something of monstrous size or power; huge creature

The budget became such a *behemoth* that observers believed the film would never make a profit.

BENEFICENT

adj (buh <u>nehf</u> ih sent)

pertaining to an act of kindness

The *beneficent* man donated the money anonymously.

BERATE

verb (bih <u>rayt</u>)

to scold harshly

When my manager found out I had handled the situation so insensitively, he *berated* me.

BILIOUS

adj (<u>bihl</u> yuhs)

ill-tempered, sickly, ailing

The party ended early when the *bilious* 5-year-old tried to run off with the birthday girl's presents.

BLASPHEMOUS

adj (<u>blaas</u> fuh muhs)

cursing, profane; extremely irreverent

The politician's offhanded comments seemed *blasphemous*, given the context of the orderly meeting.

BLATANT

adj (<u>blay</u> tnt)

completely obvious and conspicuous, especially in an offensive, crass manner

Such *blatant* advertising within the bounds of the school drew protest from parents.

BLITHELY

adv (<u>blieth</u> lee)

merrily, lightheartedly cheerful; without appropriate thought

Wanting to redecorate the office, she *blithely* assumed her co-workers wouldn't mind and moved the furniture in the space.

BOMBASTIC

adj (bahm <u>baast</u> ihk)

high-sounding but meaningless; ostentatiously lofty in style

Mussolini's speeches were mostly *bombastic*; his outrageous claims had no basis in fact.

BOVINE

adj (<u>boh</u> vien)

relating to cows; having qualities characteristic of a cow, such as sluggishness or dullness

His *bovine* demeanor did nothing to engage me.

BRAGGART

noun (<u>braag</u> uhrt)

a person who brags or boasts in a loud and empty manner

Usually the biggest *braggart* at the company party, Susan's boss was unusually quiet at this year's event.

BROACH

verb (brohch)

to mention or suggest for the first time

Sandy wanted to go to college away from home, but he didn't know how to *broach* the topic with his parents.

BUCOLIC

adj (byoo <u>kah</u> lihk)

pastoral, rural

My aunt likes the hustle and bustle of the city, but my uncle prefers a more *bucolic* setting.

BURNISH

verb (<u>buhr</u> nihsh)

to polish; to make smooth and bright

Mr. Frumpkin loved to stand in the sun and *burnish* his luxury car.

BURSAR

noun (<u>buhr</u> suhr) (<u>buhr</u> sahr)

a treasurer or keeper of funds

The *bursar* of the school was in charge of allocating all scholarship funds.

CACHE

noun (caash)

a hiding place; stockpile

It's good to have a *cache* where you can stash your cash.

CACOPHONY

noun (kuh <u>kah</u> fuh nee)

a jarring, unpleasant noise

As I walked into the open-air market after my nap, a *cacophony* of sounds surrounded me.

CALUMNY

noun (<u>kaa</u> luhm nee)

a false and malicious accusation; misrepresentation

The unscrupulous politician used *calumny* to bring down his opponent in the senatorial race.

CANTANKEROUS

adj (kaan <u>taang</u> kuhr uhs)

having a difficult, uncooperative, or stubborn disposition

The most outwardly *cantankerous* man in the nursing home was surprisingly sweet and loving with his grandchildren.

CAPTIOUS

adj (<u>kaap</u> shuhs)

marked by the tendency to point out trivial faults; intended to confuse in an argument

I resent the way he asked that *captious* question.

CATACLYSMIC

adj (<u>kaat</u> uh <u>klihz</u> mihk)

severely destructive

By all appearances, the storm seemed *cataclysmic*, though it lasted only a short while.

CATALYST

noun (<u>kaat</u> uhl ihst)

something that provokes or speeds up significant change, especially without being affected by the consequences

Technology has been a *catalyst* for the expansion of alternative education, such as home schooling and online courses.

CAUCUS

noun (<u>kaw</u> kuhs)

a closed committee within a political party; a private committee meeting

The president met with the delegated *caucus* to discuss the national crisis.

CAUSTIC

adj (<u>kah</u> stihk)

biting, sarcastic

Writer Dorothy Parker gained her reputation for *caustic* wit, and her tombstone is inscribed with a fittingly clever "Excuse my dust."

CEDE

verb (seed)

to surrender possession of something

Argentina *ceded* the Falkland Islands to Britain after a brief war.

CELERITY

noun (seh <u>leh</u> rih tee)

speed, haste

The celebrity ran past his fans with great *celerity*.

CENSORIOUS

adj (sehn <u>sohr</u> ee uhs)

critical; tending to blame and condemn

Closed-minded people tend to be *censorious* of others.

CERTITUDE

noun (<u>suhr</u> tih tood)

assurance, freedom from doubt

The witness' *certitude* about the night in question had a big impact on the jury.

CESSATION

noun (seh <u>say</u> shuhn)

a temporary or complete halt

The cessation of hostilities ensured that soldiers were able to spend the holidays with their families.

CHARY

adj (<u>chahr</u> ee)

watchful, cautious; extremely shy

Mindful of the fate of the Titanic, the captain was *chary* of navigating the iceberg-filled sea.

CHIMERICAL

adj (kie <u>mehr</u> ih kuhl) (kie <u>meer</u> ih kuhl)

fanciful; imaginary, impossible

The inventor's plans seemed *chimerical* to the conservative businessman from whom he was asking for financial support.

CIRCUITOUS

adj (suhr <u>kyoo</u> ih tuhs)

indirect, roundabout

The venue was only a short walk from the train station, but a roadblock meant I had to take a *circuitous* route.

CIRCUMVENT

verb (suhr kuhm <u>vehnt</u>)

to go around; avoid

Laura was able to *circumvent* the hospital's regulations, slipping into her mother's room long after visiting hours were over.

CLOYING

adj (<u>kloy</u> ing)

sickly sweet; excessive

When Dave and Liz got together their *cloying* affection towards one another often made their friends ill.

COAGULATE

verb (koh <u>aag</u> yuh layt)

to clot; to cause to thicken

Hemophiliacs can bleed to death from a minor cut because their blood does not *coagulate*.

COGENT

adj (<u>koh</u> juhnt)

logically forceful; compelling, convincing

Swayed by the *cogent* argument of the defense, the jury had no choice but to acquit the defendant.

COLLOQUIAL

adj (kuh <u>loh</u> kwee uhl)

characteristic of informal speech

The book was written in a *colloquial* style so it would be user-friendlier.

COMMUTE

verb (kuh <u>myoot</u>)

to change a penalty to a less severe one

In exchange for cooperating with detectives on another case, the criminal had his charges *commuted*.

COMPLACENT

adj (kuhm <u>play</u> sihnt)

self-satisfied, smug

Alfred always shows a *complacent* smile whenever he wins the spelling bee.

COMPLIANT

adj (kuhm <u>plie</u> uhnt)

submissive, yielding

The boss was unused to an assistant who spoke her mind, but he grew to respect the fact that she wasn't *compliant*.

CONCOMITANT

adj (kuh <u>kahm</u> ih tuhnt)

existing concurrently

A double-major was going to be difficult to pull off, especially since Lucy would have to juggle two papers and two exams *concomitantly*.

CONCORD

noun (<u>kahn</u> kohrd)

agreement

The sisters are now in *concord* about the car they had to share.

CONDOLE

verb (kuhn <u>dohl</u>)

to grieve; to express sympathy

My hamster died when I was in third grade, and my friends *condoled* with me and helped bury him in the yard.

CONFLAGRATION

noun (kahn fluh <u>gray</u> shuhn)

big, destructive fire

After the *conflagration* had finally died down, the city center was nothing but a mass of blackened embers.

CONFLUENCE

noun (<u>kahn</u> floo uhns)

the act of two things flowing together; the junction or meeting place where two things meet

At the political meeting, while planning a demonstration, there was a moving *confluence* of ideas between members.

CONSANGUINEOUS

adj (kahn saang <u>gwihn</u> ee uhs)

having the same lineage or ancestry; related by blood

After having a strange feeling about our relationship for years, I found out that my best friend and I are *consanguineous*.

CONSTERNATION

noun (kahn stuhr <u>nay</u> shuhn)

an intense state of fear or dismay

One would never think that a seasoned hunter would display such *consternation* when a grizzly bear lumbered too close to camp.

CONSTITUENT

noun (kuhn <u>stih</u> choo uhnt)

component, part; citizen, voter

A machine will not function properly if one of its *constituents* is defective.

CONSTRAINT

noun (kuhn <u>straynt</u>)

something that restricts or confines within prescribed bounds

Given the *constraints* of the budget, it was impossible to accomplish my goals.

CONTEMPTUOUS

adj (kuhn <u>tehmp</u> choo uhs)

scornful; expressing contempt

The diners were intimidated by the waiter's *contemptuous* manner.

CONTENTIOUS

adj (kuhn <u>tehn</u> shuhs)

quarrelsome, disagreeable, belligerent

The *contentious* gentleman in the bar ridiculed anything anyone said.

CONTIGUOUS

adj (kuhn <u>tihg</u> yoo uhs)

sharing a boundary; neighboring

The two houses had *contiguous* yards so the families shared the landscaping expenses.

CONTINENCE

noun (<u>kahn</u> tih nihns)

self-control, self-restraint

Lucy exhibited impressive *continence* in steering clear of fattening foods, and she lost 50 pounds.

CONVALESCE

verb (kahn vuhl <u>ehs</u>)

to recover gradually from an illness

After her bout with malaria, Tatiana needed to *convalesce* for a whole month.

CONVERGENCE

noun (kuhn <u>vehr</u> juhns)

the state of separate elements joining or coming together

A *convergence* of factors led to the tragic unfolding of World War I.

COQUETTE

noun (koh <u>keht</u>)

a flirtatious woman

The librarian could turn into a *coquette* just by letting her hair down and changing the swing of her hips.

COTERIE

noun (<u>koh</u> tuh ree)

an intimate group of persons with a similar purpose

Judith invited a *coterie* of fellow stamp enthusiasts to a stamp-trading party.

COUNTERVAIL

verb (kown tuhr <u>vayl</u>)

to act or react with equal force

In order to *countervail* the financial loss the school suffered after the embezzlement, the treasurer raised the price of room and board.

COVERT

adj (koh <u>vuhrt</u>)

secretive, not openly shown

The *covert* military operation wasn't disclosed until weeks later after it was determined to be a success.

CULL

verb (kuhl)

to select, weed out

You should *cull* the words you need to study from all the flash cards.

CUMULATIVE

adj (<u>kyoom</u> yuh luh tihv)

increasing, collective

The new employee didn't mind her job at first, but the daily petty indignities had a *cumulative* demoralizing effect.

CURT

adj (kuhrt)

abrupt, short with words

The grouchy shop assistant was *curt* with one of her customers, which resulted in a reprimand from her manager.

DEARTH

noun (duhrth)

a lack, scarcity, insufficiency

The *dearth* of supplies in our city made it difficult to survive the blizzard.

DEBACLE

noun (dih <u>baa</u> kuhl)

a sudden, disastrous collapse or defeat; a total, ridiculous failure

It was hard for her to show her face in the office after the *debacle* of spilling coffee on her supervisor—three times.

DECLAIM

verb (dih <u>klaym</u>)

to speak loudly and vehemently

At Thanksgiving dinner, our grandfather always *declaims* his right, as the eldest, to sit at the head of the table.

DEFAMATORY

adj (dih <u>faam</u> uh tohr ee)

injurious to the reputation

The tabloid was sued for making *defamatory* statements about the celebrity.

DEMAGOGUE

noun (<u>deh</u> muh gahg) (<u>deh</u> muh gawg)

a leader, rabble-rouser, usually appealing to emotion or prejudice

The dictator began his political career as a *demagogue*, giving fiery speeches in town halls.

DENIZEN

noun (<u>dehn</u> ih zihn)

an inhabitant, a resident

The *denizens* of the state understandably wanted to select their own leaders.

DERIDE

verb (dih <u>ried</u>)

to laugh at contemptuously, to make fun of

As soon as Jorge heard the others *deriding* Anthony, he came to his defense.

DIFFUSE

verb (dih <u>fyooz</u>)

to spread out widely, to scatter freely, to disseminate

They turned on the fan, but all that did was *diffuse* the cigarette smoke throughout the room.

DIGRESS

verb (die <u>grehs</u>)

to turn aside, especially from the main point; to stray from the subject

The professor repeatedly *digressed* from the topic, boring his students.

DILAPIDATED

adj (dih <u>laap</u> ih dayt ihd)

in disrepair, run down

Rather than get discouraged, the architect saw great potential in the *dilapidated* house.

DILUVIAL

adj (dih <u>loo</u> vee uhl)

pertaining to a flood

After she left the water running in the house all day, it looked simply *diluvial*.

DISCOMFIT

verb (dihs <u>kuhm</u> fiht)

to disconcert, to make one lose one's composure

The class clown enjoyed *discomfiting* her classmates whenever possible.

DISCRETE

adj (dih <u>skreet</u>)

individually distinct, separate

What's nice about the CD is that each song functions as a *discrete* work and also as part of the whole compilation.

DISINGENUOUS

adj (<u>dihs</u> ihn <u>jehn</u> yoo uhs)

giving a false appearance of simple frankness; misleading

It was *disingenuous* of him to suggest that he had no idea of the requests made by his campaign contributors.

DISINTERESTED

adj (dihs <u>ihn</u> trih stihd) (dihs <u>ihn</u> tuh reh stihd)

fair-minded, unbiased
A fair trial is made possible by the selection of *disinterested* jurors.

DISPASSIONATE

adj (dihs <u>paash</u> ih niht)

unaffected by bias or strong emotions; not personally or emotionally involved in something

Ideally, photographers should be *dispassionate* observers of what goes on in the world.

DISSIDENT

adj (<u>dihs</u> ih duhnt)

disagreeing with an established religious or political system

The *dissident* had been living abroad and writing his criticism of the government from an undisclosed location.

DOCTRINAIRE

adj (dahk truh <u>nayr</u>)

rigidly devoted to theories without regard for practicality; dogmatic

The professor's manner of teaching was considered *doctrinaire* for such a liberal school.

DOGGED

adj (<u>daw</u> guhd)

stubbornly persevering
The police inspector's *dogged* determination helped him catch the thief.

DOLEFUL

adj (<u>dohl</u> fuhl)

sad, mournful

Looking into the *doleful* eyes of the lonely pony, the girl yearned to take him home.

DOUR

adj (<u>doo</u> uhr) (<u>dow</u> uhr)

sullen and gloomy; stern and severe

The *dour* hotel concierge demanded payment for the room in advance.

EFFLUVIA

noun (ih <u>floo</u> vee uh)

waste; odorous fumes given off by waste

He took out the garbage at 3 A.M. because the *effluvia* had begun wafting into the bedroom.

ELEGY

noun (<u>eh</u> luh jee)

a mournful poem, usually about the dead

A memorable *elegy* was read aloud for the spiritual leader.

ELUDE

verb (ee <u>lood</u>)

to avoid cleverly, to escape the perception of

Somehow, the runaway *eluded* detection for weeks.

EMOLLIENT

adj (ih <u>mohl</u> yuhnt)

soothing, especially to the skin

After being out in the sun for so long, the *emollient* cream was a welcome relief on my skin.

EMULATE

verb (<u>ehm</u> yuh layt)

to strive to equal or excel, to imitate

Children often *emulate* their parents.

ENCUMBER

verb (ehn <u>kuhm</u> buhr)

to weigh down, to burden

She brought only her laptop to the cabin, where she wrote *unencumbered* by the distractions of the city.

ENJOIN

verb (ehn <u>joyn</u>)

to direct or impose with urgent appeal, to order with emphasis; to forbid

Patel is *enjoined* by his culture from eating the flesh of a cow, which is sacred in India.

EPOCHAL

adj (<u>ehp</u> uh kuhl) (ehp <u>ahk</u> uhl)

momentous, highly significant

The Supreme Court's *epochal* decision will no doubt affect generations to come.

EPONYMOUS

adj (ih <u>pahn</u> uh muhs)

giving one's name to a place, book, restaurant

Macbeth was the *eponymous* protagonist of Shakespeare's play.

EQUIVOCATE

verb (ih <u>kwihv</u> uh kayt)

to avoid committing oneself in what one says, to be deliberately unclear

Not wanting to implicate himself in the crime, the suspect *equivocated* for hours.

ERSATZ

adj (uhr <u>sahtz</u>)

being an artificial and inferior substitute or imitation

The *ersatz* strawberry shortcake tasted more like plastic than like real cake.

ESCHEW

verb (ehs <u>choo</u>)

to shun; to avoid (as something wrong or distasteful)

The filmmaker *eschewed* artifical light for her actors, resulting in a stark movie style.

ESPOUSE

verb (ih <u>spowz</u>)

to take up and support as a cause; to marry

Because of his religious beliefs, the preacher could not *espouse* the use of capital punishment.

ESPY

verb (ehs <u>peye</u>)

to catch sight of, glimpse

Amidst a crowd in black clothing, she *espied* the colorful dress that her friend was wearing.

EUPHEMISM

noun (<u>yoo</u> fuh mihz uhm)

an inoffensive and agreeable expression that is substituted for one that is considered offensive

The funeral director preferred to use the *euphemism* "passed away" instead of the word "dead."

EUTHANASIA

noun (yoo thun <u>nay</u> zhuh)

the practice of ending the life of hopelessly ill individuals; assisted suicide

Euthanasia has always been the topic of much moral debate.

EXCORIATE

verb (ehk <u>skohr</u> ee ayt)

to censure scathingly; to express strong disapproval of

The three-page letter to the editor *excoriated* the publication for printing the rumor without verifying the source.

EXPONENT

noun (<u>ehk</u> spoh nuhnt)

one who champions or advocates

The vice president was an enthusiastic *exponent* of computer technology.

EXPOUND

verb (ihk <u>spownd</u>)

to explain or describe in detail

The teacher *expounded* on the theory of relativity for hours.

EXPUNGE

verb (ihk <u>spuhnj</u>)

to erase, eliminate completely

The parents' association *expunged* the questionable texts from the children's reading list.

EXTIRPATE

verb (<u>ehk</u> stuhr payt)

to root out, eradicate, literally or figuratively; to destroy wholly

The criminals were *extirpated* after many years of investigation.

EXTRAPOLATION

noun (ihk <u>strap</u> uh lay shuhn)

using known data and information to determine what will happen in the future, prediction

Through the process of *extrapolation*, we were able to determine which mutual funds to invest in.

EXTRINSIC

adj (ihk <u>strihn</u> sihk) (ihk <u>strihn</u> zihk)

external, unessential; originating from the outside

"Though they are interesting to note," the meeting manager claimed, "those facts are *extrinsic* to the matter under discussion."

EXTRUDE

verb (ihk <u>strood</u>)

to form or shape something by pushing it out, to force out, especially through a small opening

We watched in awe as the volcano *extruded* molten lava.

FACETIOUS

adj (fuh <u>see</u> shuhs)

witty, humorous

Her *facetious* remarks made the uninteresting meeting more lively.

FACILE

adj (<u>faa</u> suhl)

easily accomplished; seeming to lack sincerity or depth; arrived at without due effort

Given the complexity of the problem, it seemed a rather *facile* solution.

FALLACIOUS

adj (fuh <u>lay</u> shuhs)

tending to deceive or mislead; based on a fallacy

The *fallacious* statement "the earth is flat" misled people for many years.

FEBRILE

adj (<u>fehb</u> ruhl) (<u>fee</u> bruhl)

feverish, marked by intense emotion or activity

Awaiting the mysterious announcement, there was a *febrile* excitement in the crowd.

FECKLESS

adj (<u>fehk</u> lihs)

ineffective, worthless

Anja took on the responsibility of caring for her aged mother, realizing that her *feckless* sister was not up to the task.

FEIGN

verb (fayn)

to pretend, to give a false appearance of

Though she had discovered they were planning a party, she *feigned* surprise so as not to spoil the festivities.

FERAL

adj (<u>fehr</u> uhl)

suggestive of a wild beast, not domesticated

Though the animal-rights activists did not want to see the *feral* dogs harmed, they offered no solution to the problem.

FICTIVE

adj (<u>fihk</u> tihv)

fictional, relating to imaginative creation

She found she was more productive when writing *fictive* stories rather than autobiographical stories.

FILIBUSTER

verb (<u>fihl</u> ih buhs tuhr)

to use obstructionist tactics, especially prolonged speech making, in order to delay something

The congressman read names from the phonebook in an attempt to *filibuster* a pending bill.

FITFUL

adj (<u>fiht</u> fuhl)

intermittent, lacking steadiness; characterized by irregular bursts of activity

Her *fitful* breathing became cause for concern, and eventually, she phoned the doctor.

FLIPPANT

adj (<u>flihp</u> uhnt)

marked by disrespectful lightheartedness or casualness

Her *flippant* response was unacceptable and she was asked again to explain herself.

FLOUT

verb (flowt)

to scorn, to disregard with contempt

The protestors *flouted* the committee's decision and hoped to sway public opinion.

FODDER

noun (<u>fohd</u> uhr)

raw material, as for artistic creation, readily abundant ideas or images

The governor's hilarious blunder was good *fodder* for the comedian.

FOREGO

verb (fohr <u>goh</u>)

to precede, to go ahead of

Because of the risks of the expedition, the team leader made sure to *forego* the climbers.

FORGO

verb (fohr <u>goh</u>)

to do without, to abstain from

As much as I wanted to *forgo* statistics, I knew it would serve me well in my field of study.

FORMIDABLE

adj (<u>fohr</u> mih duh buhl) (fohr <u>mih</u> duh buhl)

fearsome, daunting; tending to inspire awe or wonder
The wrestler was not very big, but his skill and speed made him a *formidable* opponent.

FORTITUDE

noun (<u>fohr</u> tih tood)

strength of mind that allows one to encounter adversity with courage

Months in the trenches exacted great *fortitude* of the soldiers.

FORTUITOUS

adj (fohr <u>too</u> ih tuhs)

by chance, especially by favorable chance

After a *fortuitous* run-in with an agent, Roxy won a recording contract.

FRENETIC

adj (freh <u>neht</u> ihk)

frantic, frenzied

The employee's *frenetic* schedule left him little time to socialize.

FULSOME

adj (<u>fool</u> suhm)

abundant; flattering in an insincere way

The king's servant showered him with *fulsome* compliments in hopes of currying favor.

FURLOUGH

noun (<u>fuhr</u> loh)

a leave of absence, especially granted to soldier or a prisoner

After seeing months of combat, the soldier received a much-deserved *furlough*.

FURTIVE

adj (<u>fuhr</u> tihv)

sly, with hidden motives

The *furtive* glances they exchanged made me suspect they were up to something.

GALVANIZE

verb (<u>gaal</u> vuh niez)

to shock; to arouse awareness

The closing down of another homeless shelter *galvanized* the activist group into taking political action.

GAMELY

adv (<u>gaym</u> lee)

spiritedly, bravely

The park ranger *gamely* navigated the trail up the steepest face of the mountain.

GAUCHE

adj (gohsh)

lacking social refinement

Snapping one's fingers to get a waiter's attention is considered *gauche*.

GRANDILOQUENCE

noun (graan <u>dihl</u> uh kwuhns)

pompous talk; fancy but meaningless language

The headmistress was notorious for her *grandiloquence* at the lectern and her ostentatious clothes.

GREGARIOUS

adj (greh <u>gaar</u> ee uhs)

outgoing, sociable

Unlike her introverted friends, Susan was very *gregarious*.

GROTTO

noun (<u>grah</u> toh)

a small cave

Alone on the island, Philoctetes sought shelter in a *grotto*.

HARANGUE

verb (huh <u>raang</u>)

to give a long speech

Maria's parents *harangued* her when she told them she'd spent her money on magic beans.

HEDONIST

noun (<u>hee</u> duhn ihst)

one who pursues pleasure as a goal

Michelle, an admitted *hedonist*, lays on the couch eating cookies every Saturday.

HEGEMONY

noun (hih <u>jeh</u> muh nee)

the domination of one state or group over its allies

When Germany claimed *hegemony* over Russia, Stalin was outraged.

HERETICAL

adj (huh <u>reh</u> tih kuhl)

departing from accepted beliefs or standards, oppositional

At the onset of the Inquisition, the *heretical* priest was forced to flee the country.

HIATUS

noun (hie <u>ay</u> tuhs)

a gap or interruption in space, time, or continuity

After a long *hiatus* in Greece, the philosophy professor returned to university.

HISTRIONICS

noun (hihs tree <u>ahn</u> ihks)

deliberate display of emotion for effect; exaggerated behavior calculated for effect

With such *histrionics*, she should really consider becoming an actress.

HUBRIS

noun (<u>hyoo</u> brihs)

excessive pride or self-confidence

Nathan's *hubris* spurred him to do things that many considered insensitive.

HUSBAND

verb (<u>huhz</u> buhnd)

to manage economically; to use sparingly

The cyclist paced herself at the start of the race, knowing that if she *husbanded* her resources she'd have the strength to break out of the pack later on.

HYPOCRITE

noun (<u>hih</u> puh kriht)

one who puts on a false appearance of virtue; one who criticizes a flaw he in fact possesses

What a *hypocrite*: He criticizes those who wear fur but then he buys for himself a leather shearling coat.

IGNOBLE

adj (ihg <u>noh</u> buhl)

having low moral standards, not noble in character; mean

The photographer was paid a princely sum for the picture of the self-proclaimed ethicist in the *ignoble* act of pick-pocketing.

ILLUSORY

adj (ih loo suhr ee) (ih loos ree)

producing illusion, deceptive

The desert explorer was devastated to discover that the lake he thought he had seen was in fact *illusory*.

IMBIBE

verb (ihm bieb)

to receive into the mind and take in, absorb

If I always attend class, I can *imbibe* as much knowledge as possible.

IMPASSIVE

adj (ihm pahs sihv)

absent of any external sign of emotion, expressionless

Given his *impassive* expression, it was hard to tell whether he approved of my plan.

IMPERIOUS

adj (ihm pihr ee uhs)

commanding, domineering; urgent

Though the king had been a kind leader, his daughter was *imperious* and demanding during her rule.

IMPERTURBABLE

adj (ihm puhr tuhr buh buhl)

unshakably calm and steady

No matter how disruptive the children became, the babysitter remained *imperturbable*.

IMPLACABLE

adj (ihm play kuh buhl) (ihm plaa kuh buhl)

inflexible; not capable of being changed or pacified

The *implacable* teasing was hard for the child to take.

IMPORTUNATE

adj (ihm <u>pohr</u> chuh niht)

troublesomely urgent; extremely persistent in request or demand

Her *importunate* appeal for a job caused me to grant her an interview.

IMPRECATION

noun (ihm prih <u>kay</u> shuhn)

a curse

Spouting violent *imprecations*, Hank searched for the person who had vandalized his truck.

IMPUDENT

adj (<u>ihm</u> pyuh duhnt)

marked by cocky boldness or disregard for others

Considering the judge had been lenient in her sentence, it was *impudent* of the defendant to refer to her by her first name.

IMPUGN

verb (ihm <u>pyoon</u>)

to call into question; to attack verbally

"How dare you *impugn* my motives?" protested the lawyer, on being accused of ambulance chasing.

IMPUTE

verb (ihm <u>pyoot</u>)

to lay the responsibility or blame for, often unjustly

It seemed unfair to *impute* the accident on me, especially since they were the ones who ran the red light.

INCANDESCENT

adj (ihn kahn <u>dehs</u> uhnt)

shining brightly

The *incandescent* glow of the moon made it a night I'll never forget.

INCARNADINE

adj (ihn <u>kaar</u> nuh dien) (ihn <u>kaar</u> nuh dihn)

red, especially blood red

The *incarnadine* lipstick she wore made her look much older than she was.

INCHOATE

adj (ihn <u>koh</u> iht)

being only partly in existence; imperfectly formed

For every page of the crisp writing that made it into the final book, Jessie has 10 pages of *inchoate* rambling that made up the first draft.

INCIPIENT

adj (ihn <u>sihp</u> ee uhnt)

beginning to exist or appear; in an initial stage

The *incipient* idea seemed brilliant, but they knew it needed much more development.

INCORRIGIBLE

adj (ihn <u>kohr</u> ih juh buhl)

incapable of being corrected or amended; difficult to control or manage

"You're *incorrigible*," yelled the frustrated mother to her son, in the middle of his third tantrum of the day.

INCREDULOUS

adj (ihn <u>krehj</u> uh luhs)

unwilling to accept what is true, skeptical

The Lasky children were *incredulous* when their parents told them they were moving to Alaska.

INDOMITABLE

adj (ihn <u>dahm</u> ih tuuh buhl)

incapable of being conquered

Climbing Mount Everest would seem an *indomitable* task, but it has been done many times.

INGRATIATE

verb (ihn <u>gray</u> shee ayt)

to gain favor with another by deliberate effort, to seek to please somebody so as to gain an advantage

The new intern tried to *ingratiate* herself with the managers so that they might consider her for a future job.

INHERENT

adj (ihn <u>hehr</u> ehnt)

involving the essential character of something, built-in, inborn

The class was dazzled by the experiment and as a result more likely to remember the *inherent* scientific principle.

INQUEST

noun (<u>ihn</u> kwehst)

an investigation, an inquiry

The police chief ordered an *inquest* to determine what went wrong.

INSENSATE

adj (ihn <u>sehn</u> sayt) (ihn <u>sehn</u> siht)

lacking sensibility and understanding, foolish

The shock of the accident left him *insensate*, but after some time, the numbness subsided and he was able to tell the officer what had happened.

INSOLENT

adj (<u>ihn</u> suh luhnt)

insultingly arrogant, overbearing

After having spoken with three *insolent* customer service representatives, Shelly was relieved when the fourth one sympathized with her complaint.

INSULAR

adj (<u>ihn</u> suh luhr) (<u>ihn</u> syuh luhr)

characteristic of an isolated people, especially having a narrow viewpoint

It was a shock for Kendra to go from her small high school, with her *insular* group of friends, to a huge college with students from all over the country.

INSUPERABLE

adj (ihn <u>soo</u> puhr uh buhl)

incapable of being surmounted or overcome

Insuperable as though our problems may seem, I'm confident we'll come out ahead.

INTER

verb (ihn <u>tuhr</u>)

to bury

After giving the masses one last chance to pay their respects, the leader's body was *interred*.

INTERLOCUTOR

noun (ihn tuhr <u>lahk</u> yuh tuhr)

ones who takes part in conversation

Though always the *interlocutor*, the professor actually preferred that his students guide the class discussion.

INTERNECINE

adj (ihn tuhr <u>nehs</u> een)

mutually destructive; equally devastating to both sides

Though it looked as though there was a victor, the *internecine* battle benefited no one.

INTERREGNUM

noun (ihn tuhr <u>rehg</u> nuhm)

a temporary halting of the usual operations of government or control

The new king began his reign by restoring order that the lawless *interregnum* had destroyed.

INTIMATION

noun (ihn tuh <u>may</u> shuhn)

a subtle and indirect hint

Abby chose to ignore Babu's *intimation* that she wasn't as good a swimmer as she claimed.

INTRACTABLE

adj (ihn traak tuh buhl)

not easily managed or manipulated

Intractable for hours, the wild horse eventually allowed the rider to mount.

INTRANSIGENT

adj (ihn traan suh juhnt) (ihn traan zuh juhnt)

uncompromising, refusing to abandon an extreme position

His *intransigent* positions on social issues cost him the election.

INTREPID

adj (ihn trehp ihd)

fearless, resolutely courageous

Despite freezing winds, the *intrepid* hiker completed his ascent.

INUNDATE

verb (ihn uhn dayt)

to cover with a flood; to overwhelm as if with a flood

The box office was *inundated* with requests for tickets to the award-winning play.

INVETERATE

adj (ihn veht uhr iht)

firmly established, especially with respect to a habit or attitude

An *inveterate* risk-taker, Lori tried her luck at bungee-jumping.

IRASCIBLE

adj (ih raas uh buhl)

easily angered, hot-tempered

One of the most *irascible* barbarians of all time, Attila the Hun ravaged much of Europe during his time.

IRONIC

adj (ie rahn ihk)

poignantly contrary or incongruous to what was expected

It was *ironic* to learn that shy Wendy from high school grew up to be the loud-mouth host of the daily talk show.

IRREVERENT

adj (ih <u>rehv</u> uhr uhnt)

disrespectful in a gentle or humorous way

Kevin's *irreverent* attitude toward the principal annoyed the teacher but amused the other children.

ITINERANT

adj (ie <u>tihn</u> uhr uhnt)

wandering from place to place; unsettled

The *itinerant* tomcat came back to the Johansson homestead every two months.

JETTISON

verb (<u>jeht</u> ih zuhn) (<u>jeht</u> ih suhn)

to discard, to get rid of as unnecessary or encumbering

The sinking ship *jettisoned* its cargo in a desperate attempt to reduce its weight.

JOCULAR

adj (<u>jahk</u> yuh luhr)

playful, humorous

The *jocular* old man entertained his grandchildren for hours.

JUNTA

noun (<u>hoon</u> tuh) (<u>juhn</u> tuh)

a small governing body, especially after a revolutionary seizure of power

Only one member of the *junta* was satisfactory enough to be elected once the new government was established.

KISMET

noun (<u>kihz</u> meht) (<u>kihz</u> miht)

destiny, fate

When Eve found out that Garret also played the harmonica, she knew their meeting was *kismet*.

LAMPOON

verb (laam <u>poon</u>)

to ridicule with satire

The mayor hated being *lampooned* by the press for his efforts to improve people's politeness.

LARGESS

noun (laar <u>jehs</u>)

generous giving (as of money) to others who may seem inferior

She'd always relied on her parent's *largess*, but after graduation, she had to get a job.

LAUDABLE

adj (<u>law</u> duh buhl)

deserving of praise

Kristin's dedication is *laudable*, but she doesn't have the necessary skills to be a good paralegal.

LAX

adj (laaks)

not rigid, loose; negligent

Because our delivery boy is *lax*, the newspaper often arrives sopping wet.

LECHEROUS

adj (<u>lehch</u> uh ruhs)

lewd, lustful

The school board censored the movie because of its portrayal of the *lecherous* criminal.

LEVITY

noun (<u>leh</u> vih tee)

an inappropriate lack of seriousness, overly casual

The joke added needed *levity* to the otherwise serious meeting.

LEXICON

noun (<u>lehk</u> sih kahn)

a dictionary; a stock of terms pertaining to a particular subject or vocabulary

The author coined the term Gen-X, which has since entered the *lexicon*.

LIBERTARIAN

noun (lih buhr <u>tehr</u> ee uhn)

one who advocates individual rights and free will

The *libertarian* was always at odds with the conservatives.

LIBERTINE

noun (<u>lihb</u> uhr teen)

a free thinker, usually used disparagingly; one without moral restraint

The *libertine* took pleasure in gambling away his family's money.

LICENTIOUS

adj (lih <u>sehn</u> shuhs)

immoral; unrestrained by society

Conservative citizens were outraged by the *licentious* exploits of the free-spirited artists living in town.

LILLIPUTIAN

adj (lihl ee <u>pyoo</u> shun)

very small

Next to her Amazonian roommate, the girl seemed *lilliputian*.

LIMBER

adj (<u>lihm</u> buhr)

flexible, capable of being shaped

After years of doing yoga, the elderly man was remarkably *limber*.

LITHE

adj (lieth)

moving and bending with ease; marked by effortless grace

The dancer's *lithe* movements proved her to be a rising star in the ballet corps.

LOQUACIOUS

adj (loh <u>kway</u> shuhs)

talkative

She was naturally *loquacious*, which was always a challenge when she was in a library or movie theater.

MACABRE

adj (muh <u>kaa</u> bruh) (muh <u>kaa</u> buhr)

having death as a subject; dwelling on the gruesome

Martin enjoyed *macabre* tales about werewolves and vampires.

MACROCOSM

noun (<u>maak</u> roh cahz uhm)

the whole universe; a large-scale reflection of a part of the greater world

Some scientists focus on a particular aspect of space, while others study the entire *macrocosm* and how its parts relate to one another.

MALAISE

noun (maa <u>layz</u>)

a feeling of unease or depression

During his presidency, Jimmy Carter spoke of a "national *malaise*" and was subsequently criticized for being too negative.

MALAPROPISM

noun (<u>maal</u> uh prahp ihz uhm)

the accidental, often comical, use of a word which resembles the one intended, but has a different, often contradictory meaning

Everybody laughed at the *malapropism* when instead of saying "public broadcasting" the announcer said "public boredcasting."

MALEDICTION

noun (maal ih <u>dihk</u> shun)

a curse, a wish of evil upon another

The frog prince looked for a princess to kiss him and put an end to the witch's *malediction*.

MALEVOLENT

adj (muh <u>lehv</u> uh luhnt)

exhibiting ill will; wishing harm to others

The *malevolent* gossiper spread false rumors with frequency.

MALFEASANCE

noun (maal <u>fee</u> zuhns)

wrongdoing or misconduct, especially by a public official

Not only was the deputy's *malfeasance* humiliating, it also spelled the end of his career.

MALLEABLE

adj (<u>maal</u> ee uh buhl)

easily influenced or shaped, capable of being altered by outside forces

The welder heated the metal before shaping it because the heat made it *malleable.*

MANNERED

adj (<u>maan</u> uhrd)

artificial or stilted in character

The portrait is an example of the *mannered* style that was favored in that era.

MASOCHIST

noun (<u>maas</u> uhk ihst)

one who enjoys being subjected to pain or humiliation

Only a *masochist* would volunteer to take on this nightmarish project.

MAVERICK

noun (<u>maav</u> rihk) (<u>maav</u> uh rihk)

an independent individual who does not go along with a group

The senator was a *maverick* who was willing to vote against his own party's position.

MAWKISH

adj (<u>maw</u> kihsh)

sickeningly sentimental

The poet hoped to charm his girlfriend with his flowery poem, but its *mawkish* tone sickened her instead.

MEGALOMANIA

noun (mehg uh loh may nee uh)

obsession with great or grandiose performance

Many of the Roman emperors suffered from severe *megalomania*.

MELLIFLUOUS

adj (muh lihf loo uhs)

having a smooth, rich flow

She was so talented that her *mellifluous* flute playing transported me to another world.

MICROCOSM

noun (mie kruh kahz uhm)

a small scale representation of a larger system

This department is in fact a *microcosm* of the entire corporation.

MILIEU

noun (mihl yoo)

the physical or social setting in which something occurs or develops, environment

The *milieu* at the club wasn't one I was comfortable with, so I left right away.

MISANTHROPE

noun (mihs ahn throhp)

a person who hates or distrusts mankind

Scrooge was such a *misanthrope* that even the sight of children singing made him angry.

MISNOMER

noun (mihs noh muhr)

an error in naming a person or place

Iceland is a *misnomer* since it isn't really icy; the name means "island."

MISSIVE

noun (mihs ihv)

a written note or letter

Priscilla spent hours composing a romantic *missive* for Elvis.

MITIGATE

verb (<u>miht</u> ih gayt)

to make less severe, make milder

A judge may *mitigate* a sentence if it's decided that the crime was committed out of necessity.

MODICUM

noun (<u>mahd</u> ih kuhm)

a small portion, limited quantity

I expect at least a *modicum* of assistance from you on the day of the party.

MOLLIFY

verb (<u>mahl</u> uh fie)

to soothe in temper or disposition

A small raise and increased break time *mollified* the unhappy staff, at least for the moment.

MORDANT

adj (<u>mohr</u> dnt)

biting and caustic in manner and style

Roald Dahl's stories are *mordant* alternatives to bland stories intended for kids.

MORES

noun (<u>mawr</u> ayz)

fixed customs or manners; moral attitudes

In keeping with the *mores* of ancient Roman society, Nero held a celebration every weekend.

MOROSE

adj (muh <u>rohs</u>) (maw <u>rohs</u>)

gloomy, sullen

After hearing that the internship had been given to someone else, Lenny was *morose* for days.

MOTE

noun (moht)

a small particle, speck

Monica's eye watered, irritated by a *mote* of dust.

MUTABILITY

noun (myoo tuh <u>bihl</u> uh tee)

the quality of being capable of change, in form or character; susceptibility of change

The actress lacked the *mutability* needed to perform in the improvisational play.

MYOPIC

adj (mie <u>ahp</u> ihk) (mie <u>oh</u> pihk)

lacking foresight, having a narrow view or long-range perspective

Not wanting to spend a lot of money up front, the *myopic* business owner would likely suffer the consequences later.

NEBULOUS

adj (<u>neh</u> <u>byoo</u> luhs)

vague, undefined

The candidate's *nebulous* plans to fight crime made many voters skeptical.

NECROMANCY

noun (<u>nehk</u> ruh maan see)

the practice of communicating with the dead in order to predict the future

The practice of *necromancy* supposes belief in survival of the soul after death.

NEFARIOUS

adj (nih <u>fahr</u> ee uhs)

intensely wicked or vicous

Nefarious deeds are never far from an evil-doer's mind.

NEONATE

noun (<u>nee</u> uh nayt)

a newborn child

The *neonate* was born prematurely so she's still in the hospital.

NIHILISM

noun (<u>nie</u> hihl iz uhm)

belief that traditional values and beliefs are unfounded and that existence is useless; belief that conditions in the social organization are so bad as to make destruction desirable

Robert's *nihilism* expressed itself in his lack of concern with the norms of moral society.

NOMENCLATURE

noun (<u>noh</u> muhn klay chuhr)

a system of scientific names

In botany class, we learned the *nomenclature* used to identify different species of roses.

NON SEQUITUR

noun (nahn <u>sehk</u> wih tuhr)

a statement that does not follow logically from anything previously said

After the heated political debate, her comment about cake was a real *non sequitur*.

NOVEL

adj (<u>nah</u> vuhl)

new and not resembling anything formerly known

Piercing any part of the body other than the earlobes was *novel* in the 1950s, but now it is quite common.

OBDURATE

adj (<u>ahb</u> duhr uht)

stubbornly persistent, resistant to persuasion

The president was *obdurate* on the matter, and no amount of public protest could change his mind.

OBFUSCATE

verb (<u>ahb</u> fyoo skayt)

to confuse, make obscure

Benny always *obfuscates* the discussion by bringing in irrelevant facts.

OBSTINATE

adj (<u>ahb</u> stih nuht)

unreasonably persistent

The *obstinate* journalist would not reveal his source, and thus, was jailed for 30 days.

OLFACTORY

adj (ohl <u>faak</u> tuh ree)

relating to the sense of smell

Whenever she entered a candle store, her *olfactory* sense was awakened.

OLIGARCHY

noun (<u>oh</u> lih gaar kee)

a government in which a small group exercises supreme control

In an *oligarchy*, the few who rule are generally wealthier and have more status than the others.

ONUS

noun (<u>oh</u> nuhs)

a burden, an obligation

Antonia was beginning to feel the *onus* of having to feed her friend's cat for the month.

OPINE

verb (oh <u>pien</u>)

to express an opinion

At the "Let's Chat Talk Show," the audience member *opined* that the guest was in the wrong.

OPPORTUNIST

noun (aap ore <u>too</u> nist)

one who takes advantage of any opportunity to achieve an end, with little regard for principles

The *opportunist* wasted no time in stealing the idea and presenting it as his own.

OPPROBRIOUS

adj (uh <u>proh</u> bree uhs)

disgraceful, shameful

She wrote an *opprobrious* editorial in the newspaper about the critic who tore her new play to shreds.

ORNERY

adj (<u>ohr</u> nuh ree)

having an irritable disposition, cantankerous

My first impression of the taxi driver was that he was *ornery*, but then he explained that he'd just had a bad day.

OSCILLATE

verb (<u>ah</u> sihl ayt)

to swing back and forth like a pendulum; to vary between opposing beliefs or feelings

The move meant a new house in a lovely neighborhood, but she missed her friends, so she *oscillated* between joy and sadness.

OSSIFY

verb (<u>ah</u> sih fie)

to change into bone; to become hardened or set in a rigidly conventional pattern

The forensics expert ascertained the body's age based on the degree to which the facial structure had *ossified*.

OSTRACIZE

verb (<u>ahs</u> truh size)

to exclude from a group by common consent

Feeling *ostracized* from her friends, Tabitha couldn't figure out what she had done.

OUST

verb (owst)

to remove from position by force; eject

After President Nixon so offensively lied to the country during Watergate, he was *ousted* from office.

PAEAN

noun (<u>pee</u> uhn)

a tribute, a song or expression of praise

He considered his newest painting a *paean* to his late wife.

PALATIAL

adj (puh <u>lay</u> shuhl)

relating to a palace; magnificent

After living in a cramped studio apartment for years, Alicia thought the modest one bedroom looked downright *palatial*.

PALIMPSEST

noun (<u>pahl</u> ihmp sehst)

an object or place having diverse layers or aspects beneath the surface

Years ago, paper was very expensive, so the practice was to write over previous words, creating a *palimpsest* of writing.

PALPABLE

adj (<u>pahlp</u> uh buhl)

capable of being touched or felt; easily perceived

The tension was *palpable* as I walked into the room.

PALTRY

adj (<u>pawl</u> tree)

pitifully small or worthless

Bernardo paid the ragged boy the *paltry* sum of 25 cents to carry his luggage all the way to the hotel.

PANACHE

noun (puh <u>nahsh</u>)

flamboyance or dash in style and action

Leah has such *panache* when planning parties, even when they're last-minute affairs.

PANDEMIC

adj (paan <u>deh</u> mihk)

occurring over a wide geographic area and affecting a large portion of the population

Pandemic alarm spread throughout Colombia after the devastating earthquake.

PANEGYRIC

noun (paan uh <u>geer</u> ihk)

elaborate praise; formal hymn of praise

The director's *panegyric* for the donor who kept his charity going was heart-warming.

PARADIGM

noun (<u>paar</u> uh diem)

an outstandingly clear or typical example

The new restaurant owner used the fast-food giant as a *paradigm* for expansion into new locales.

PARAGON

noun (<u>paar</u> uh gon)

a model of excellence or perfection

She's the *paragon* of what a judge should be: honest, intelligent, and just.

PARAMOUNT

adj (<u>paar</u> uh mownt)

supreme, of chief importance

It's of *paramount* importance that we make it back to camp before the storm hits.

PARE

verb (payr)

to trim off excess, reduce

The cook's hands were sore after she *pared* hundreds of potatoes for the banquet.

PARIAH

noun (puh <u>rie</u> ah)

an outcast

Once he betrayed those in his community, he was banished and lived the life of a *pariah*.

PATENT

adj (<u>paa</u> tehnt)

obvious, evident

Moe could no longer stand Frank's *patent* fawning over the boss and so confronted him.

PATHOGENIC

adj (paa thoh <u>jehn</u> ihk)

causing disease

Bina's research on the origins of *pathogenic* microorganisms should help stop the spread of disease.

PATRICIAN

adj (puh <u>trih</u> shuhn)

aristocratic

Though he really couldn't afford an expensive lifestyle, Claudius had *patrician* tastes.

PATRONIZE

verb (<u>pay</u> troh niez)

to act as patron of, to adopt an air of condescension toward; to buy from

LuAnn *patronized* the students, treating them like simpletons, which they deeply resented.

PECULATE

verb (<u>pehk</u> yuh layt)

to embezzle

These days in the news, we read more and more about workers *peculating* the system.

PECUNIARY

adj (pih <u>kyoon</u> nee <u>ehr</u> ee)

relating to money

Michelle's official title was office manager, but she ended up taking on a lot of *pecuniary* responsibilities such as payroll duties.

PELLUCID

adj (peh <u>loo</u> sihd)

transparently clear in style or meaning, easy to understand

Though she thought she could hide her ulterior motives, they were *pellucid* to everyone else.

PENCHANT

noun (<u>pehn</u> chehnt)

an inclination, a definite liking

After Daniel visited the Grand Canyon, he developed a *penchant* for travel.

PENITENT

adj (<u>peh</u> nih tehnt)

expressing sorrow for sins or offenses, repentant

Claiming the murderer did not feel *penitent*, the victim's family felt his pardon should be denied.

PENURY

noun (<u>pehn</u> yuh ree)

an oppressive lack of resources (as money), severe poverty

Once a famous actor, he eventually died in *penury* and anonymity.

PEREGRINATE

verb (<u>pehr</u> ih gruh nayt)

to travel on foot

It has always been a dream of mine to *peregrinate* from one side of Europe to the other with nothing but a backpack.

PHALANX

noun (<u>fay</u> laanks)

a compact or close-knit body of people, animals, or things

A *phalanx* of guards stood outside the prime minister's home day and night.

PHILISTINE

noun (<u>fihl</u> uh steen)

a person who is guided by materialism and is disdainful of intellectual or artistic values

The *philistine* never even glanced at the rare violin in his collection but instead kept an eye on its value and sold it at a profit.

PHILOLOGY

noun (fih <u>lahl</u> uh jee)

the study of ancient texts and languages

Philology was the predecessor to modern-day linguistics.

PHLEGMATIC

adj (flehg <u>maa</u> tihk)

having a sluggish, unemotional temperament

His writing was energetic but his *phlegmatic* personality wasn't suited for television, so he turned down the interview.

PIQUE

verb (peek)

to arouse anger or resentment in; provoke

His continual insensitivity *piqued* my anger.

PLAINTIVE

adj (<u>playn</u> tihv)

expressive of suffering or woe, melancholy

The *plaintive* cries from the girl trapped in the tree were heard by all.

PLATITUDE

noun (<u>plaa</u> tuh tood)

overused and trite remark

Instead of the usual *platitudes*, the comedian gave a memorable and inspiring speech to the graduating class.

PLEBEIAN

adj (plee <u>bee</u> uhn)

crude or coarse; characteristic of commoners

After five weeks of rigorous studying, the graduate settled in for a weekend of *plebeian* socializing and television watching.

PLUCKY

adj (<u>pluh</u> kee)

courageous; spunky

The *plucky* young nurse dove into the foxhole, determined to help the wounded soldier.

POLITIC

adj (<u>pah</u> luh tihk)

shrewd and crafty in managing or dealing with things

She was wise to curb her tongue and was able to explain her problem to the judge in a respectful and *politic* manner.

POLYGLOT

noun (<u>pah</u> lee glaht)

a speaker of many languages

Ling's extensive travels have helped her to become a true *polyglot*.

PORE

verb (pohr)

to read studiously or attentively

I've *pored* over this text, yet I still can't understand it.

PORTENTOUS

adj (pohr <u>tehn</u> tuhs)

foreshadowing, ominous; eliciting amazement and wonder

Everyone thought the rays of light were *portentous* until they realized a nine-year-old was playing a joke on them.

POSIT

verb (<u>pohz</u> iht)

to assume as real or conceded; propose as an explanation

Before proving the math formula, we needed to posit that *x* and *y* were real numbers.

POTABLE

adj (<u>poh</u> tuh buhl)

suitable for drinking

Though the water was *potable*, it tasted terrible.

POTENTATE

noun (<u>poh</u> tehn tayt)

a ruler; one who wields great power

Alex was much kinder before he assumed the role of *potentate*.

PRECARIOUS

adj (prih <u>caa</u> ree uhs)

lacking in security or stability; dependent on chance or uncertain conditions

Given the *precarious* circumstances, I chose to opt out of the deal completely.

PRECIPITOUS

adj (pree <u>sih</u> puh tuhs)

steeply; hastily

At the sight of the approaching helicopters, Private Johnson *precipitously* shot a flare into the air.

PRESAGE

noun (<u>preh</u> sihj)

something that foreshadows; a feeling of what will happen in the future

The demolition of the Berlin Wall was a *presage* to the fall of the Soviet Union.

PRESTIDIGITATION

noun (<u>prehs</u> tih <u>dihj</u> ih <u>tay</u> shuhn)

a cleverly executed trick or deception; sleight of hand

My hunch was that he won the contest not so much as a result of real talent, but rather through *prestidigitation*.

PRETERNATURAL

adj (pree tuhr <u>naach</u> uhr uhl)

existing outside of nature; extraordinary; supernatural

We were all amazed at her *preternatural* ability to recall smells from her early childhood.

PRIMEVAL

adj (priem <u>ee</u> vuhl)

ancient, primitive

The archaeologist claimed that the skeleton was of *primeval* origin, though in fact it was the remains of a modern-day monkey.

PRODIGAL

adj (<u>prah</u> dih guhl)

recklessly extravagant, wasteful

The *prodigal* expenditures on the military budget during a time of peace created a stir in the Cabinet.

PROFFER

verb (<u>prahf</u> uhr)

to offer for acceptance

The deal *proffered* by the committee satisfied all those at the meeting, ending a month-long discussion.

PROGENITOR

noun (proh <u>jehn</u> uh tuhr)

an ancestor in the direct line, forefather; founder

Though his parents had been born here, his *progenitors* were from India.

PROLIFERATE

verb (proh <u>lih</u> fuhr ayt)

to grow by rapid production of new parts; increase in number

The cancer cells *proliferated* so quickly that even the doctor was surprised.

PROMULGATE

verb (<u>prah</u> muhl gayt)

to make known by open declaration, proclaim

The publicist *promulgated* the idea that the celebrity had indeed gotten married.

PROPENSITY

noun (proh <u>pehn</u> suh tee)

a natural inclination or preference

She has a *propensity* for lashing out at others when stressed, so we leave her alone when she's had a rough day.

PROSAIC

adj (proh <u>say</u> ihk)

relating to prose (as opposed to poetry); dull, ordinary

Simon's *prosaic* style bored his writing teacher to tears, though he thought he had an artistic flair.

PROSCRIBE

verb (proh <u>skrieb</u>)

to condemn or forbid as harmful or unlawful

Consumption of alcohol was *proscribed* in the country's constitution, but the ban was eventually lifted.

PROSTRATE

adj (<u>prah</u> strayt)

lying face downward in adoration or submission

Lying *prostrate* awaiting the Pope, a car splashed me with water.

PROVINCIAL

adj (pruh <u>vihn</u> shuhl)

limited in outlook, narrow, unsophisticated

Having grown up in the city, Anita sneered at the *provincial* attitudes of her country cousins.

PROXY

noun (<u>prahk</u> see)

a person authorized to act for someone else

In the event the stock shareholder can't attend the meeting, he'll send a *proxy*.

PSEUDONYM

noun (<u>soo</u> duh nihm)

a fictitious name, used particularly by writers to conceal identity

Though George Eliot sounds as though it's a male name, it was the *pseudonym* that Marian Evans used when she published her classic novel *Middlemarch*.

PUGILISM

noun (<u>pyoo</u> juhl ih suhm)

boxing

Pugilism has been defended as a positive outlet for aggressive impulses.

PUISSANT

adj (<u>pwih</u> sihnt) (<u>pyoo</u> sihnt)

powerful

His memoir was full of descriptions of *puissant* military heroics, but most were exaggerations or outright lies.

PUNCTILIOUS

adj (puhngk <u>tihl</u> ee uhs)

concerned with precise details about codes or conventions

The *punctilious* student never made spelling errors on her essays.

PUNDIT

noun (<u>puhn</u> diht)

one who gives opinions in an authoritative manner

The *pundits* on television are often more entertaining than the sitcoms.

PURLOIN

verb (<u>puhr</u> loyn)

to steal

The amateur detective Dupin found the *purloined* letter for which the police had searched in vain.

PURPORT

verb (puhr <u>pohrt</u>)

to profess, suppose, claim

Brad *purported* to be an opera lover, but he fell asleep at every performance he attended.

RANCOR

noun (<u>raan</u> kuhr)

bitter hatred

Having been teased mercilessly for years, Herb became filled with *rancor* toward those who had humiliated him.

RANKLE

verb (<u>raang</u> kuhl)

to cause anger and irritation

At first the kid's singing was adorable, but after 40 minutes it began to *rankle*.

RAPACIOUS

adj (ruh <u>pay</u> shuhs)

taking by force; driven by greed

Sea otters are so *rapacious* that they consumer 10 times their body weight in food every day.

RAPT

adj (raapt)

deeply absorbed

The story was so well performed that the usually rowdy children were *rapt* until the final word.

RAREFY

verb (rayr uh fie)

to make rare, thin, or less dense

The atmosphere *rarefies* as altitude increases, so the air atop a mountain is too thin to breathe.

RAZE

verb (rayz)

to tear down, demolish

The house had been *razed*; where it once stood, there was nothing but splinters and bricks.

REACTIONARY

adj (ree aak shuhn ayr ee)

marked by extreme conservatism, especially in politics

The former radical hippie had turned into quite a *reactionary*, and the press tried to expose her as a hypocrite.

RECAPITULATE

verb (ree kuh pihch yoo layt)

to review by a brief summary

After the long-winded president had finished his speech, his assistant *recapitulated* for the press the points he had made.

RECIDIVISM

noun (rih sihd uh vih zihm)

a tendency to relapse into a previous behavior, especially criminal behavior

According to statistics, the *recidivism* rate for criminals is quite high.

REFRACT

verb (rih fraakt)

to deflect sound or light

The crystal *refracted* the rays of sunlight so they formed a beautiful pattern on the wall.

REFUTE

verb (rih <u>fyoot</u>)

to contradict, discredit

She made such a persuasive argument that nobody could *refute* it.

RELEGATE

verb (<u>reh</u> luh <u>gayt</u>)

to send into exile, banish; assign

Because he hadn't scored any goals during the season, Abe was *relegated* to the bench for the championship game.

REMISSION

noun (rih <u>mih</u> shuhn)

a lessening of intensity or degree

The doctor told me that the disease had gone into *remission*.

REMUNERATION

noun (rih <u>myoo</u> nuh ray shuhn)

payment for goods or services or to recompense for losses

You can't expect people to do this kind of boring work without some form of *remuneration*.

REPLETE

adj (rih <u>pleet</u>)

abundantly supplied, complete

The gigantic supermarket was *replete* with consumer products of every kind.

REPOSE

noun (rih <u>pohz</u>)

relaxation, leisure

After working hard every day in the busy city, Mike finds his *repose* on weekends playing golf with friends.

REPREHENSIBLE

adj (rehp ree <u>hehn</u> suh buhl)

blameworthy, disreputable

Lowell was thrown out of the bar because of his *reprehensible* behavior toward the other patrons.

REPROVE

verb (rih <u>proov</u>)

to criticize or correct, usually in a gentle manner

Mrs. Hernandez *reproved* her daughter for staying out late and not calling.

REQUITE

verb (rih <u>kwiet</u>)

to return or repay

Thanks for offering to lend me $1,000, but I know I'll never be able to *requite* your generosity.

RESCIND

verb (rih <u>sihnd</u>)

to repeal, cancel

After the celebrity was involved in a scandal, the car company *rescinded* its offer of an endorsement contract.

RESILIENT

adj (rih <u>sihl</u> yuhnt)

able to recover quickly after illness or bad luck; able to bounce back to shape

Psychologists say that being *resilient* in life is one of the keys to success and happiness.

RESOLUTE

adj (<u>reh</u> suh <u>loot</u>)

marked by firm determination

Louise was *resolute*: She would get into medical school no matter what.

RESPLENDENT

adj (rih splehn dihnt)

splendid, brilliant

The bride looked *resplendent* in her gown and sparkling tiara.

REVILE

verb (rih veye uhl)

to criticize with harsh language, verbally abuse

The artist's new installation was *reviled* by critics who weren't used to the departure from his usual work.

RHETORIC

noun (reh tuhr ihk)

the art of speaking or writing effectively; skill in the effective use of speech

Lincoln's talent for *rhetoric* was evident in his beautifully expressed Gettysburg Address.

RIFE

adj (rief)

abundant prevalent especially to an increasing degree; filled with

The essay was so *rife* with grammatical errors that it had to be rewritten.

ROSTRUM

noun (rahs truhm)

an elevated platform for public speaking

Though she was terrified, the new member of the debate club approached the *rostrum* with poise.

SACCHARINE

adj (saa kuh ruhn)

excessively sweet or sentimental

Geoffrey's *saccharine* poems nauseated Lucy, and she wished he'd stop sending them.

SACRILEGIOUS

adj (saak rih lihj uhs)

impious, irreverent toward what is held to be sacred or holy

It's considered *sacrilegious* for one to enter a mosque wearing shoes.

SALACIOUS

adj (suh <u>lay</u> shuhs)

appealing to sexual desire

His television character was wholesomely funny, so audiences who saw his stand-up comedy routine were shocked by how *salacious* his jokes were.

SALIENT

adj (<u>say</u> lee uhnt)

prominent, of notable significance

His most *salient* characteristic is his tendency to dominate every conversation.

SANCTIMONIOUS

adj (<u>saangk</u> tih <u>moh</u> nee uhs)

hypocritically devout; acting morally superior to another

The *sanctimonious* columnist turned out to have been hiding a gambling problem that cost his family everything.

SATIATE

verb (<u>say</u> shee ayt)

to satisfy (as a need or desire) fully or to excess

After years of journeying around the world with nothing but backpacks, the friends had finally *satiated* their desire to travel.

SATURNINE

adj (<u>saat</u> uhr nien)

cold and steady in mood, gloomy; slow to act

Her *saturnine* expression every day made her hard to be around.

SAVANT

noun (suh <u>vahnt</u>)

a person of learning; especially one with knowledge in a special field

The *savant* so impressed us with his knowledge that we asked him to come speak at our school.

SCRUPULOUS

adj (<u>skroop</u> yuh luhs)

acting in strict regard for what is considered proper; punctiliously exact

After the storm had destroyed their antique lamp, the Millers worked to repair it with *scrupulous* care.

SEAMY

adj (<u>see</u> mee)

morally degraded, unpleasant

The tour guide avoided the *seamy* parts of town.

SECULAR

adj (<u>seh</u> kyoo luhr)

not specifically pertaining to religion, relating to the world

Although his favorite book was the Bible, the archbishop also read *secular* works such as mysteries.

SEDITION

noun (seh <u>dih</u> shuhn)

behavior that promotes rebellion or civil disorder against the state

Li was arrested for *sedition* after he gave a fiery speech in the main square.

SEMINAL

adj (<u>seh</u> muhn uhl)

influential in an original way, providing a basis for further development; creative

The scientist's discovery proved to be *seminal* in the area of quantum physics.

SEQUESTER

verb (suh <u>kweh</u> stuhr)

to set apart, seclude

When juries are *sequestered*, it can take days, even weeks, to come up with a verdict.

SERAPHIC

adj (seh <u>rah</u> fihk)

angelic, sweet

Selena's *seraphic* appearance belied her nasty, bitter personality.

SIMIAN

adj (<u>sih</u> mee uhn)

apelike; relating to apes

Early man was more *simian* in appearance than is modern man.

SINECURE

noun (<u>sien</u> ih kyoor)

a well-paying job or office that requires little or no work

The corrupt mayor made sure to set up all his relatives in *sinecures* within the administration.

SOBRIQUET

noun (<u>soh</u> brih <u>kay</u>) (<u>soh</u> brih <u>keht</u>)

a nickname

One of former president Ronald Reagan's sobriquets was *The Gipper*.

SOJOURN

noun (<u>soh</u> juhrn)

a temporary stay, visit

After graduating from college, Iliani embarked on a *sojourn* to China.

SOLICITOUS

adj (suh <u>lih</u> sih tuhs)

anxious, concerned; full of desire, eager

Overjoyed to see the pop idol in her very presence, the *solicitous* store owner stood ready to serve.

SOPHOMORIC

adj (sahf <u>mohr</u> ihk)

exhibiting great immaturity and lack of judgment

After Sean's *sophomoric* behavior, he was grounded for weeks.

SPARTAN

adj (<u>spahr</u> tihn)

highly self-disciplined; frugal, austere

When he was in training, the athlete preferred to live in a *spartan* room, so he could shut out all distractions.

SPECIOUS

adj (<u>spee</u> shuhs)

having the ring of truth but actually being untrue; deceptively attractive

After I followed up with some research on the matter, I realized that the charismatic politician's argument had been *specious*.

SPORTIVE

adj (<u>spohr</u> tihv)

frolicsome, playful

The lakeside vacation meant more *sportive* opportunities for the kids than the wine tour through France.

SQUALID

adj (<u>skwa</u> lihd)

filthy and degraded as the result of neglect or poverty

The *squalid* living conditions in the building outraged the new tenants.

STALWART

adj (<u>stahl</u> wuhrt)

marked by outstanding strength and vigor of body, mind, or spirit

The 85-year old went to the market every day, impressing her neighbors with her *stalwart* routine.

STASIS

noun (<u>stay</u> sihs)

a state of static balance or equilibrium; stagnation

The rusty, ivy-covered World War II tank had obviously been in *stasis* for years.

STINT

verb (stihnt)

to be sparing or frugal; to restrict with respect to a share or allowance

Don't *stint* on the mayonnaise, because I don't like my sandwich too dry.

STIPULATE

verb (<u>stihp</u> yuh <u>layt</u>)

to specify as a condition or requirement of an agreement or offer

The contract *stipulated* that if the movie was never filmed, the actress got paid anyway.

STRATIFY

verb (<u>straa</u> tuh fie)

to arrange or divide into layers

Schliemann *stratified* the numerous layers of Troy, an archeological dig that remains legendary.

STRIDENT

adj (<u>strie</u> dehnt)

loud, harsh, unpleasantly noisy

The traveler's *strident* manner annoyed the flight attendant, but she managed to keep her cool.

STRINGENT

adj (<u>strihn</u> guhnt)

imposing severe, rigorous standards

Many people found it difficult to live up to the *stringent* moral standards imposed by the Puritans.

STYMIE

verb (<u>stie</u> mee)

to block or thwart

The police effort to capture the bank robber was *stymied* when he escaped through a rear window.

SUBTERRANEAN

adj (<u>suhb</u> tuh <u>ray</u> nee uhn)

hidden, secret; underground

Subterranean tracks were created for the trains after it was decided they had run out of room above ground.

SULLY

verb (<u>suh</u> lee)

to tarnish, taint

With the help of a public-relations firm, he was able to restore his *sullied* reputation.

SUPERFLUOUS

adj (soo <u>puhr</u> floo <u>uhs</u>)

extra, more than necessary

The extra recommendations Jake included in his application were *superfluous*, as only one was required.

SUPERSEDE

verb (<u>soo</u> puhr <u>seed</u>)

to cause to be set aside; to force out of use as inferior, replace

Her computer was still running version 2.0 of the software, which had long since been *superseded* by at least three more versions.

SUPPLANT

verb (suh <u>plaant</u>)

to replace (another) by force, to take the place of

The overthrow of the government meant a new leader to *supplant* the tyrannical former one.

SURMOUNT

verb (suhr <u>mownt</u>)

to conquer, overcome

The blind woman *surmounted* great obstacles to become a well-known trial lawyer.

SYBARITE

noun (<u>sih</u> buh riet)

a person devoted to pleasure and luxury

A confirmed *sybarite*, the nobleman fainted at the thought of having to leave his palace and live in a small cottage.

TACTILE

adj (<u>taak</u> tihl)

producing a sensation of touch

The Museum of Natural History displays objects for people to touch so that they have a *tactile* understanding of how different peoples and animals lived.

TANTAMOUNT

adj (<u>taan</u> tuh mownt)

equal in value or effect

If she didn't get concert tickets to see her favorite band, it would be *tantamount* to a tragedy.

TAUTOLOGICAL

adj (<u>tawt</u> uh <u>lah</u> jih kuhl)

having to do with needless repetition, redundancy

I know he was only trying to clarify things, but his *tautological* statements confused me even more.

TAWDRY

adj (<u>taw</u> dree)

gaudy, cheap, showy

The performer changed into her *tawdry* costume and stepped onto the stage.

TEMERITY

noun (<u>teh</u> mehr ih tee)

unreasonable or foolhardy disregard for danger, recklessness

I offered her a ride since it was late at night, but she had the *temerity* to say she'd rather walk.

TEMPESTUOUS

adj (tehm <u>pehs</u> choo uhs)

stormy, turbulent

Our camping trip was cut short when the sun shower we were expecting turned into a *tempestuous* downpour.

TEMPORAL

adj (<u>tehmp</u> ore uhl)

having to do with time

The story lacked a sense of the *temporal*, so we couldn't figure out if the events took place in one evening or over the course of a year.

TENACIOUS

adj (teh <u>nay</u> shuhs)

tending to persist or cling; persistent in adhering to something valued or habitual

For years, against all odds, women *tenaciously* fought for the right to vote.

TENET

noun (<u>teh</u> niht)

a principle, belief, or doctrine accepted by members of a group

One of the *tenets* of Islam is that it is not acceptable to eat pork.

TENUOUS

adj (<u>tehn</u> yoo uhs)

having little substance or strength; flimsy, weak

Francine's already *tenuous* connection to her cousins was broken when they moved away and left no forwarding address.

TERSE

adj (tuhrs)

concise, brief, free of extra words

Her *terse* style of writing was widely praised by the editors, who had been used to seeing long-winded material.

THWART

verb (thwahrt)

to block or prevent from happening; frustrate, defeat the hopes or aspirations of

Thwarted in its attempt to get at the bananas inside the box, the chimp began to squeal.

TITULAR

adj (<u>tihch</u> yoo luhr)

existing in title only; having a title without the functions or responsibilities

Carla was thrilled to be voted Homecoming Queen until somebody explained that the *titular* honor didn't mean she could boss anybody around.

TOADY

noun (<u>toh</u> dee)

one who flatters in the hope of gaining favors

The king was surrounded by *toadies* who rushed to agree with whatever outrageous thing he said.

TORTUOUS

adj (<u>tohr</u> choo uhs)

having many twists and turns; highly complex

To reach the remote inn, the travelers had to negotiate a *tortuous* path.

TOUT

verb (towt)

to praise or publicize loudly or extravagantly

She *touted* her skills as superior to ours, though in fact, we were all at the same level.

TRAJECTORY

noun (truh <u>jehk</u> tuh ree)

the path followed by a moving object, whether through space or otherwise; flight

The *trajectory* of the pitched ball was interrupted by an unexpected bird.

TRANSIENT

adj (<u>traan</u> see uhnt)

passing with time, temporary, short-lived

The reporter lived a *transient* life, staying in one place only long enough to cover the current story.

TRANSITORY

adj (<u>traan</u> sih <u>tohr</u> ee)

short-lived, existing only briefly

The actress' popularity proved *transitory* when her play folded within the month.

TREMULOUS

adj (<u>treh</u> myoo luhs)

trembling, timid; easily shaken

The *tremulous* kitten had been separated from her mother.

TROUNCE

verb (trowns)

to beat severely, defeat

The inexperienced young boxer was *trounced* in a matter of minutes.

TRUCULENT

adj (<u>truhk</u> yuh lehnt)

disposed to fight, belligerent

The bully was initially *truculent* but eventually stopped picking fights at the least provocation.

TURGID

adj (<u>tuhr</u> jihd)

swollen as from a fluid, bloated

In the process of osmosis, water passes through the walls of *turgid* cells, ensuring that they never contain too much water.

TUTELAGE

noun (<u>toot</u> uh lihj)

guardianship, guidance

Under the *tutelage* of her older sister, the young orphan was able to persevere.

UNCANNY

adj (uhn <u>kaa</u> nee)

so keen and perceptive as to seem supernatural, peculiarly unsettling

Though they weren't related, their resemblance was *uncanny*.

UNCONSCIONABLE

adj (uhn <u>kahn</u> shuhn uh buhl)

unscrupulous; shockingly unfair or unjust

After she promised me the project, the fact that she gave it to someone else is *unconscionable*.

UNFROCK

verb (uhn <u>frahk</u>)

to dethrone, especially of priestly power

Any priest caught breaking his oath would certainly be *unfrocked*.

USURY

noun (<u>yoo</u> zuh ree)

the practice of lending money at exorbitant rates

The moneylender was convicted of *usury* when it was discovered that he charged 50 percent interest on all his loans.

VARIEGATED

adj (<u>vaar</u> ee uh <u>gayt</u> ehd)

varied; marked with different colors

The *variegated* foliage of the jungle allows it to support thousands of animal species.

VEHEMENTLY

adverb (<u>vee</u> ih mehnt lee)

marked by extreme intensity of emotions or convictions

She *vehemently* opposed the closing of the neighborhood garden, and was even arrested for protesting when the bulldozers came.

VERACITY

noun (vuhr <u>aa</u> sih tee)

accuracy, truth

She had a reputation for *veracity*, so everyone believed her version of the story.

VERBOSE

adj (vuhr <u>bohs</u>)

wordy

The DNA analyst's answer was so *verbose* that the jury had trouble grasping his point.

VERITABLE

adj (<u>vehr</u> iht uh buhl)

being without question, often used figuratively

My neighbor was a *veritable* goldmine of information when I was writing my term paper on the Civil Rights era because she had been a student organizer and protester.

VERNACULAR

noun (vuhr <u>naa</u> kyoo luhr)

everyday language used by ordinary people; specialized language of a profession

Preeti could not understand the *vernacular* of the south, where she had recently moved.

VERNAL

adj (<u>vuhr</u> nuhl)

related to spring; fresh

Bea basked in the balmy *vernal* breezes, happy that winter was coming to an end.

VICARIOUSLY

adverb (vie <u>kaar</u> ee uhs lee)

felt or undergone as if one were taking part in the experience or feelings of another

She lived *vicariously* through the characters in the adventure books she was always reading.

VILIFY

verb (<u>vih</u> lih fie)

to slander, defame

As gossip columnists often *vilify* celebrities, they're usually held in low regard.

VIM

noun (vihm)

vitality and energy

The *vim* with which she worked so early in the day explained why she was so productive.

VINDICATE

verb (<u>vihn</u> dih kayt)

to clear of blame; support a claim

Tess felt *vindicated* when her prediction about the impending tornado came true.

VIRULENT

adj (<u>veer</u> yuh luhnt)

extremely poisonous; malignant; hateful

Alarmed at the *virulent* press he was receiving, the militant activist decided to go underground.

VISCERAL

adj (<u>vihs</u> uhr uhl)

instinctive, not intellectual; deep, emotional

When my twin was wounded many miles away, I, too, had a *visceral* reaction.

VITUPERATE

verb (vih <u>too</u> puhr ayt)

to abuse verbally, berate

Vituperating someone is never a constructive way to effect change.

VOCIFEROUS

adj (voh <u>sih</u> fuhr uhs)

loud, noisy

Amid the *vociferous* protests of the members of parliament, the prime minister continued his speech.

VOLLEY

noun (<u>vah</u> lee)

a flight of missiles; round of gunshots

The troops fired a *volley* of bullets at the enemy, but they couldn't be sure how many hit their target.

VOLUBLE

adj (<u>vahl</u> yuh buhl)

talkative, speaking easily, glib

The *voluble* man and his reserved wife proved the old saying that opposites attract.

WAN

adj (wahn)

sickly pale

The sick child had a *wan* face, in contrast to her rosy-cheeked sister.

WANTON

adj (<u>wahn</u> tuhn)

undisciplined, unrestrained; reckless

The townspeople were outraged by the *wanton* display of disrespect when they discovered the statue of the town founder covered in graffiti.

WAX

verb (waaks)

to increase gradually; to begin to be

The moon was *waxing*, and would soon be full.

WIELD

verb (weeld)

to exercise authority or influence effectively

For such a young congressman, he *wielded* a lot of power.

WILY

adj (<u>wie</u> lee)

clever; deceptive

Yet again, the *wily* coyote managed to elude the ranchers who wanted it dead.

WINSOME

adj (<u>wihn</u> suhm)

charming, happily engaging

Dawn gave the customs officers a *winsome* smile, and they let her pass without searching her bags.

WORST

verb (wuhrst)

to gain the advantage over; to defeat

The North *worsted* the South in America's Civil War.

WRY

adj (rie)

bent or twisted in shape or condition; dryly humorous

Every time she teased him, she shot her friends a *wry* smile.

YEN

noun (yehn)

a strong desire, craving

Pregnant women commonly have a *yen* for pickles.

ZENITH

noun (<u>zee</u> nihth)

the point of culmination; peak

The diva considered her appearance at the Metropolitan Opera to be the *zenith* of her career.

ZEPHYR

noun (<u>zeh</u> fuhr)

a gentle breeze; something airy or unsubstantial

The *zephyr* from the ocean made the intense heat on the beach bearable for the sunbathers.

Note for International Students

If you are an international student considering attending an American university, you are not alone. Nearly 600,000 international students pursued academic degrees at the undergraduate, graduate, or professional school level at U.S. universities during the 2004–2005 academic year, according to the Institute of International Education's Open Doors report. Almost 50 percent of these students were studying for a bachelor's or first university degree. This number of international students pursuing higher education in the United States is expected to continue to grow. Business, management, engineering, and the physical and life sciences are particularly popular majors for students coming to the United States from other countries.

If you are not a U.S. citizen and you are interested in attending college or university in the United States, here is what you'll need to get started.

- If English is not your first language, you'll probably need to take the TOEFL® (Test of English as a Foreign Language) or provide some other evidence that you are proficient in English. Colleges and universities in the United States will differ on what they consider to be an acceptable TOEFL score. A minimum TOEFL score of 213 (550 on the paper-based TOEFL) or better is often required by more prestigious and competitive institutions. Because American undergraduate programs require all students to take a certain number of general education courses, all students—even math and computer science students—need to be able to communicate well in spoken and written English.

- You may also need to take the SAT® or the ACT®. Many undergraduate institutions in the United States require both the SAT and TOEFL for international students.

- There are over 3,400 accredited colleges and universities in the United States, so selecting the correct undergraduate school can be a confusing task for anyone. You will need to get help from a good advisor or at least a good college guide that gives you detailed information on the different schools available. Since admission to many undergraduate programs is quite competitive, you may want to select three or four colleges and complete applications for each school.

- You should begin the application process at least a year in advance. An increasing number of schools accept applications year round. In any case, find out the application deadlines and plan accordingly. Although September (the fall semester) is the traditional time to begin university study in the United States, you can begin your studies at many schools in January (the spring semester).

- In addition, you will need to obtain an I-20 Certificate of Eligibility from the school you plan to attend if you intend to apply for an F-1 Student Visa.

*All test names used in this section are registered trademarks of their respective owners.

KAPLAN ENGLISH PROGRAMS*

If you need more help with the complex process of university admissions, assistance preparing for the SAT, ACT, or TOEFL, or help building your English language skills in general, you may be interested in Kaplan's programs for international students.

Kaplan English Programs were designed to help students and professionals from outside the United States meet their educational and career goals. At locations throughout the United States, international students take advantage of Kaplan's programs to help them improve their academic and conversational English skills, raise their scores on the TOEFL, SAT, ACT, and other standardized exams, and gain admission to the schools of their choice. Our staff and instructors give international students the individualized attention they need to succeed. Here is a brief description of some of Kaplan's programs for international students:

General Intensive English

Kaplan's General Intensive English course is the fastest and most effective way for students to improve their English. This full-time program integrates the four key elements of language learning—listening, speaking, reading and writing. The challenging curriculum and intensive schedule are designed for both the general language learner and the academically bound student.

TOEFL and Academic English

Our world-famous TOEFL course prepares you for the TOEFL and also teaches you the academic language and skills needed to succeed in a university. Designed for high-intermediate to advanced-level English speakers, our course includes TOEFL-focused reading, writing, listening, speaking, vocabulary, and grammar instruction.

General English

Our General English course is a semi-intensive program designed for students who want to improve their listening and speaking skills without the time commitment of an intensive program. With morning class time and flexible computer lab hours throughout the week, our General English course is perfect for every schedule.

Take your SAT prep to the next level with Kaplan Premier Tutoring

Personal Attention. Convenience. Proven Results.

See the difference that one-on-one in-home tutoring can make on the SAT or the ACT. Call today for a free consultation.